D1565616

Chaos Organization and Disaster Management

PUBLIC ADMINISTRATION AND PUBLIC POLICY

A Comprehensive Publication Program

Executive Editor

JACK RABIN
Professor of Public Administration and Public Policy
School of Public Affairs
The Capital College
The Pennsylvania State University—Harrisburg
Middletown, Pennsylvania

Chaos Organization and Disaster Management

Alan Kirschenbaum
Technion–Israel Institute of Technology
Haifa, Israel

MARCEL DEKKER, INC.   NEW YORK · BASEL

Library of Congress Cataloging-in-Publication Data
A catalog record for this book is available from the Library of Congress.

ISBN: 0-8247-4715-1

This book is printed on acid-free paper.

Headquarters
Marcel Dekker, Inc., 270 Madison Avenue, New York, NY 10016, U.S.A.
tel: 212-696-9000; fax: 212-685-4540

Distribution and Customer Service
Marcel Dekker, Inc., Cimarron Road, Monticello, New York 12701, U.S.A.
tel: 800-228-1160; fax: 845-796-1772

Eastern Hemisphere Distribution
Marcel Dekker AG, Hutgasse 4, Postfach 812, CH-4001 Basel, Switzerland
tel: 41-61-260-6300; fax: 41-61-260-6333

World Wide Web
http://www.dekker.com

The publisher offers discounts on this book when ordered in bulk quantities. For more information, write to Special Sales/Professional Marketing at the headquarters address above.

Current printing (last digit):

10 9 8 7 6 5 4 3 2 1

PRINTED IN THE UNITED STATES OF AMERICA

Dedication

This book took form over a long period of time. It started with my involvement with a small group of individuals dedicated to preparing guidelines for the Israeli population to survive both a conventional and nonconventional war. It evolved into developing a behavioral disaster management unit in Israel's Home Front Command. This involvement put me face to face with practical issues and inherent organizational conflicts found in disaster management. To the men and women who were part of this effort goes my wholehearted appreciation.

And then there is my family and best critic and friend, Elka. Without her perseverance and that of my children, the disruption to our family life, which I imposed in developing my ideas and writing them down, would have made completing this book very unlikely. To Yossi, Gila, and Eliezer, I can only wish a safer world. To my grandchildren, peace.

Two guiding principles laid the foundation for writing this book. The first originated in an ancient Talmudic saying.

ללמדך, שכל המאבד נפש אחת מישראל, מעלה עליו הכתוב, כאילו אבד עולם מלא: וכל המקים נפש אחת מישראל, מעלה עליו הכתוב כאילו קים עולם מלא.

מסכת סנהדרין, סדר נזיקין , פרק ד' משנה ה'

(Therefore a single man was created) to teach you that if anyone destroys a single soul from the children of man, The Scripture considers him as though he destroyed a whole world, and if someone rescues a single soul from the

children of man the Scripture considers him as though he had saved a whole world.—Talmud, Tractate Sanhedrin

The second principle on the benefit of organizing chaos.

בראשית ברא אלקים את השמים ואת הארץ: והארץ היתה תהו ובהו
וחשך על פני תהום ורוח אלקים מרחפת על פני המים: ויאמר אלקים יהי
אור ויהי אור: וירא אלוקים את האור כי טוב.....

בראשית פקר א', א-ד.

In the beginning, G-d created the heaven and earth. Now the earth was unformed and void and darkness was upon the face of the deep, and the spirit of G-d hovered over the face of the waters. And G-d said, 'Let there be light'. And there was light. And G-d saw the light, that it was good.—Old Testament, Genesis I

Preface

There can be little doubt that organized disaster behaviors are an inherent trait among people throughout the world and throughout history. In the past, organized disaster behaviors were primarily in reaction to life-threatening events arising in the natural environment. These reactions reflected our adaptive ability in an often chaotic natural world to initiate organized social survival skills. They have stood us in good stead for millennia. Today, we face disasters of our own making. In the urbanized world, this adaptive process has led us to transfer these traditional disaster behaviors into formal organizations. In the past, disaster organizing was focused in the family and community whereas today it is mainly in the hands of civil servants in large complex public administrations. This transition did not take place overnight, but it has radically altered how we, the potential victims of disaster, have come to see and react to them. Despite the transition to formalized disaster management organizations, it is extremely difficult to ignore the millenium of acquired survival knowledge that has been passed down, tested, modified, and eventually institutionalized into the very fabric of our societies. It is equally difficult to ignore the social outcomes of these survival lessons as they express themselves in an ongoing "friction" with formalized disaster management. No doubt, this disagreement will become exacerbated and be with us for many years to come.

The rise of public sector administration, however, has its dangers. By putting all our eggs in the "disaster management organization" basket, we run the risk of having them all smashed. There is enough hard evidence today to suggest that this may be taking place. The question is why? My arguments for this trend point an accusing finger at the built-in organizational conflicts typical of public sector disaster management. My basic argument throughout this book is that they have disenfranchised the very people whom they are supposed to help. This is compounded by an unclear understanding of basic behavioral concepts associated with disasters, such as "preparedness," and the absence of a decisive means to measure an organization's effectiveness. In a further effort to understand why disaster management organizations have been failing us, I took the potential victim's point of view. What I found was a wide chasm between how disaster management experts and potential victims of disaster see the world of disasters. I found that traditional forms of disaster behavior are alive and well, that risk perceptions do not match those of the experts; and that the final decision maker for surviving disasters is not the disaster manager but a family's "mother hen." In short, public sector disaster agencies do not come even close to fulfilling their basic goals as service organizations. They have focused on their own needs and not those of their clients. They see the world through organization prisms and not through the eyes of the potential victim.

Discovering these faults led me to re-examine the community's role in preparing individuals and families for disaster. My original argument that we should refocus our attention on the community and family social roots of disaster behavior could now be evaluated. By viewing disaster communities in terms of their social networks, and not simply physical areas, I soon realized that traditional disaster behaviors are deeply embedded in social bonds we develop. Bonds within our families, with neighbors and friends, and through general community social activities are the active building blocks that affect how we look at and react to disasters. Such networks were found to be a critical stepping-stone in initiating preparedness activities, a measure of our chances for survival. In short, I reaffirmed the centrality of social networks within disaster communities as critical predictors of disaster behavior.

Now I faced the dilemma of how to approach disaster management outside the province of public sector bureaucratic organizations. This led me to explore the possibility of privatization. The pros and cons of privatization have filled books. Yet, I had actual responses from households in a national field study (in Israel) that showed that a substantial proportion of people would purchase disaster services in the private market. What better indication than this—where most of these services are provided with little or no cost—that privatization is a feasible alternative to public sector disaster management. Putting all this together as a "program" for action, I suggested a "General Social Process Model of Disaster Management." My point was to suggest how, through alternative privatization strategies, we can increase our ability to survive disasters by focusing on the social processes inherent in disaster communities and the crucial role played by mothers in implementing appropriate disaster behaviors. Unlike unsubstantiated ideological or organizational strategies available today, the social process model is the outcome of a step-by-step empirical analysis of actual disaster behaviors. This, in and of itself, distinguishes its approach and potential contribution in the area of disaster management.

Overall, my quest in writing this book was to go beyond temporary fads, buzz words, or ideological arguments and provide a methodological and empirical platform from which to initiate a critical analysis of disaster management. The model, which I have proposed in the last chapter, is not an ideological position. It is drawn from a sophisticated empirical analysis of an unusual and comprehensive set of data. This means the social process model is, like all research models, open to criticism using the general rules of scientific testing and revalidation. My hope is that others will do this, as it will move the area of disaster management from one dependent on slogans to one supported by an empirically based understanding of disaster behavior. With this knowledge, disaster managers will have a solid foundation from which to initiate organizational and managerial activities that will strengthen disaster behaviors associated with survival—in short, to save people's lives.

Alan Kirschenbaum

Contents

1

Creating Disasters

TAXES AND DISASTERS

Disasters and emergencies appear to be as inevitable as taxes; so too is our ongoing effort to cope with them. The ability to cope lies deep in our primordial past, which has taught us that "organizing" is the most efficient and effective means to survive (Kauffman 1994). Most of this organizing takes place without our really being cognizant that it is a special type of behavior. It seems the most natural thing to do when facing danger, channeling us to improvise defensive types of behaviors that over time are reinforced in our families, small groups, and communities. Whenever an outside threat such as a disaster occurs or is likely to occur signals and social cues are set in motion that prompt internal social group cohesion. The most amazing thing about this process is that it seems never-ending. In the last ten years, 4777 natural (not technological or industrial) disasters have occurred, killing more than 880,000 people. In addition they have affected the property, health, and jobs of about 1.9 billion people and inflicted economic losses of around $685 billion to the world's economies (UN Reliefweb 2002).*

The apparent chaos and threatening nature of disasters—as unusual, uncontrollable, and many times unpredictable events—facilitated the development of organizational means to restore order and normalcy. The fact that there is strength in numbers and that group and community strength

1

accumulates when individuals cooperate has apparently been one of the most effective means of coping and surviving. In most cases the latent organizational structures that have evolved over thousands of years to mitigate disasters lay dormant and were only activated when needed. When we humans were still wanderers, our small, compact communities moved to better hunting or grazing grounds when faced with a drought or seasonal changes. With agricultural settlement and town life came the oldest types of "first responders," volunteer firefighters, who in actuality were simply neighbors helping each other out. Each new situation brought with it creative forms of disaster behaviors that were evaluated over time and eventually incorporated into that community. These same latent organizing behaviors appear today in a variety of ways and have embedded themselves in our social activities.

The reason this process repeated itself over and over again is because first and foremost societies are in the business of surviving. Survival becomes problematic when its members are killed or injured, when its economic viability is thwarted, or when the fabric of everyday life is tattered (Miller et al. 1999; Janney et al. 1977). It is at these times that we dig deep into those wellsprings of disaster experiences we learned over thousands of years. It is extremely important to recognize that the activation of these latent but tried and true "disaster-oriented" organizational social skills was essential to increase the survival function of the group or community (Paton and Johnston 2001). This ability to organize has shown itself to be effective in practically all manner of social and political behavior, from helping neighbors to winning a war. In most cases this meant the participation of the entire group or community so as to reaffirm and strengthen social bonds, clarify the division of labor, and most important, set in motion practical means to overcome the

---

* As stated in Pelling et al. (2002): "Reported disaster frequency has doubled every ten years since 1960, with 96% of all deaths from natural disasters occurring in the global south. The annual average financial loss caused by natural disasters, accidents, technological accidents, and urban fires, estimated between 1991 and 2000 in US$ millions at constant 2000 prices, was 234 in Africa, 21,293 in the Americas, 40,346 in Asia, 17,930 in Europe, and 1178 in Oceania. Individual annual losses fluctuate greatly, with 1995 being the worst year on record, when 0.7% of global GDP was lost to natural disasters. All disaster loss estimates need to be viewed with caution. They are compiled from government reports and insurance statements with no common methodology and little transparency in their calculation. Moreover, they account only for loss of physical assets and indicate nothing of the full scale of personal loss and livelihood disruption, which is proportionately higher in less developed countries. Low human development countries average more than 1000 deaths per disaster but less than US$100 million loss, compared with high human development countries, that average less than ten deaths but over US$600 million in losses per disaster. Such losses are difficult for any economy to absorb but for developing countries, they can be devastating. Hurricane Mitch is said to have set back development in Nicaragua by 20 years."

various types of disasters that are always about to occur (Dynes 1998). One should not be deceived into thinking that these latent organizational qualities are a thing of the past. Just take a look at a small part of a U.S. government report describing the organization plans that emerged after the terrorist attack on the Pentagon in Washington, D.C. This report came after a "spontaneous" evacuation of thousands of employees immediately after the Pentagon attack by terrorists and the recognition that the officials did not "control" the situation.

> The federal government has created a new procedure for evacuating federal employees in Washington in the case of possible terrorist attacks on the nation's capital. The protocol, which took effect in May, tells who can decide to evacuate federal employees from agencies and how the government will communicate the decision to employees and to city and state agencies that would be affected by a mass exodus of civil servants from Washington. It is an attempt to improve on the ad hoc process used on Sept. 11. (Jason http://www. govexec.com/dailyfed 14.8.02).

These forms of disaster organizing have for centuries been an inherent part of a community's social structure. Today, most of these social functions have been excised and replaced by public sector agencies dominated by external noncommunity public administrations. What was once the province of the community is now in the hands of local government. In some rare cases these overlap, but the difference lies primarily in the form of organization; be it fellow community members or government bureaucrats. I will argue—and make every effort to demonstrate—that the consequences of this change have increased the vulnerability of communities to the vagaries of disasters.

HISTORICAL ORGANIZING FORMS

The historical forms of organizations dealing with disaster events (before, during, and after) reflect how well we have adapted to the sources of disasters (from natural to man-made), as well as how we utilize social capital in minimizing disruption. It is easy to imagine how our ancestors, living in caves or wandering the plains, developed the means to cope with and survive what were then considered natural events—even those that we today consider disasters (such as floods, fires, and extreme weather conditions). The process of adaptation, migration, and inventiveness were all used in conjunction with adaptive forms of organization to maximize survival. The result has been a type of organizational disaster subculture that emerged when disaster threats were perceived to be eminent (Granot 1996). This pattern of community participation in the development and activation of organized behavior to face disasters has remained in place over thousands of years (Oliver-Smith 1986).

Unlike most other social adaptive processes, which run headlong into the force of "tradition", disaster behavior is much more dynamic. Disasters are not everyday events, nor are any two disasters exactly alike, requiring that we deal with them in a more flexible and fine-tuned manner. Categories of disasters do have a basic common denominator that sets the framework in how we deal with them, however. These commonalities in their physical appearance, frequency, and destructive powers provide a rule of thumb as to how to act. What we apparently have done is use these grassroot disaster behaviors of "normal" disasters as a benchmark for survival. A good example of this might be a situation in which the residents in a river valley accustomed to annual spring flooding would gauge an upcoming flood and make appropriate preparations. The villagers' "usual" preparations might be adjusted because of a winter of unusually heavy snow, moving their livestock and valuables to even higher ground and joining with their neighbors in a community effort to reinforce flood barriers. In general, the villagers simply utilize past experiences with flooding as a springboard to enhance their disaster behaviors. Once the flood is over, these experiences will (if successful) be incorporated into these villagers' disaster behavior repertoire.

The institutionalization of organized behavior in the face of disasters must be seen in light of the extended time span over which it occurred. This time span reinforced, refined, and culturally embedded such behavior into our psyches; it became part of everyday life. As time went on, however, small groups and communities grew, dispersion led to cultural differences, and technological advances were made. Both population growth and domesticated agriculture led to newer organizational forms. These organizational forms accommodated to the culture that generated them (Roth 1970). Nation-states evolved from tribes, urban centers evolved from rural villages, and commercial trade overpowered barter or subsistence markets. What did not change was the occurrence of disasters. What *did* change was the frequency and severity of disasters, especially with the urbanization of populations (Quarantelli 1999; Institute of Civil Engineers 1995). Individuals, groups, and communities not only faced the wrath of nature, but also unknown types of disasters fashioned by their changing social, political, and economic environment (Blaikie et al. 1994). This historical change forced people to face disasters of their own making (Quarantelli 1993; Cuthbertson and Nigg 1987). In particular, there arose the potential risks associated with technological disasters (Perrow 1984).

With most societies rapidly undergoing modernization came the first faltering but consistent steps at alternative organizational forms to specifically deal with disasters. These steps followed the historical pattern of mass migrations and urban growth, both of which threw millions of rural peoples into concentrated urban geographic areas. This concentration of so many people into increasingly dense urban areas set the stage for all types of potential disasters unknown in an agrarian society, including those from disease and fire. Now, in one short moment, large numbers of people could be directly affected by a disaster. We need only to remind ourselves of the Chicago fire over a century ago or even the Kobe earthquake in Japan just a few years ago. What emerged from these first stages of modernization were the initial attempts at socially designed steps to adapt disaster behavior to a new environment which, for the most part, continued to be the local community (Quarantelli 1985). The reason was that the early stages of urban development were characterized by social patterns still influenced by village life but on a grander scale. Throughout this reorganization process, however, there emerged an underlying theme that shifted emphasis from local community survival toward artificially designed organizations.

FROM COMMUNITY TO BUREAUCRACY

Modernization, it seems, was the proverbial straw that broke the camel's back by transferring community-based "disaster organizing" into the hands of the nation-state. This process started fairly late in human history—less than 300 years ago—just before the industrial revolution and global population explosion, yet it marked a watershed in the organizational forms of survival with the appearance of specialized suborganizations whose objectives were primarily focused on mitigating, coping, and resolving the emergence of natural and man-made disasters.

This type of specialization reflected the general trend toward adaptive reorganization to modernization. It also fostered the emergence of new definitions of disasters (Gilbert 1998). One result was that after thousands of years of trail and error, bureaucratic organizations replaced traditional groups and small communities as the main source of disaster organizing. This displacement had a significant impact on what was defined as a disaster. All at once, a combination of organizational, social, and physical qualities associated with the collapse of cultural protection became the key components for disaster definitions (Dombrowsky 1998). For example, forest fires or floods— once considered natural events—were socially redefined as disasters. Industrial output, once a key in measuring progress, was now redefined as hazmat disasters for producing potential toxic wastes (Edelstein 1988). The natural cycle of hurricanes, tornados, and floods became disasters as people defied nature and migrated to those areas associated with this phenomenon. Now we have flood, tornado, and hurricane "victims." Then there are the actuarial definitions, which count the numbers of dead or injured or the amount of property destroyed or damaged as guidelines to determine whether a disaster occurred or not (Gordon 1982). The most recent redefinition has come in the wake of the September 11, 2001, terrorist attack on the Twin Towers and the Pentagon. A recent newspaper announcement stated, for example, "On October 1, the National Center for Health Statistics will begin using new classifications for terrorism-related deaths and injuries" (*New York Times* September 10, 2002). I am sure that such redefinitions will continue on a parallel path with disaster management organizations' needs for growth and power. In most cases, these redefinitions reflect a transition in the belief that man had the ability to more rationally assess the risk associated with the control of the environment and the future (Rogers 1997).

With the transfer of disaster management into public bureaucracies came the inevitable intervention of politics. In the United States, a disaster has occurred when the president says it has. In nations that have not set aside funds to compensate victims and that barely can reconstruct basic infrastructure, declarations of disasters are less forthcoming. When the World Bank or United Nations intends to provide "disaster funds," disasters are more likely to be declared. Apparently politics and disasters make good bedfellows! Here is a comment made during a heated discussion among emergency managers in an E-mail chat group that lets us look at how politics and bureaucracy interact.

> ...at what point (should) the President declare a disaster. After 2 decades we have learned a lot about which events require federal intervention. The trend has been a clear increase in the number of declarations since the Stafford Act went into effect. More clear definitions could lead to more consistent federal response and more clarity in the system as to when federal mechanisms are employed (Richard August 19, 2002).

ORGANIZATIONAL FORMS

To better understand this change, it is helpful to study the evolution of adaptive mechanisms that were operative over thousands of years. To do so, we need to make several assumptions. We start off by assuming that the primordial group survival behavior remains intact as a viable collective force countering threats against societal continuance (Torry 1979). This means that it is latent behavior embedded in most types of social groups. These groups may be organic in nature, emerging during times of need, or groups already in place in the community under the rubric of general welfare groups. For example, case studies have shown that one of the most prevalent types of helping behaviors during disasters is taking in displaced families or persons or helping those who have experienced the loss of property, have been injured, or have experienced the death of a family member. These are emergent types of behaviors that move from being latent to active during disasters. There are also emergent behaviors such as those we see among first responders. Here I refer to voluntary ambulance drivers, firefighters, or search and rescue teams, which are activated within a predesigned framework. When a disaster occurs (or is about to occur), these individuals join existing groups. The key to these types of behaviors is a flexible social network interwoven into the community that allows the emergence of organized group behaviors in cases of disasters.

Second, we assume that such organizational behavior before, during, and after disasters would be honed over time to maximize efficiency and effectiveness. The time-honored learning curve of experience should, according to this assumption, winnow out what not to do and select behavior crucial for survival. Resident farmers of Iceland know where *not* to build on the basis of past stories of avalanches passed down through generations. Residents of Tiberius, Israel, have learned to plant shade trees on the side of their homes, thus maximizing shade. Builders have learned to design earthquake-resistant homes, shipbuilders safer and more stable ships, and so on. Trial and error over centuries, along with modern technology and information systems, have all been integrated into these social networks.

To say that this process was entirely rational clashes with what we know about human "nature." What I *do not* assume is that the implementation of these organizational forms and complimentary behaviors to cope and manage disasters have been consistently rational (Fisher 1998). The diversity of social relationships that emerge from different cultures, finding expression in individual, family, and community behaviors, can at times perplex even the most ardent believer in rational behavior. Slights, grudges, revenge, jealousy, and love are all part of the human makeup that plays a part in how we organize. Even the most rationally created organizations are not entirely rational.

This last point is poignant for organizations are devices built and dependent upon a diversity of people reflecting both rational and nonrational behaviors (Daft 1998). In order to understand the implications and relevance of this duality for disaster management, the impediments on organizational behavior will need to be examined. To do so, I will first contrast community models of disaster management to those prevalent in complex bureaucratic organizations. Both will be reviewed in terms of organization behavior employed to adapt to social disruptions created by the physical environment. This means looking at both "natural" organizational social adaptations found in community settings and "artificial," purposeful organizing devices that are associated with bureaucratic structures.

COMMUNITY MODELS

Communities are organized social units. As such, they have the flexibility to adapt to change, and accommodate their physical and social environment. They represent the cumulative social assets of small-group interdependent relations built on family–clan, friendship, and economic networks. Commonality is based on being ecologically distinct into natural and/or social areas (Hawley 1950). On this basis, they represent one of the major mechanisms for societal survival, development, and growth. In such communities, disasters are socially constructed normative situations when efforts are made "to protect and benefit some social resource whose existence is perceived to be threatened" (Dynes 1998). The uncanny way in which collective community action occurs prior to, during, or after a disaster demonstrates the power of organic, indigenous organizing (Comfort 1994; Oliver-Smith 1986; Schware 1982). Studies of disasters involving communities point out the varied ways local populations organize not only to help their neighbors, but also to revitalize and reconstruct the social basis of their communities (Drabek 1986). One such recent study in Japan focused on the emergence of such self-organizing groups in the midst of a technically advanced, densely populated metropolitan region (Comfort 1996). This type of independent organizing occurred even when "disaster authorities" were mandated to do this job.

The key to understanding this type of organizing rests at the very heart of basic social processes, during which simple interactions lead to normative behavior. These behaviors form repetitive patterns that are institutionalized over time. From here, the force of tradition takes over, and with it the inherent capability for what has been recently called self-organization. One part of this process, as I have argued, involves survival. Survival behaviors developed over long periods have also become institutionalized, emerging as organized community group behavior during crises (Dynes et al. 1990; Parr 1970; Quarantelli and Dynes 1970). Such self-organizing behaviors in the face of disaster represent one type of emergent community response. As the concept of community is universal, being ubiquitous in highly urbanized as well as rural-dominated societies, disaster behavior depends on the dynamic social structure of the community. To view community in this context is to tease out those long dormant survival behaviors that increase survival chances. More important, as these survival behaviors are indigenous and organic to communities in contrast to artificial or exogenous organizational implants, the expected chances for survival and reconstruction of the community's social fabric should be greater when undisturbed. In addition, case studies of how communities utilize their social assets during and after a disaster demonstrate the strength of social groups within communities. A large and varied number of disaster case studies support this viewpoint (National Hazards Research Center 2000).

ORGANIZATIONAL MODELS

If this is the case, why has there emerged an alternative disaster management system associated with public administration? To begin to answer this question requires examining the basis for such an alternative organization. As I argued, the shift from community to state brought with it a similar shift of disaster management from the community into complex bureaucratic public sector organizations. The most palatable reason appears to be that such an organizational framework seemed the natural outgrowth of the modernization process. It reflected the philosophy embedded in science, namely controlled change, and afforded a rational approach to disaster management. Such an approach found its way into public administration disaster management as a curious combination of styles. By examining them, we will not only learn how disaster organizing is structured, but also the mechanisms, flaws, and constraints built into it. (See Table 1.)

Rational System Approach

One of the most pervasive explanations for the basis of organizing behavior has emerged from the *rational system* approach. This approach assumes a high degree of rationality in human behavior that is directed toward purposeful goal seeking. Given this approach, the organizing ability of modern man to deal with disasters should generate a foolproof disaster management organization capable of dealing with every imaginable type of disaster. The emergent structure that would evolve is likely to have the classic characteristics of what we call today a bureaucracy: a hierarchical structure, authority associated with the office, defined power relationships, and a top-down chain of command. This approach toward organizing has several variants. One focuses on the scientific rational utilization of the individual, who is seen as a cog in a well-oiled machine. Frederick Taylor's classic "scientific management" approach represents this viewpoint. Another approach sees various types of generic societal authorities as the basis for goal attainment in bureaucratic structures. (See Weber's study of bureaucracy.) A third emphasizes the rational use of administrative directives. Henry Fayol's fourteen

TABLE 1 Major Contributors of Organizational Models

Rational models	Natural system	Open system
Fredrick Taylor	Elton Mayo	Norbert Weiner
Max Weber	Chester Barnard	Walter Buckley
Henry Fayol	Philip Selznick	
Marsh and Simon	Talcot Parsons	

principles of administrative management exemplify this perspective. In addition, a fourth approach by Robert Marsh and Herbert Simon claim that it is a highly formalistic framework with rational options for decision makers that forms the basis for organizational success. The underlying theme of all these organizational forms is that rational behavior determines the best structure, means, and processes through which the organization attains the groups' goals. Within this ideal structure, rational decisions take place that expedite performance.

Natural Systems Approach

On the face of it, such a logical organized structure should work! The rational approach in organizing behavior, however, disregarded many nonrational human characteristics. In a sense the "ideal" rational man faced the not so rational person enmeshed in the complexities of social life. Taking this cue, organizational researchers forcefully argued that organizations mirrored the social dynamics inherent in societies. The champions of this perspective developed what is now called the "natural systems" approach. These included proponents such as Elton Mayo (human relations), Chester Barnard (cooperative systems), Philip Selznick (institutional), and Talcot Parsons (social systems) (Scott 1995). Their arguments were simple. The artificial rational system of organizations was contingent upon (but not entirely replaced by) the foibles and frailty of human social relationships. Organizational relationships developed according to the rules imposed by societies and went beyond strict rationality. Loves, preferences, hatred, and jealousy were all part of the formula in social relationships. Informal social structures could comfortably live alongside formal bureaucratic hierarchies and informal leaders alongside formal officers. Departmental or personal conflict of interests could undermine rationally constructed chains of command and authority. In short, the ability to rationally organize did not always guarantee that success was inevitable or that goal attainment would be efficient and effective. Proponents of human resource management considerably enhanced this theme to the point at which employees' nonrational "needs" overwhelmed organizational goals. The bottom line was that understanding organizations required unraveling the mechanisms by which social behavior becomes organized. In a large sense, the natural systems approach revived the idea that organizing behavior was a "natural" component of society and certainly an inherent means to enhance survival in the face of disasters.

Open System

An extension of the natural system was appropriately designated the "open system" approach. This is because it became increasingly clear to organizational theorists that viewing organizations as closed, independent systems did not match reality. This led to the development of the open system approach. If organizations mirrored the culture in which they arose, this had to include cross-organizational relationships. What evolved was an approach that viewed organizations as subsystems within larger systems, emphasizing the importance of the organization's external environment and the interdependence between organizations. This perspective found strong support in the writings of Norbert Weiner (cybernetics) and Walter Buckley (modern systems theory). In its large sweep, this approach forced many to see the social and structural dynamics of organizations to be part of a larger set of organized social relationships. All at once organizational systems were seen as having interlocking, subordinate, and competitive parts; cross-organizational relationships appeared in the exchange of goods and services, changes in one subordinate system affected other systems, and internal structure depended on supply and demand made by other organizations. This was an important contribution to understanding organizations. The implications were that organizations, the goals of which were to confront disasters or emergencies, could no longer be seen as independent of their social, organizational, or environmental roots. This meant the possibility of a window of opportunity to reintroduce the community as a subset of the larger disaster management organization system. The social system approach has raised the possibility of interorganizational dissonance, however (and not only cooperation), which as we will see has become a key operative element in the way public administration manages disasters (Kouzmin et al. 1995).

ORGANIZING CHAOS

As we have seen, there are three approaches to understanding the workings of organizations; the rational, natural, and open system approaches. By matching them to how disasters are organized through the alternative disaster management models—community versus public administration—we can gain some notion of how chaos is organized and then managed. Ideally, the community model represents the historic primodial-disaster organizing mechanisms for survival. Community-based disaster management would in this model organize chaos by involving organic, flexible, and consensual social subsystems. In contrast, disaster management influenced by rational, natural, and open systems would be more characteristic of the bureaucratic public administration system prevalent today (*Public Administration Review* 1985). Disaster related chaos, from this perspective, would be quantified and pigeonholed. We thus have two opposing perspectives of how chaos can be organized.

The winner in this contest is the bureaucratic public administration system. It overwhelmingly dominates disaster management in both developed and developing nations (WHO 1994). In addition, the appeal of public administration to manage disasters is supported by a rational new-science philosophy that claims the ability to control, predict, and manage our material, social, and even religious lives. To this end, the institutional organization of chaos has become identified with public administration (WHO 1994). Under the rubric of modern science and rationalizing organizations, the natural content and social meaning of disasters was abandoned. What resulted were their artificial classification and conceptual description, which were based on statistical estimates and probabilities (Gordon 1982). By fitting disasters into the framework of science and by making order of chaotic but reoccurring natural phenomenon, public policy administrators created an artificial but systematic means of controlling, predicting, and managing disasters (U.S. General Accounting Office 1991). Simultaneously, this perspective also influenced how the potential and actual victims of disasters would be viewed (Quarantelli 1998). They too could be classified scientifically and managed. Now damage control could be objectively evaluated and recovery policies dehumanized (Gunn 1992).

There are advantages, however, in the way public administrations organize chaos. From an academic perspective, such organizing provides the building blocks for empirically testing theoretical propositions. This process sets in motion a means to objectify and collect quantitative data alongside qualitative anthropological material. The results have been fairly impressive, based on the recent increase in serious academic and practitioner publications in the area of *disaster* management. A quick Internet search under the key word disaster will pull up hundreds of sites and dozens of publications. Of equal importance has been the creation of national and global data banks (International Red Cross 1997), centers focusing on disaster studies, information clearinghouses, in-depth studies of specific disasters, and laboratory experiments (Anderson and Woodrow 1989). The great advantage of trying to make sense out of disasters from a physical and social perspective is that it allows us to view disasters from a broad perspective (Kent 1987), but as I will point out, these advantages in data and information generation, which were created within the walls of public administrations, can easily go awry within the very auspices of these same public agencies (McEntire 1997).

INFORMATION AND DISASTER MANAGEMENT

In general, the expansion of traditional forms of public administration has gone hand in hand with the demand for more and better information. Such information seeking has several advantages. Not only does it provide a justification for providing public sector jobs; it also creates information pools that offer a legitimate basis for policy development and operational decisions. For both politicians and bureaucrats, judgments backed up by numbers are a more legitimate means to make decisions than political opinions. In the case of the early development of disaster management as a single issue at the federal level, data collection became a paramount organizational goal. Scientifically dedicated data collection increasingly replaced generic community sources of information. The dedications for quantitative information was accelerated by the fact that disasters are highly visible, require immediate solutions, and do not go away. The great hope is that a mountain of facts can mitigate the unknown quality of disasters and especially be used as a means to persuade people to follow organizational guidelines. The extent of this goal can be seen in the dialogue among emergency managers (EMs) on the International Association of Emergency Manager E-mail group.

> How can we (EMs) plan without information? Intelligent planning includes reviewing and sorting information from as many sources as possible in order to create an operational plan appropriate to one's jurisdiction. I know that sometimes the amount of information we all receive is extremely time consuming. Reviewing and sorting out that which may apply is a very laborious task, but how else can we be "current" when the questions will be asked (Richard EMC August 2002)?

The result was a feedback loop that led to a need for more accurate data (Kelly 1995). Creating information pools formed primary organizational goals. Although some research was initiated, the emphasis was on the technical aspect of information gathering as the primary tool to outfox disasters. As I pointed out, more information and facts were an illusion for control. The assumption was that disasters could be avoided, mitigated, and dealt with more efficiently and effectively when more information was available (Neal 1993). The logical step in many disaster management organizations was therefore to put such information and data searches high on the priority list of organizational goals. One result of these data collection efforts has been the creation of global data banks, centralized electronic library collections, research and training centers, and local information centers. These data pools also have a political use. Professional politicians either ignore or use them when convenient. When funds are needed from central government banks, the data inevitably cry out of the impending disaster. When compensation is to be given, these same *facts* tend to reduce the damage assessments!

HIDDEN POLITICAL AGENDA

Collecting "hard facts" has an additional consequence: it gives legitimacy to the disaster agency, as people have a tendency to believe "facts." Just look under the surface of "fact finding," however, and you will find the "public" of public sector disaster management organizations. This hidden political agenda is really nothing new, but takes on an added dimension in the case of disasters. Doing a poor job can have explosive political consequences on public trust (or disdain), both in the short and long terms, and certainly for politicians, who depend on votes. In countries in which disaster management is run and controlled by a nondemocratic government, voting may be irrelevant, but demonstrations and rebellion are critical. In democracies, voter dissatisfaction can topple governments, and even, as was the case for the Federal Emergency Management Agency (FEMA) in the United States, lead to a change in leadership and organizational structure. This is happening again today, partly in response the September 11 terrorist attack on the Twin Towers and the Pentagon, with FEMA being incorporated into the newly created Homeland Security Department. The national and local politics that have become part and parcel of public organizations in disaster management are an extremely sensitive issue. The reason may lie in the enormous budgets that are allocated for disaster compensation to victims of disasters and the chain of profits that are involved in the mitigation and recovery stages of disasters. Billions of dollars are involved. What is particularly relevant today above and beyond such natural disasters as floods, hurricanes, typhoons, earthquakes, or wildfires, is the more immediate threat of terror and security, which seems to have taken on a life of its own. The politicians of old could live with local regional natural disasters that affected specific population sectors. Now, however, the terror threat seems to have gotten out of hand as it crosses the accepted boundaries by threatening the safety, health, and economic well-being of whole nations. It is for this reason that there are signs of greater political intervention in what was once touted to be a professional organization. Some candid emergency managers expressed their feelings on the way they see their job and on how national and local politics annoy them. Let me just cite a few of the many comments made by disaster managers.

> Seems like right now there are too many folks without a clue mixed in with too many decisions based on politics, not on safety systems knowledge. It makes for a very bad situation that is only going to get worse as more of the same keeps getting added to the mix (Bob September 2002).

> Our security policies have little to do with security and much to do with keeping the special interests happy. Remember, 2002 is the "midterm" election year with respect to the Bush administration. The absolute top priority in the Federal government right now is acquiring or retaining slim majorities in Congress and winning as many statehouses as possible (Dave September 2002).

Another demonstration that "interoperability" isn't a technical problem...it's a political one (Art August 2002).

I wager that New York Office of Emergency Management is not the only city/county EM agency that has those type of problems [sic; political intervention]. It seems that EM continues to be the victim of "peacetime priorities" (we're not a priority until an emergency) and political personalities (Steven September 2002).

What these quotes suggest is another level of organizational conflict, that between the professional disaster managers and their political mentors; so not only are there built-in conflicts inherent in formal bureaucratic organizations, but also those imposed from external sources, namely politicians. In recognition of these heavy constraints on what disaster managers portray as the best way to save lives, researchers have attempted to examine another approach to ways in which public administrators may be able to deal more effectively with disaster management. It is to this that I now turn my attention.

NEW PUBLIC MANAGEMENT

The recent development of the New Public Management (NPM) approach to making public administrations more responsive to the potential and actual victims of disasters has brought about a glimmer of hope that such advantages would come to fruition. The basic assumption is that measures commonly employed in the private sector could be transferred and utilized in the public sector (Vigoda 2002). Of these the primary is "performance" measures. By obtaining quantitative measures of performance, it is hoped that public sector agencies will be able to have transparent standards by which to measure their effectiveness and thereby be more responsive to the public. In the search for such performance measures, proponents have argued that full use would be made of related sciences, which would then be implemented in practice by using the latest performance-linked managerial techniques.

This perspective, however, depends on how performance is to be measured. In fact, it is the Achilles' heel of this perspective, as public sector performance measures are a far cry from the bottom line "performance–profit" measures inherent in the competitive private sector. The industrial engineering and organizational/managerial behavior literature on performance measures has to some degree dealt with white-collar occupations—the predominant work group in public sector jobs—but it has rarely touched the public sector. One reason is that public sector administration is a monopoly-protected labor market in which the objective measure, "profit," is derived from and dependent on political policy instead of actual bottom-line profits. Profit enters public administration only in terms of budgets derived from various public sources (e.g., taxes), therefore performance is limited to attaining political or social rather than economic profit objectives. If and when these political, social, and economic policies do converge, however, public sector disaster management may be successful in preventing and mitigating disasters. The degree to which this can happen remains clouded in a number of issues. The primary one, I suggest, has to do with the organizational structure of disaster management agencies.

DISASTER MANAGEMENT ORGANIZATIONS

While disasters have been coterminous with humankind over the millenniums, non-community-based disaster organization are relatively new. At mid-twentieth century, it was nearly impossible to point to specific organizations (or job positions) whose task was to manage disasters (except those that were war-or conflict-related). The only notable exceptions have been local community-based fire and police (and of course militia) organizations throughout the world; disaster prevention and mitigation remained in the hands of local communities. In the United States, this appears to have remained mainly intact (Rubin 1981; Mileti and Sorenson 1987; Stallings and Schepart 1987). In less urbanized and industrialized nations, this pattern continued even into the latter part of the twentieth century. With the Second World War came a surge of interest in both disaster research and prevention (Form and Nosow 1958; Fritz 1957). This interest emerged primarily in Western urban and industrialized nations and was "imposed" through the dominance of training programs on less developed countries (Quarantelli 1986). It seems reasonable to conjecture that the vast organizational experience gained during the war and the threat of nuclear destruction upon the civilian population engendered this thrust of interest. Natural and technological disasters continued to occur and were sporadically studied (Charles and Kim 1988). For the most part, disasters were seen as the problem of local communities (Quarantelli 1995). Within a short period of time, however, the intervention of public authorities at the federal level or by central governments (e.g., military) became predominant. It was at this point that even local community organizations started to take on the formal bureaucratic characteristics of their larger federal big brother. In the United States, this metamorphous was even mandated in law (FEMA 1999).

Until this point, most disasters were seen as a scientific challenge. Technical solutions were the way disasters were defined. Dams could control floods. Fires could be controlled by water distribution points, building materials, and sprinkler systems; earthquakes by building codes; and tornadoes and hurricanes by weather warning systems. Apparently it was much easier to look for technical solutions to the symptoms of disasters than seek their generic social cause. Even terrorism has fallen under the sway of this type of thinking. Take as an example a new product being marketed to emergency and disaster managers as a way to counter terrorism: "The hub of the program is…a "war room" of sorts that allows users to better comprehend complex issues and situations. The program utilizes advanced computers, display systems and software tools that simulate an attack based on real and projected data" (Sandia National Laboratories posted August 23, 2002).

Some of the disaster managers soon began to realize that the "gadgets and toys," as they called the wonder pill technology, may not be the best way to deal with disasters. Without them, however, especially in the area of communications, organizational coordination in complex disaster situations would be extremely difficult. They also provided a highly visible physical expression of doing something. Having pop-up computer screens and state-of-the-art wireless communicators can be very impressive, so rather than rock the boat, heavy resources continually flowed into the technological solutions. This did not, however, meet the pleasure of some disaster managers, who began to verbalize the beginning of a trend questioning technical solutions for disasters. One, for example, raised this sensitive issue before his colleagues.

> I'm interested in the this concept/equipment for reasons others are probably not. With all the funding that is suddenly available and the amount of equipment that is being purchased for the sake of spending, has anyone tested the equipment in the various setting that it is intended for? On 9/11 some of the best systems available failed because it was more important to have the look, than the function. To be somewhat "tongue & cheek" is this "toys for boys or gadgets for girls?" Coming from the emergency medical side, which trauma/ems has a total federal funding of 3.5 million, does this help the people and environment we are suppose to be helping or simply make us look good (Robert 2002)?

It started to become clear in the late 1980s that technical solutions were not enough and that disasters involved complex social and psychological components, so a new direction was sought for avoiding, mitigating, and preparing for disasters. This search concentrated primarily on socially based information (Quarantelli 1988). Public administrators who had to deal with disasters sought "cookbook" solutions that represented the path of least resistance in understanding disaster behavior (Charles and Kim 1988; Quarantelli 1997), but when this proved too complex, they typically relied on the existing organizational structure and interorganizational relationships to deal with these problems. For the most part, lip service was given to the part that citizens had a hand in their own survival and safety during disasters. In reality, ready-made organizational solutions were used. The results were mediocre, to say the least (Granot 1999; Tierney 1985; U.S. General Accounting Office 1991). Falling back to an organizational solution, public sector disaster managers again sought salvation through better organized information systems at both a national and an international level. Technology was hailed to be at the heart of this information solution. Fixed in the heart of public administrations was the belief that access to better and more up-to-date and reliable data would—through their rational organizational structure—provides the answers to preventing and mitigating disasters. When all else failed, compensation became the tool used most often to disguise failures at prevention. Even as early as the 1980s questions were being raised about the claim that disasters resulted in a net economic gain for the impacted areas (Chang, 1984). (See Figure 1.)

In a short time it became apparent that the ability of government-sponsored organizations to deal with disasters did not live up to this rational scientific promise (Platt and McMullen 1979); some studies began to show the downside of public administrative intervention into local disasters (McLuckiel 1975; Hirose 1979; Heathcote 1980; Sylves 1991; Olson et al. 2000). What was frightening about these case studies was that they had little if any impact on how public disaster management was approached. In time, however, more concern was put on approaches that favored natural and open system approaches—factors that put an emphasis on the social sciences. It was at this point that social science research (primarily sociology) in the area of disasters began to develop and increasingly affect public sector public disaster managers in public administrations (Drabek 1986). Journals, research groups, and professional specialization began to appear. The turn of this present century saw the creation of a new professional group called "disaster managers." This group received professional certification, could attain a specialized college degree, and most important, could find employment. The criteria for such certification was initiated and to a large degree controlled by the bureaucratic public administrators who dealt with disaster management, however (FEMA 1999). The end result is disaster managers who are similar to each other in terms of their managerial perspective, knowledge, and operational skills.

It can be assumed that the increase of disaster management professionals was driven by market forces—primarily the availability of jobs. These job slots were more often than not created and supported by public sector funding. Most local authorities have (or need) a position for such professionals (LACDE 2000). The expectation was that these professionals would simply be clones of their big brothers in federal-level positions. The certification program, however, was to a great extent influenced by social scientists,

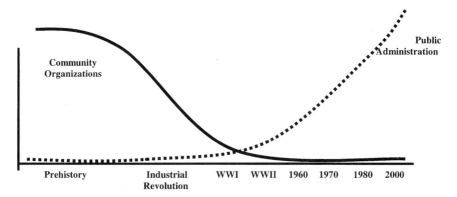

FIGURE 1 Historical development of public sector disaster management organizations.

who dominated the disaster research field and controlled academic certification. Disasters were now seen not only through the eyes of the (potential victims but also within the context of the community's social organization. Disasters were being moved out of the technical sphere and redefined as the product of the community and its social organization (Quarantelli 1998). Such a perspective were counter to the organizational standard operating procedure of public administrators (i.e., centralized, formalistic decision making on the basis of bureaucratic criteria). In fact, this process exacerbated the already built-in structural friction inherent in public administrations by trying to move the focus of attention to the victims 'rather than the organizations' needs.

This trend in humanizing disasters was supported by the mass media, which emphasized "human interest" stories as well as portrayals of the bureaucratic nature of the disaster management agencies (Fisher 1998). Unfortunately, the mass media, both newspapers and movies, tended to emphasize behaviors that went counter to empirical research! These portrayals have— despite their fictitious nature—persisted even until today. For example, the following is the reaction of a disaster manager in a recent newspaper article:

> The scientific research over the last forty years or so is unambiguous: panic is rare, very much less common than it's supposed or than it's depicted in fiction. So why, in the face of all the evidence, does the imagined threat of panic command such loyalty? In disaster movies and other fiction there's an easy, technical explanation available: Vivid physical behavior...screaming, flailing about and such...is simply easier to express on film or in writing than the quiet, "flat-

tened" affect more typical of real people in dire circumstances. Physical excitement is easier to communicate to the audience...so dramatic necessity trumps realism (Art, August 2002).

The combination of internal organizational faults along with mass media provided the extra push that was needed to move disaster management toward looking at the victims. Suffice it to say here that the historical development of disaster managers has been from clan and community leaders in the past to certified professionals in the bureaucratic organizations of today. This transformation reflects the types of events that are now defined as disasters and the belief in complex organizations as the solution to modern society's problems. Such a transformation and its impact has had global ramification. It is to this that I now turn.

GLOBAL DISASTER MANAGEMENT

One of the major symbolic acts removing disaster management from the community to large public administration organizations was the declaration by the United Nations at the end of the twentieth century of the "decade of the disaster." Disaster management became global; financial resources along with the establishment of numerous associate and consortium organizations sprang up. Mass media took up the cause with every major and minor disaster reported worldwide. Disaster myths were created and perpetuated by the mass media (Fisher 1998). Until this global agenda was declared, environmental issues were still in their infancy and the number of research or consulting organizations that focused on disasters was extremely small (Myers 1993). The establishment of disaster research units (mainly university-affiliated) and disaster management units in public administrations only became visible in the second half of the century in the late 1950s). By 2000, the number of disaster-related organizations had grown exponentially. The U.S. government alone has no fewer than twenty-six major agencies and dozens of regional offices dealing with disasters. There are an additional ninety-five specialized units established for differing disaster situations. To this can be added eighty U.S. domestic nongovermental organizations (NGOs). This number can be used as a rough indication of the same process occurring throughout the Western world.

The distribution of disaster-related *global*-based agencies (NGOs and public) likewise grew, comprising over ninety major public agencies with offices throughout the world. This pattern of the globalization of disaster management also strengthened the hold of public administration on the area of disasters. It has also led to interagency conflicts (Granot 1999) and problems of coordination (McEntire 1997), as well as territorial imperatives, turf wars (International Red Cross 1997), and competition (Kent 1987). What was apparent at the national or state level—at which public administrations dominated the definition of disaster, who was qualified to be a disaster victim, what help would be afforded, and so on—was now extended at the global level by other forms of public administration in different guises. As several critical reports have noted, the results have been at the same mediocre levels of disaster management (on a larger scale), where in some cases such "assistance" was more detrimental than helpful (Kent 1987)! The most visible of these have been associated with the droughts in Africa, where NGOs and international aid have actually harmed more people than they have helped.

BUILT-IN CONFLICT

The question that I raise here is why public administration organizations have fared so poorly in the field of disaster management. The fundamental answer lies in the built-in conflicts inherent in such organizations. These conflicts have plagued formal complex organizations throughout the ages and have become more acute today with their greater transparency. This built-in conflict stems from the nature of artificially created structures based on rational systems when confronted by the informal structures that pervade them. Anyone who has ever worked in an organization very quickly learns ways of getting around and through the red tape by going outside the formal and official way of behaving. Sometimes a quick phone call, talk over a cup of coffee, or meeting at the local pub or at social affairs can get more done in a few minutes than fifty official meetings. This is because on the one hand the formal structure is bureaucratic and rule-oriented, where centralized decisions based on rational mechanical authority are prevalent. Such a structure demands organizational behavior that is organization-oriented rather than client-oriented, whereby bureaucratic structure forms a distinct internal labor market independent of outside competitors and is internally rewarded (Di-Prete 1989). In short, follow the rules and keep your head down. Putting all of this into the words of an emergency manager seems a good way to demonstrate the frustration of working within the walls of a disaster agency.

> For those who appreciate irony, before the "gold rush" we in EM (emergency management) found most bureaucrats and politicians busy pointing at others when it came to accepting (or avoiding) responsibility. Now, it is politically incorrect to fail to include a high level fire official from any and all activity. Based on my "endless loop" experience, the next group to enjoy largesse will be non-

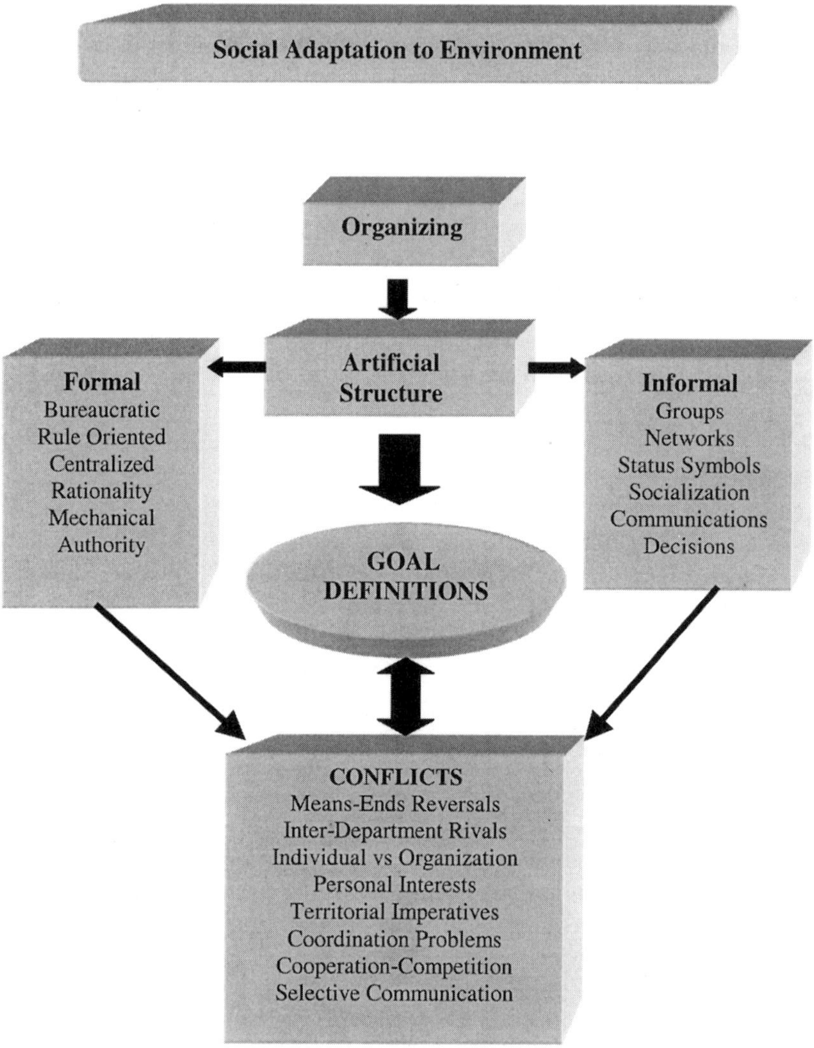

Social Adaptation to Environment

Organizing

Formal
Bureaucratic
Rule Oriented
Centralized
Rationality
Mechanical
Authority

Artificial
Structure

Informal
Groups
Networks
Status Symbols
Socialization
Communications
Decisions

GOAL
DEFINITIONS

CONFLICTS
Means-Ends Reversals
Inter-Department Rivals
Individual vs Organization
Personal Interests
Territorial Imperatives
Coordination Problems
Cooperation-Competition
Selective Communication

FIGURE 2   How built-in conflicts evolve in bureaucratic organizations.

response level Health officials. Then LE [local emergency] will re-enter the loop. Then a RADEF [radioactive emergency fallout] scare will resurrect the old "tin hat an arm band" group and around and around we go. Bottom line: remind them all that people die when appropriate resources are not applied rapidly and effectively, no matter what label they choose to assign to the source of the threat. Good luck in getting them together (Bill Jul, 2002).

These issues are only a small part of the problem. As disaster management agencies are only one (small) but bifurcated unit within a larger bureaucratic public administration, they face a multitude of intra-and inter-organizational conflicts: to coordinate or seek cooperation (Hills 1994); to resolve the confusion over their role and function by other administrators (Perry 1995); and to coordinate both their disparate and conflicting management practices (Sylves 1991; Cosgrave 1997) and their legal problems of authority (Drabek et al. 1981; Adams 1981). The most damaging for the potential disaster victims is that within such formal bureaucratic structures, effectiveness may come to be measured in terms of interdepartmental power relationships and not services rendered. This is a crucial problem, for the one thing that such disaster agencies rarely do is take a measure of their effectiveness. This issue will be taken up in more detail in Chapter 4. (See Figure 2.)

This built-in conflict between the formal and informal social structures within bureaucratic public administrations has a number of negative consequences on the effectiveness of disaster management. Placing these conflicting factors within the organizational framework of disaster management's goals creates many of the nonrational behaviors so often associated with organizations (Gordon 1996). Some of the more distinctive types of conflicts involve disputes concerning means and ends, individual versus organizational goals, territorial (and/or departmental) imperatives, cooperation in contrast to competition, the selective flow of information, and even personal interests versus administrative directives (Daft 1998). More often than not the conflicts are built on personal likes and dislikes, favoritism, discrimination, and even jealousies. These built-in conflicts have become increasingly more visible as public agencies are becoming more transparent. They are extremely detrimental to disaster management as expectations and dependence from their major stakeholders—the potential "victims" of disasters—grows.

COMMUNITY CONSENSUS

On the other hand, communities are the natural outcome of human organizing. They are pervasive throughout the world, organic in nature, composed of indigenous populations, and structured on the basis of family and economic strata (Quarantelli 1998). Communities are not only found in rural areas but can exist within the midst of large urban centers. Unlike bureaucratic structures that exemplify public administrations, however, a community's structure is kept intact mainly through a social process of consensus building (Ross 1967). This process is continually renewed through basic social interactions that foster symbolic identification and attachment to the community. Some of these encompass family and friendship networks, social and voluntary group formation, and economic investment and interdependencies. This consensus lays the basic foundation for cooperative action on the part of its members. Embedding into this process the time-honed disaster survival experiences gained from the past (as they are socially defined by the community), we find an organizational framework on instant alert and well prepared for dealing with a disaster and coping with its results. This has been most poignant in the generation of emergent norms that have laid dormant during disasters (Neal and Phillips 1995). Some recent research on how disaster-related decisions are made clearly points out how neighbors and neighborhood institutions affect behavior (Kirschenbaum 1996). In fact, there has been a recent glut of papers, books, and even U.S. federal programs that have renewed the efforts to bring disaster management down to the community level (Drabek 1986; FEMA 2000; LACDE 2000). These efforts have built their assumptions on the fact that at the community level policy decisions are already built into the social structure. (See Figure 3.)

The other side of the coin, however, is that certain types of community-based disasters require external intervention that is only available through

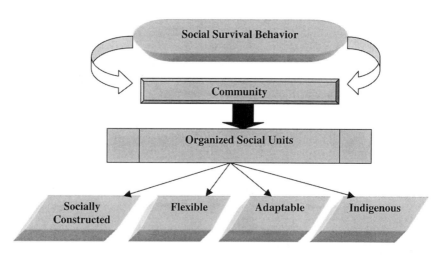

FIGURE 3 Characteristics of community model for community disaster management.

public sector or NGO support (Haider et al. 1991; Haas et al. 1977). Most of these situations are truly mass disasters that affect an entire community and lay waste the social (and economic) basis for coping. It is at this point that outside help is necessary, but as many a case study has shown, external help can create a dependency on the giving organization and may stifle the long-term recovery process. In some cases, the help actually exacerbates the situation, especially in cases of draught and flooding. In others, it prolongs the recovery stage by intervening in the social reconstruction of the community (Britton 1991).

Thus, if we now compare the community and public administration models of disaster management it is possible to discern that no one model is truly ideal. Both are needed in certain circumstances to cope with disasters, yet the overwhelming evidence points toward the community model as being better equipped to socially, psychologically, and economically manage disasters. The major reason for this is that disaster management agencies located within public administrations suffer from all the inadequacies inherent in formal structured bureaucracies. This being the case, why do such disaster management units persist in dominating the field of disaster management? What is even more perplexing is, as I will now demonstrate, that such public sector units have not led to a reduction of disasters or reduced their impact.

MORE AGENCIES, MORE DISASTERS

To put my argument more sharply, the growth and expansion of disaster management in public administrations has not prevented or ameliorated disasters, but may have actually exacerbated them. I have reasoned that the built-in conflict inherent in bureaucratic disaster agencies makes such disaster goal effectiveness both a low priority and difficult to attain, and with the dominance of such public agencies in the field of disaster management, organizational behaviors reflected concern for bureaucratic rather then the victims' (and community) concerns. The results could be simplistically described as *the greater the number of disaster agencies, the more the number and severity of disasters*. To support my contention, I will make use of data collected since the turn of the century (1900–2000). These data of recorded disasters, along with the growth of disaster management agencies over the past century, should clarify this proposition. These disaster data were collected by an international disaster database agency (Centre for Research 2000) and have already been utilized by various researchers to analyze disaster in both Africa (Elberier et al. 1998) and the Arab world (Al-Madhari and Elberier 1996). In our case, the focus will be on long-term trends, to reflect the basic changes in the structure of disaster management since the twentieth century and see how they associate with actual disasters. (See Figure 4–8.)

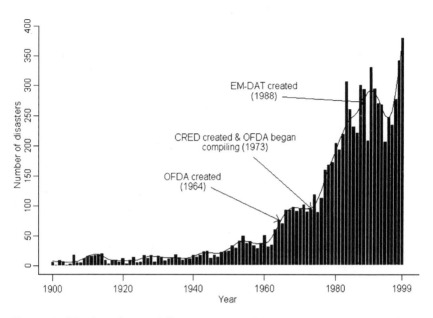

FIGURE 4 Number of natural disasters reported between 1900 and 1999. *Source*: EM-DAT: the OFDA/CRED International Disaster Database (http://www.cred.be).

As we can see in Figure 4, recordings of *natural* disasters* over the last 100 years show them to be a continuously increasing. Until the 1960s, the number recorded has more or less remained stable, between ten to fifty annually. The greatest surge in the number of recorded natural disasters appears after 1960, rising sixfold, from fewer than fifty to 300 to 350 annually by 1999. This pattern fits neatly with the growth of disaster management agencies, which occurred primarily after the 1960s. Does this mean that we are experiencing greater numbers of natural disasters or that disaster management units actually contributed to increased numbers of disasters? The answer to these questions seems to be complex, but has followed a chain of interrelated events.

This chain includes first and foremost how definitions of disasters are generated. At one time, communities socially defined disasters in terms of their communal physical and social survival. Most repetitive natural events

---

* Natural disasters include avalanches, landslides, droughts/famines/food shortages, earthquakes, epidemics/floods, scrub fires, and tropical cyclones/hurricanes/typhoons/storms/volcanoes, as well as cold waves/tsunami/insect infestations.

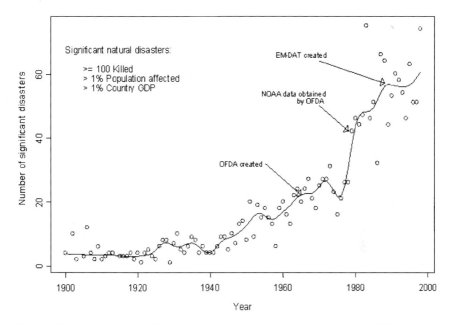

FIGURE 5 Number of significant natural disasters based on numbers killed, population affected, and GDP loss between 1900 and 2000.

would not even be considered or scrutinized as a potential disaster. Annual flooding, hurricanes, and storms were accommodated by various means to assure survival (e.g., not living in flood plains, choosing temperate climates and appropriate (building materials). Only extraordinary, life-threatening events were considered to be disasters. These same "natural" events today are defined as disasters to fit bureaucratic organizational survival needs. In this case, disaster parameters are to a large extent an artificial, bureaucratic, "make-work" definition. Generating disasters justifies an agency's existence, growth, and development. The result, as the data show, has been an increased number of disasters.

Increased numbers of disaster events after the 1960s also involved the interaction of technology with the bureaucratic need for information. Redefining disasters generated *potential* disaster events, but technology provided accessibility to them. With increasing sophistication over time in communication technology, locating bureaucratically defined disasters became more readily accessible and detailed. Weather and communication satellites as well as information and news centers provided the platform for locating and dispensing information on and about disasters. This accessibility was fed by

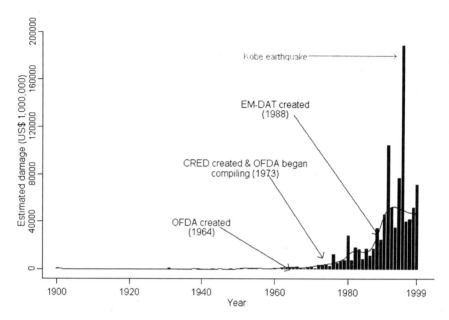

FIGURE 6 Estimated damage reported for natural disasters between 1900 and 1999. *Source*: EM-DAT: the OFDA/CRED International Disaster Database (http://www.cred.be).

the demand for such data by increasing numbers of disaster management units established in public administrations after the 1960s. By redefining disasters, having technological access to them, and utilizing this accessibility to fill data banks, disaster agencies found the goose that laid the golden egg to justify, develop, and increase organizational power. In both cases, this watershed period—the 1960s—seems to mark the point at which the full force of bureaucratic public administration overwhelmed community-based disaster management. As a result, definitions of a disaster developed from within these bureaucratic structures rather than organically from the communities affected. The result, as the data demonstrate, has been an increase in the number of disasters, and as I have pointed out, the number of disasters grew along with the number of such disaster management units created.

SEVERITY AND DISTRIBUTION

To say that this match between increased numbers of reported natural disasters and disaster management units was coincidental or artificially created faces another daunting fact; not only have the number of natural disasters

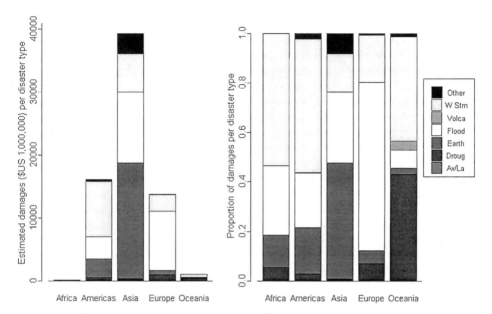

FIGURE 7   Average annual damages from natural disasters during 1989 to 1999 by continent. *Source*: EM-DAT: the OFDA/CRED International Disaster Database (http://www.cred.be).

increased, but also the number that are classified as significant. Taking a long view over the last century, disasters were measured in terms of their severity by using not only such factors as people killed but also numbers affected or their (nation's) economy dislocated. On the basis of these figures, the number of significant natural disasters has steadily grown over the last century. (See Figure 5.) It is clear that on the basis of all three measures of disaster severity the numbers follow a similar upward pattern over time. More specifically, the number of disasters in which at least 100 people were killed, 1% of the population affected, and 1% of the nation's Gross Domestic Product (GDP) lost remained stable until after World War II, and then began to steadily increase from five to ten to approximately sixty annual disaster events. This same pattern holds true when examining disaster severity in terms of estimated damage in financial terms. (See Figure 6.) Ignoring the exceptions (such as the Kobe earthquake in Japan), damages ranged from a few million in the 1960s and to billions by the end of the century. If we add to these data technological disasters (see Chart 1), we see that here, too, the number of technological disasters has increased 200% from 1970 to 1999 and seems to be hovering at over 200 per year for the last ten years.

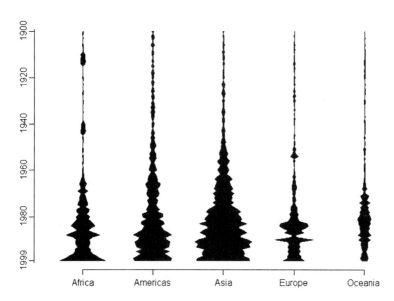

FIGURE 8 The number of natural disasters reported between 1900 and 1999 by continent. *Source*: EM-DAT: the OFDA/CRED International Disaster Database (http://www.cred.be).

MORE PEOPLE—MORE DISASTERS?

Some have argued that this pattern of increased severity and number of disasters can be explained by increasing population size and higher concentrations and density of population distribution. The argument is fairly simple, as it makes sense that when there are more people around and concentrated in smaller areas, disasters will take a greater toll than if people are more spread out. Given the data I have, this question can actually be empirically tested. To do so requires utilizing a statistical procedure called a regression. This provides a summary number that tells us which of a number of possible explanatory variables can best predict changes in a dependent variable. The dependent variable that will be focused on here is the number of reported natural disasters and deaths due to them. In this way, I can control for the impact of levels of economic development on industrial and technological disasters. In this case, there are several important independent explanatory predictor variables involved: the size of the area in which disasters took place, the size of the population involved, and an area's population density.

What made sense in terms of how population and density affected the severity of disasters did not play out in the empirical analysis. When regressing some of these factors against disaster severity measures, there seems to be

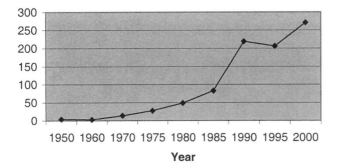

CHART 1   Number of technological disasters reported (1950–2000). *Source*: The Centre for Research on the Epidemiology of Disasters (CRED). Universite Catholique De Louvain, Brussels, Belgium.

a very ambiguous link (Centre for Research 2000). These conclusions are based on reported global disaster events from 1964 until 1998, a period in which numbers of disasters and population grew intensely. The results suggest that area size (km^2 per nation), when regressed against the number of natural disasters and deaths, shows it to be an extremely weak explanatory variable ($r^2 = 0.17, 0.14$). When looking at the impact of population size (country by country), a slightly greater but still very moderate coefficient appears ($r^2 = 0.48, 0.38$). Finally, density (km^2 by country) proves to be a fairly good explanation for the number of natural disasters and only moderate for the number of deaths ($r^2 = 0.76, 0.47$). It thus appears that at least for this time period, area and population size are not very good explanations of either the increased number of natural disasters or their severity as measured in terms of deaths.

DENSITY AND DISTRIBUTION

Density—and only in the case of the number of natural disasters—provides a somewhat better explanation for both the appearance of greater numbers and severe consequences of disasters. This is both good and bad news. While extremely difficult to obtain more detailed data, the density variables may actually reflect concentrations of population that act to trigger and exacerbate such natural disasters as flooding, droughts, food shortages, and epidemics. Concentrations of people in sensitive areas or in areas that are prone to natural disasters encourage them to happen. When you overload an area, strain its resources, or disrupt its natural defenses, you are inviting a disaster. The voluntary migration of people to cities and towns in flood plains and to metropolitan regions located on major earthquake faults are examples of where density and disasters coincide. The classic example of this phenomenon is New Orleans, where engineers devised a series of dams and flood control systems (including massive pumps), originally to offset the flooding from the Mississippi and hurricanes to maintain its commercial harbor. This led to a deterioration of the natural defenses of the city against flooding, but provided more land for building residential homes, leading to an increase in the city's population and of course to a potential disaster. It was estimated that the city would be under twenty feet of water if a hurricane directly hit the city!

If density can act as a fairly good predictor of the number of natural disasters and to some extent its severity, it would then be expected that disaster agencies would be more numerous in areas that are more prone to these types of disasters. What we do know is that disasters are not distributed evenly; no one nation can claim it gets more than its fair share of disasters. On the other hand, public sector disaster management units are not evenly distributed. The data indicate that disasters have affected all major regions of the world. Asia, however, faces the brunt of such disasters, followed in intensity by the Americas, Africa, and Europe (see Figures 7 and 8), but the concentration of public sector disaster management organizations does not seem to be related to the actual distribution of disasters. Europe tops the list, having over a third of these global agencies. North America (the United States, and Canada) houses 20%, Asia 15%, South America 9%, and Australia 8%, with India (5%), Africa (3%), and the Middle East (3%) also contributing to the total. What appears is thus close to an inverse relationship between the frequency of reported natural disasters and the number of disaster management units located in these areas.

Looking at the economic impact of these disasters provides a somewhat less clear relationship between severity and the distribution of disaster agencies. Asia, the Americas, and Europe, in that order, pay the highest price for these disasters. Africa and Oceania have experienced a fairly large number of disasters, but at little economic cost to their economies. In the case of Americas and Europe, the high cost may be due to their higher level of economic development, so that disasters exact a greater price. A flood in India may wipe out 10,000 farms, but at a much lower cost than a similar flood of only 100 farms in the United States. For this reason, the relationship between the number of disaster management agencies and the severity of these disasters may not be as direct as the number of disasters.

On the basis of these empirical data, we thus see two distinct patterns that help clarify if disaster management agencies—in their present bureaucratic form—help or hinder our survival against disasters. Testing the proposition that "the greater the number of disaster agencies, the more the number and severity of disasters," I have found that this proposition generally holds on a global basis but not a regional one. As we have seen, where disasters are more frequent, the number of public sector agencies to prevent, mitigate, and help in recovery is *least*. In terms of the severity of disasters, however, there seems to be support for the notion that despite increases in the number of public sector disaster management units since the 1960s, they have not reduced either the number or the severity of disasters.

CRITICAL ASSESSMENT

These results seem to fly in the face of what we are being told and what governments are doing, especially since September 11, but disasters are a never-ending story, and like most stories have at least two sides to them. I have deliberately chosen to emphasize the side that critically evaluates how public administration disaster management agencies have fared in preventing, mitigating, and coping with disasters. It has been argued that the recent historical maturity of such public administrative apparatuses in the field of disaster management goes counter to the centuries-old disaster survival skills that have been embedded in community social structures. These time-honored abilities to organize and hone community-based skills have been severely disrupted as a result. Partly due to the process of modernization, community-based survival skills have been transferred out of the community into public sector bureaucratic organizations. This process, based on twentieth-century organizational theories, advocated a rational approach to creating and managing service organizations. This, the argument goes, would provide the most effective and efficient means to deal with such phenomena as disasters. If this were the case however, we would expect a decrease in the number and severity of disasters with the increased numbers of such disaster management units.

Due to a built-in conflict between the formal and informal structures in complex organizations, however, such lofty goals are nearly impossible to reach. This is even more true in the bureaucratic-type organizations typified by public administrations. If we dismantle the generic term administration, such built-in conflicts include interagency or departmental rivalries, endemic problems of coordination and cooperation, means–ends reversals, distorted communications networks, and of course power politics. Public sector disaster management units thus may not fit the ideal picture that was proposed by their rational approach founders. The opposite may actually be the case, which led me to reconsider the community model as an alternative approach.

The advantages of the community model for disaster management are first and foremost their pervasiveness throughout the world. They are naturally organized, mainly based on ongoing social networks of individuals, families, and businesses, and they embody a vast historical knowledge of survival skills that become emergent in times of disasters. In most cases, communities are resilient and able to accommodate themselves to disasters. As social units, communities also suffer from internal conflicts and social disruptions that might not make the accommodation process unidirectional or smooth. The difference, however, even with these internal forms of social conflicts, is that it is a community's (and not a bureaucratic organization's) survival that is at jeopardy. The stakeholders all have an intrinsic interest to cooperate even if a disaster event leads to short-term social disruption and conflict within a community. It is only when such disasters are devastating, when all sources of internal help dissipate, that it becomes necessary to ask for external help, but here again, does this mean obtaining help from public sector disaster management units? I (and others) would argue that community-to-community help would be better.

The dominance of public sector administrations, which control disaster management units, makes this argument a moot point, however. Rarely do communities control their own destinies. With this in mind, I reviewed the growth and role of disaster management units in public administrations (both globally and national). These units, on the one hand, represented a way of organizing chaos with the goal of control and prevention. On the other hand they provided job slots for professionals whose background was primarily in the social sciences. In addition to the built-in conflicts within public administrations, disaster management agencies thus had their own special types of conflicts-advocates of the victims versus concerns of the organization. To some degree the "victims" in this conflict have made a comeback. Once again, emphasis was put on the community but not as the generic source of disaster survival. The public sector organization was simply decentralized, down-graded, and renamed as community disaster management.

There are those at the cutting edge of public administration, however, who argue that in NPM lay the foundation for a revival of public administration as a means of tackling society's many problems. They argue to make public administrations responsive to the public they serve, create an accounting system based primarily on private sector performance criteria. It is possible to make these organizational behemoths both efficient and effective. What I have argued—and the data support—is that public administration *at present*, even if we integrate NPM concepts, cannot manage disasters. For one thing, private sector bottom-line profits are not appropriate in public administrations, in which political and social policies are measures of performance. If we integrate NPM performance-based concepts into the bureaucratic vocabulary, however, particularly concepts related to "responsive to" or "facilitating" community needs, it may become possible to improve public sector disaster management. This means measuring public administration performance by the degree to which it provides and facilitates a community to *independently* prepare for, mitigate, and manage its own (potential) disasters. In this way, effective public sector disaster management agencies would be those that received disaster-related shopping lists from local communities and provided top-quality merchandise.

We thus come back to the basic question and proposition I raised. Given all the inherent conflicts in public sector disaster management units, have they helped prevent or at least mitigate disasters? Employing a historic disaster data bank, I investigated this question. My basic argument was that despite the growth in the number of public sector disaster management units, both the number and severity of disasters have increased. Using data covering a 100-year period from 1900 to 2000 and based on reported disasters, I found this to be generally true! A curious association matching increased numbers and severity of disasters with increased numbers of disaster management units emerged. Until the 1960s, the number of both natural and technological disasters remained fairly low and stable. The main point of departure occurred afterward, just when disaster management units started flourishing both in the West and as part of global organizations (U.N.). At this point there was seen a steady, strong increase in both the number and severity of disasters. Even the rationalization that increased numbers of disasters could be traced to vulnerability promulgated by population growth, and increased densities were shown to be empirically problematic.

WHAT'S NEXT?

Can it be said that public sector disaster management units instigate disasters, increase their ferocity, and boost their human and economic costs, or have these disasters been around all the time and only recently been redefined in terms of the public administrations' bureaucratic needs? The answer probably lies somewhere in between, but it is clear that the increasing numbers of disasters associated with the increased numbers of public sector disaster agencies may not be sheer coincidence. The following chapters will tell the detailed story of why this "coincidence" has occurred and in the process strengthen the arguments for community-based disaster management.

2

Preparing for the Worst

A CAMEL OR A HORSE?

Over the past several millenniums we have been adapting ourselves to an ever-changing environment that has been wrought with natural dangers. This adaptation process as a survival mechanism has not been easy. As Malthus pointed out just over 100 years ago, we were kept in check by a trade-off of population growth with food supply and natural disasters. Once the food problem was more or less solved along with major breakthroughs in controlling infectious diseases, we were left with only one "restraint"; namely, natural disasters. Who would have thought then that given our increasing control over our environments such natural disasters would have increased in number and intensity? Could it be that the "checks and balances" that Malthus spoke about are still in place despite all our efforts? Also despite all our efforts, we continue to seek ways of adding to our survival repertoire, and as I have pointed out, we now have organizations whose sole purpose is to minimize damage from various forms of disasters. These organization are for the most part bureaucratic in form and style. More recently, they have been populated by a new cadre of public servants called emergency or disaster managers, from which a whole new world of survival strategies has evolved.

One of these key planning strategies for disaster management agencies is based on imagining *worst-case scenarios* and then preparing for them. Given the type of organizations within which they are formulated, most of these plans are put into drawers or lie on shelves gathering dust. There is nothing extraordinary or new in this way in which public sector disaster management organizations handles their work, but the increased complexity and decreased control over disasters has led to creative, alternative ways to justify the organizations' existence and continuity, namely by re-emphasizing planning, an important organizational function that "makes work" and creates tangible results. Now and then these plans are taken off the shelf and simulated as tabletop games or in rare cases actually tried out in the field with the participation of relevant agencies. In many cases they simply fall apart in actual practice. Take the following example:

> Even a year after the terrorist attack on the Twin Towers, officials were admitting to organizational chaos. "To this day, the Fire Department cannot say just how many firefighters were sent into the towers, and where they died. It lost track of them, in part because some companies did not check in with chiefs. Individual firefighters jumped on overcrowded trucks, against policy. Others ordered off the fire trucks, grabbed rides in cars. Port Authority police officers also flocked to the scene, leaving posts at bridges and tunnels," Chief Morris said. "Ambulance crews converged on Lower Manhattan, leaving much of the city sparsely covered. At one point, the city's Emergency Medical Service had no ambulances for some 400 backed-up emergency calls, its senior officer on duty," Walter Kowalczyk, said later. Fire officials said that just after the collapses, more than 100 ambulances, nearly one-third of the fleet on duty, went to the buildings (*New York Times*, July 7, 2002).

Salient to these courses of action is an undercurrent of interagency jealousies and territorial competition that impinge on how these scenarios are planned. More interesting is how these plans are implemented. A recent example of this was evident in the heated controversy among disaster managers over the place of volunteers and nongovernmental organizations (NGOs) in disaster management. The controversy arose in respect to wildfires that were raging in the United States, but touched on a sensitive nerve that reflected these agencies' territorial imperatives. One E-mail writer involved in this controversy wrote, "NGO's should know their place." Another pointed an accusing finger at the "unauthorized intervention on their [volunteers] part" that "disrupted the efforts of professionals to get on top of things."

The other side of the coin is the restrictions placed on disaster managers by their organizations' internal administrative practices that affect both decision making and performance. Frequent exhortations to follow the lines of command, adhere to the rules, fill out the proper forms, creating positive work summaries, cover oneself, and so on reflect the sometimes onerous weight put on individuals in these organizations. This would be particularly true in the case of a disaster professional whose training and knowledge might lead to a decision that would directly clash with administrative orders. As disaster management agencies are dependent on public sector largess and are wedged into a competitive bureaucratic labyrinth, dreams of comprehensive preparedness for worst-case scenarios are rarely (if ever) fulfilled.

Despite these constrictions on disaster managers, however, there are counterbalancing forces driving organizations to grow, expand, and exercise power. The result, as numerous case studies have shown, can lead to an artificial and sometimes virtual reality in which the well-intentioned plans so laboriously worked on simply breakdown in the face of the demands of actual disasters. As I noted above, look at what happened on 9/11 in New York City when homicidal bombers used commercial aircraft to destroy the Twin Towers. At another level, it can also lead to focusing on creating worst-case scenarios and preparedness plans for events whose likelihood of occurring are close to nil. As one disaster manager justified this practice in a chat group exchange of ideas: "Isn't the job of an emergency manager based on paranoia? We look at any and every possible scenario (the what if's) and develop some type of contingency plan for the just in case. So, what some call paranoia, I call preparedness" (Maury, May 2002).

All these efforts made within the framework of public sector disaster agencies have been justified as a means to save human lives, yet given what we know about organizational dynamics, goals can sometimes be marginalized while the administrative means can become ends in themselves. Instead of goals directed toward preparing for, mitigating, or preventing disasters, the means—all the committees, interdisciplinary study teams, and technological facilitators—become the prime focus of the organization. If and when this happens there is the danger that public image and political expedience might overshadow professional competence; wide-screen Power Point projectors replace critical analysis. One possible result, as many organizational researchers have pointed out, will be that resources and efforts are channeled into enhancing the organization rather than attaining goals set up to save lives. What have we attained? Nothing less than the proverbial camel that was planned as a horse—worst-case disaster scenarios made to fit the demands of the bureaucratic organization. The result is a "compromised" preparedness or mitigation plan. In short order, preparing for a worst-case plan is by organizational default transformed at the best of times into a "medium level"-case disaster plan! At the worst of times it is transformed into a useless set of directives. While this is perhaps a great accomplishment within the constraints put on public sector disaster managers, in the end the potential victims are the ones who pay the bill in terms of life and property.

SHAKY GROUNDS

The actual basis for creating a preparedness plan for a worst-case scenario tends to lean on very shaky and sometime erroneous theoretical and empirical fundamentals. Ask ten disaster managers what preparedness means to them and you will probably get fifteen different answers. In fact, as I will shortly point out, this is actually the case! This inconsistency is usually not taken seriously, however, and at most times is dismissed as the province of researchers and theoreticians who have little practical experience with the "real world." This "divide" between researchers and practitioners is more artificial then real and reflects an ostrichlike attitude on the part of practitioners to face difficult conceptual issues that have direct practical implications. Such an attitude is legitimized by numerous case studies that are brought in to highlight real-world situations and point out what are considered critical problem areas despite their inherent discrepancies and disputed application. An example of this is the emphasis on "communications." Take the following piece of information that was transmitted on the International Association of Emergency Managers (IAEM) E-mail service carrier recently:

> The ARRL [Amateur Radio Relay League] will receive a $181,900 homeland security grant from the US government to train Amateur Radio operators in emergency communications. In my urban county we have responders on VHF, UHF and 800, and almost no one have the capacity to talk to everyone. (In fact, I can't really think of ANYONE that can!) (IAEM E-mail June 2002).

It is assumed that these amateur volunteer radio operators will act as an alternative means of communicating when normal paths are blocked or destroyed, but communicating with whom, themselves? To warn people of impending disasters? Not likely. More probably they will act as substitutes for officials and will pass on information among the various disaster agencies. Just look at what one disaster manager says about the problems of talking to one another! While there is certainly an acute need to coordinate disaster operations, there may be an even greater need to communicate with the victims of disasters, both in terms of warnings and vital information for their well-being and safety, yet the "practical" is nothing less than ethnocentric—directed entirely toward the needs of the disaster organizations. It ignores the victims, and by doing so, it also ignores the research that has been done on the social and psychological aspects of warning systems and informal communications networks, all of which have proven to be significant in reducing loss of life and property (Burkhart 1994). Is practical thus really practical?

Not surprisingly, most of the problem areas that are consistently brought up by disaster managers are related to organizational issues, especially interorganizational conflicts and problems related to coordination. Take the following reaction to the purse strings being opened by the U.S. government: "Any one who has been observing the largess of the public purse in Washington already knows that this is flowing from multiple agencies. Some times different division of the same department with conflicting requirements attached to funds, want to accomplish the same thing" (IAEM E-mail June 2002).

Not unexpectedly, these informal anecdotes are supported by case study analyses. Unfortunately, such remarks among the expert disaster management profession are followed by simplistic platitudes and advice concerning how to rectify basic organizational processes, all of which is based on a limited understanding of these processes. For example

> The current tunnel vision that exists in the federal government is its usual reactionary attitude to any event. That is pass legislation and throw money at it. Don't take the time to really analyze what the situations are and what should be done, instead throw money first and then figure out what to do.

> I remember those days when the emphasis was on Civil Defense, and the agency was overly occupied by overly-military oriented managers...we do not want to go back that way, believe me.

In addition, such statements as the need for better coordination and communications appear again and again, yet how to actually bring them about comes down to very personal experiences, as expressed in such statements as "in my organization we do such and such—" and "I know of someone who said that—" or "from my experience—."

More disturbing is that rarely if ever do we find critical thinking about the basic concepts that are the foundation for increasing the effectiveness of disaster management. The original goal of preparing for the worst-case scenario seems to take a back seat. What is even more disturbing is that the meaning of core concepts in disaster management, in particular the concept of "preparedness," is taken for granted; there is no universal consensual agreement as to its meaning. Without first understanding the conceptual and empirical basis of what preparedness is, disaster managers and researchers will continue to struggle with all kinds of organizational solutions that under the right conditions might be of some help but uner the wrong conditions may exacerbate the suffering of people and reduce survival chances.

WHAT IS PREPAREDNESS?

For a considerable time, perhaps out of convenience, both disaster researchers and managers have relied heavily on accepted but empirically ambivalent disaster management concepts. These concepts have guided practitioners and have been sanctified in the classic disaster management foursome code of *mitigation, preparedness, response, and recovery* (Lindell and Perry 1992). Without a doubt, preparedness appears to be the key to opening up the disaster black box precisely because of its impact on activities linked to mitigation, response, and recovery. This makes historical sense, as preparedness evolved from generic social behaviors based on group adaptive survival patterns in the face of natural disasters over thousands of years (Kirschenbaum 2001b). Today, however, the concept of preparedness has been transformed from community survival patterns into the rhetoric of formalized bureaucratic organizations (Tierney 1989; Smith and Dowell 2000). Not surprisingly, the use of the concept by disaster managers has come to reflect organizational activity framed by syntax defined by public administration goals (Sylves and Waugh 1996; Casper 1985). For example, the use of the term preparation plans usually relates to how well the disaster agency is prepared and *not* the potential disaster victims. Just take the following proposal suggesting guidelines for chief administrators to prepare their localities. Notice that all the effort is directed toward making the organizational structure more effective! Not a word is directed toward how this increased effectiveness will be of benefit to the potential disaster victims.

> Preparation Guidelines is a self-assessment tool that was prepared especially for use by the chief administrator (elected or appointed) of a local government...it consisted of reviewing the operations of more than 300 local government emergency management agencies, and developing dozens of on-site case studies of local government emergency management operations. The end result was the development of 20 key characteristics that were found to contribute to an effective local government emergency management organizational structure (IAEM E-mail).

SURVIVING

This emphasis on the "organization" was not always the case, however. The concept of preparedness has its origins in culturally bound survival behavior, usually linked to specific locations and influenced by a community's social structure. Organizing was an integral part of preparing, but there is no getting away from the fact that a large part of these survival behaviors developed in tandem with environmental and climatic conditions, leading to the peculiar form of disaster behavior. For example, finding water became a specialty of desert dwellers, fishing for those living near the sea, farming for those living on rich land, and hunting for those whose survival depended on accommodating themselves to forest areas. As such, being prepared, as an integral part of the survival process, would mean different things to different peoples in different cultures (DeVries 1995). For those living in Iceland, preparing would mean being ready for snow avalanches, in India being ready for floods, in Japan being ready for earthquakes, and so on. If we extrapolate today, disaster organizations are another stage in the adaptive process, and we, the potential victims of disasters, now have to find ways to not only survive disasters but also the organizations that are designated to deal with them.

The likelihood that the concept of preparedness reflects both environmental and cultural diversity is reflected by its many shades of definitions. For us, living in what seems to be an increasingly urbanized world and inundated by the by-products of industry and increased competition for basic life-giving raw materials, survival has taken on a new face; namely, new types of disasters. A few thousand years ago, the only type of technological or industrial disasters related to perhaps simple types of cottage manufacturing—a loom breaking or dyeing material spilling. Today, the situation has radically changed; we face nuclear reactor meltdowns and accidental release of toxic gases or plague materials along with the natural disasters that have been with us since time immemorial. The importance of preparedness still remains with us, however. As one disaster manager recently acknowledged from an organizational perspective: "I have to say that the time to study bioterrorism is not after a lethal outbreak occurs, but beforehand. Preparedness is not response, but the ability to respond" (Tom, June 2002).

EVOLVING MEANINGS

For this reason, the meaning of preparedness has evolved from its organic origins in the community to bureaucratic organizations. Today, for example, preparedness is being defined in "cookbook" fashion (Charles and Kim 1988) as well as in terms of physical objects or activities (FEMA 2000). In some cases preparedness is synonymous with disaster scenario plans and their concomitant logistic or technical ramifications (Kelly 1995). For all these various definitions—which reflect our own survival challenges-rarely has this generic concept been framed as part of a larger theoretical paradigm. What is clearly missing is a consensual agreement among researchers and by implication managers of the conceptual definition of preparedness, one dictated by empirically based theory and *not* bureaucratic expediency.

A cursory view of the scientific literature shows that researchers have indeed sought a theoretical basis for defining preparedness. For example, Perry et al. (1981) have argued that preparedness depends on a community's level of recognizing danger and its potential risk to lives and property. Others have sought a more empirical basis of preparedness (Gillespie and Streeter 1987), pointing out the cultural bias inherent in the meaning of preparedness (Quarantelli 1986) and even differentiating its perception from actual activities associated with it (Russell et al. 1995). Some researchers have found links between levels of preparedness and individual sociodemographic characteristics, social networks, and past disaster-related experiences (Lindell and Perry 2000). Yet I would like to suggest that all these attempts to define and measure preparedness still remain unsatisfactory, as they are particularistic in nature, reflecting one discipline or another and imbedded in Western thought and formalistic organizational forms. If so, where do we start to unravel the meaning of preparedness?

WHOSE DEFINITION?

A glance at the Oxford English Dictionary's definition of preparedness is a telling story in itself. It formally defines the concept as to make ready, put together, and equip both things and people. The impression (from other definitions found in various other dictionaries) is that the concept originated as a military term stressing the level of organizational readiness to defend oneself or to attack an enemy. It is not surprising, then, that what has evolved today are definitions that are mainly dominated by organizational concerns flowing from rational bureaucratic structures and to some extent with small group social networking processes (Quarantelli 1985).

It is difficult to disregard the etiology of disaster preparedness, as it has led in its wake to a variety of definitional approaches. Most are categorized in terms of *attributes* of preparedness, namely its physical or technological components. As attributes, preparedness is defined in terms of standardized "lists" of goods, materials, and services aimed at preparing for a variety of disasters (FEMA 2000). From this come all those "how to be prepared in case of" suggestions that are widely published in both the popular press and Web sites; so if you live in a high-risk tornado area, dig a deep hole and build yourself an underground shelter. Also, keep water, food, batteries, a radio, and a first aid kit handy. These attributes are synonymous with the meaning and measure of preparedness.

Others have operationalized preparedness in terms of a format dictated by scenario planning. The "what if" is followed by "what to do," and finally by "how to do it." This type of planning is endemic among disaster managers, as it allows them to see ahead and be prepared for all contingencies. This perspective favors planning for the worst-case scenario, defining these plans as an integral part of preparedness (Linkie 2000). The what-if and how-can planning scenario has even evolved as a means of increasing the levels of "protected, self-reliant, and sustainable communities" (Paton et al. 2000). Simulations and training exercises have become the hallmark of this perspective, with built-in contingency scenarios and alternative plans for multifaceted disasters. In some cases, it also includes initiating predisaster activities (e.g., simulation/training exercises), and not only mitigating the sources of disaster (Tarn et al. 1998; Nja-Ove 1997). Take, for example, the following advice given during an open discussion of the role that intelligence against terrorism should play for disaster managers.

> The nature of emergency management in dealing with terrorism is largely responsive, rather than proactive. It is difficult to begin mitigation activities when one does not know what to mitigate against. We know what to do with a tornado, hurricane, earthquake, aircraft crash, etc. The more we learn about the numerous groups, what they target, and their attack methods will allow us to create better prevention techniques that are applicable on the local scale. Raw intelligence serves this purpose as what is done overseas normally can be done just as easily over here (E-mail, IAEM, August 8, 2002).

An additional group of definitions stresses the social–psychological processes involved in preparedness (Enders 2001). Preparedness is defined as concrete behaviors evolving from perceptions that individuals and groups develop in the face of disasters; it is ongoing dynamic social process influenced by both cognitive and group-related factors. In fact, this perspective has been closely associated with the adaptive mechanisms that we as humans have employed over time to create many of the survival disaster behaviors that are part and parcel of our daily lives. It is closely related to those disaster researchers who define preparedness in terms of socially based events. Understanding and predicting individual–small group interactions and relationships is, in their perspective, a means toward understanding the meaning of disaster preparedness (Norris et al. 1999). In short, they argue that disasters are really social constructs from which we take our cue about how to prepare for them. Here, an emphasis has been on awareness, risk perceptions, motivation, interactive social networks, and leadership (Tatano 1999; Britkov and Sergeev 1998). This broad band of social phenomena associated with how preparedness is defined is remarkable for the fact that it refocuses attention onto the potential victims rather than on the organizations.

Researchers who favor technological meanings of preparedness stress attributes associated with macrolevel technological infrastructure as power sources, backup systems, communications, logistics (Fiedrich et al. 2000; Heaney et al. 2000), and integrated information and computer technology systems (Jayaraman and Chandrosekhar, 1997). Anything technological is considered the basis for defining what it is to be prepared. This approach is quite utilitarian in that it does not make the pretense to define preparedness, and only contributes another component to its definition. In addition, who could be *against* technology? It provides, on the surface, an "easy fix" to complex human-based problems and is extremely well matched for organizational solutions. As one of the most often heard complaints among disaster managers is the problem with communications, what better way to solve this than by newer, faster, and more expensive communications equipment! Let me give you just a few examples of the types of technological toys that disaster managers seek.

> Target Notification services will provide residents with, "immediate and timely notification of emergencies such as natural disasters, missing children, or civil disturbances".... serving nearly 3 million telephone numbers. The service can be activated using a Web-based interface or by telephoning a call center.

> Emergency Mobile (EM) vehicle will be used in a support capacity. This vehicle would be equipped with an onboard computer, fax, printer, wireless Internet connection w/ a hardwire backup, multiple channel radio(s), portable radios, battery powered hand lights, and the Township EOC. I would also include duplicate copies of reference materials from our Emergency Operations Center.

DOUBLE MEANINGS

These diverse definitions of preparedness not only mean a lack of consensus as to its meaning, but in practical terms confusion in implementing preparedness behaviors for saving lives and property. *Depending upon which definition is chosen, the choice of preparedness measures can result in different empirical inputs and expected behavioral outcomes.* Simply put the choice of one definition over another predisposes what we look for (inputs) and therefore affects what we will find (output). For example, preparation for fires in urban high-rise buildings has led to the installation of fire doors on and between floors. This technical preparedness solution is only good, however, if people keep the fire doors closed! By fire safety standards, therefore, the building is safe as it is prepared for the outbreak of fire, but if we define fire preparedness in terms of human behavior, it should include an awareness of the need to close the fire door, a familiarity with the escape routes, and other avoidance measures (smoke) that define preparedness. The existence of fire doors thus does not necessarily mean high levels of fire preparedness for the behavioral scientist. The troubling outcome here is that for the fire department the building is safe. For the disaster manager who chooses another definition of preparedness, the evaluation of safety might be different.

There are other areas in which preparedness definitions differ. Take warning systems, for example Here, too, it may depend on the eye of the beholder, be it internal organizational warnings or external warnings to potential disaster victims. Study after study has shown that despite all the technological advancement in warning systems—be they sirens, mobile units, radio, or TV or Internet links—they are far from effective. Take the following typical internal organizational warning communications problem as an example:

> The problem with "trickle down" is not limited to just "local yokels." There are some institutional problems within the FBI. The local office found during the Fall, Winter of 01–02 they could find out faster from CNN that the Atty Gen or someone else was releasing information than they could from internal channels (Eric, August 8, 2002).

At the other end of the spectrum are communicating warnings to evacuate in the face of floods and hurricanes, fires, and toxic spills. Here, too such warnings have been consistently ignored by fairly large numbers of those in danger (at least as determined by authorities!). Seeking a solution has led concerned people to expand the meaning of what a warning is.

> ... (conference) unanimously called for the creation of a public–private partnership aimed at improving the delivery of timely and accurate emergency information to people at risk. The mission of the new organization is to improve the delivery of warnings and emergency information to the public through better education, research, standards creation and policy recommendations (IAEM, E-mail).

MISPLACED CONCRETENESS

From a strictly methodological point of view, different definitions have a direct consequence on the external validity and internal reliability of the concept. More simply, does preparedness mean what it is supposed to mean to everybody? Is its meaning consistent for everyone? With the variety of definitions being claimed as sacred, it is no wonder that the concept of preparedness is in deep methodological trouble. Anyone can stake a claim as to what preparedness is about, do research, and come to conclusions, but with no consensus on its meaning and measure, it is virtually impossible to compare studies or results, as each is based on a different measure. There is also the risk of falling into the trap of what is called "misplaced concreteness" if preparedness is composed of a number of independent subcategories. Emphasis will be put on one aspect of preparedness to the detriment of the others, leading to a biased set of results and conclusions.

Let me take an example from the disaster literature, namely the term community, which has numerous nuances and meanings, all of which contribute to its general meaning (e.g., a physical area, a social area, a psychological mental map, or a group of people with common interests). Choosing one or more of these subdefinitions would mean only getting a small piece of the general concept. The result would be an emphasis on one set of empirical predictor variables (e.g., a physical area) to the exclusion of other(s). This would consequently narrow the meaning of the concept and a priori determine its empirical outcome. In our example, my definition based on the physical assets of a community would exclude social networks, co-operative use of resources, and so on, missing out on a whole range of social processes that are an integral part of community life and disaster behaviors. This is also true for preparedness. In practical terms, disaster practitioners may have to face the critical issue of choosing what represents preparedness, as each choice has its own organizational and behavioral consequences and what they choose will have a direct impact on our lives. The question I raise now is why not find a compatible definition that is agreeable to everyone?

A BETTER MOUSETRAP

The argument that preparedness has multiple meanings and is measured in different ways does not excuse us from seeking what some people like to call a better mousetrap. To invent that better mousetrap, however, requires two basic and somewhat novel methodologies. Both are based on a lot of common sense but are backed up by empirically derived data and sophisticated statistical analysis. First and foremost, it should be clear that like most generalized concepts the concept of preparedness, which will determine the effectiveness of a worst-case plan, needs some pulling apart. To do so there is need for a working model that disaggregates the general construct of pre-paredness into initial intuitive conceptual categories. Taking the research literature as a guide here, four such categories are obvious, namely those based on the (1) physical attributes, (2) emphasis on knowledge, (3) planning component, and (4) aspects of protective behavior of preparedness. This approach, building on findings of previous empirical research (Gillespie and Streeter 1987; Russell et al. 1995), allows for the addition of other alternative subcategories of meanings. For example, it is possible to theoretically include such facets as access to technology, communications networks, and social psychological perceptions. For the moment, however, let us relate to the four named above.

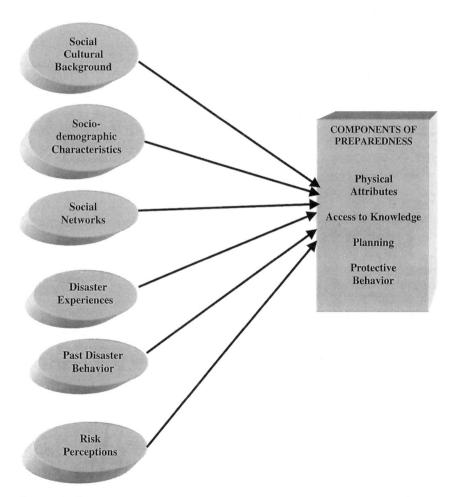

FIGURE 1 Proposed theoretical working model of preparedness.

The disaster literature further suggests there are at least six major categories of independent predictor variables. Such variables provide individuals with alterative generic social sources of reference which guide them in developing their definitions of preparedness. Choices, for example, may be due to individual personal preferences. It is very possible that thing-oriented types of persons, for example, see preparedness in its full-blown technical glory. For those who are "people-oriented" among us, we might perceive of preparedness in a more social way, one that connects us to the opinions of our family and neighbors. As our working model suggests, other considerations must be taken into account, particularly the social/cultural background or setting within which we define preparedness. Concern for avalanches in Iceland, for example, may not evoke the same preparedness concerns as Japanese fears of earthquakes. Similarly, situations of war and terror cannot be equated to naturally occurring disasters. In addition are those elements that reflect who we are, our sociodemographic characteristics, the intensity and types of social networks we are engaged in, our past experiences with emergency and/or disaster situations, and how we perceive of the risks involved in various types of disasters. All these (and probably more) find their way into how we define and perceive of preparedness. (See Figure 1.)

GENERATING PROPOSITIONS

A series of propositions can be generated from the suggested working model. Propositions are a way in which serious people explore possible relationships between variables. For example, take the following proposition. Anyone having been physically exposed to the horrific World Trade Center terrorist attack will be more prepared for such attacks in the future than those who only heard of it secondhand. If I find this to be true, I would then want to know to what degree it is true or if there are other circumstances that could moderate this relationship, such as the age or sex of the person; perhaps women are more affected than men, or younger persons more than older ones.

The basic assumption upon which these propositions are based is that preparedness has discrete subcategories of measurable meanings, so that when a person says he or she is prepared, their preparedness refers to very specific kinds of behaviors. For example, Mr. X says he is prepared for the next terrorist attack on the United States, as he has purchased an automatic weapon. Mr. Y also says he is prepared, but he has prepared a special room against biochemical weapons. This same type of problem of consensual definitions also plagues scientists. Previous research has commonly examined preparedness as a single overall construct (Larrson and Enander 1997) or divided it into an activity or perception (Russel, et al. 1995), making it extremely difficult to set in place specific propositions for the hypothesized subcategory components. Under the *assumption* that each of the preparedness constructs has a distinct set of predictors, however, I can go out on a limb and suggest a series of propositions that can be tested. The advantage here is that these propositions also provide an analytical path to look more closely at the construct of preparedness, thereby creating a platform for an agreed-upon universal definition.

The propositions are fairly straightforward. What is not as clear is the direction or strength of the associations. It is expected, for instance, that basic sociodemographic characteristics of the household sample heads, such as age, education, and income level, will have a dissimilar impact on each subcomponent of preparedness. To get this point across let me provide a simple example. Its possible to argue on the one hand that older people will be more prepared than younger ones as the result of their greater life experiences, making them more wary of what could possibly happen. Of course, it could go the opposite way, with younger persons being more prepared since they have much more to lose and are more cognizant of what's going on around them. This kind of duality in the direction of the propositions applies to all these variables and can only be resolved through an empirical evaluation.

In addition, the social networks that we accumulate throughout our lives through interactions with family, friends, and neighbors certainly influence how we view the world and potential disasters. Also accounted for is our previous involvement in actual disaster preparations or having had the misfortunate of experiencing a disaster. Finally, there is the individual's evaluation of the perceived risk of a disaster actually occurring, which might vary for one or more components of preparedness.

WHOSE PREPAREDNESS?

The adage that *one's elixir may be another's poison* also applies to construct building. In this context, preparedness as perceived by disaster managers is probably a far cry from that of those who find themselves at the receiving end of disasters. Why the difference? The answer is complex, but has to do with the antecedents of how chaos is organized. Disaster managers are "organizational men"; they are practitioners working in a public sector bureaucratic and formalistic organization. They cannot help but be influenced by their organization's milieu. This includes their perceptions, attitudes, and organizational behavior toward disaster management, and affects how they see the world of disaster. It defines for them what preparedness is, but only in organizational terms. It should therefore come as little surprise that the definition of preparedness by disaster managers may differ substantially from that of ordinary citizens. Just look at what was said at a recent meeting of such disaster managers.

> At a meeting of hundreds of emergency management professionals from 35 states and several other countries. . . . Particularly troubling, said Thomas Von Essen, the city's former fire commissioner, was that politicians who should be working to prevent or respond to the next terrorist attack were instead engaged in a political fight in Washington over the events leading up to the last one (New York Times, May 22, 2002).

For us, the potential victims of disasters, being prepared may have a lot to do with how we perceive the risks that disasters will actually occur. If we feel that they are high, we may do a number of things. We might go out and get those things that will make us better prepared, take the time to get better informed, or discuss the issue with family members, but if we think the risks are low, we might simply put off doing anything. Not so with disaster managers, whose livelihood depends on preparing their organizations for disasters. What they perceive to be preparedness for the worst case may not be what the rest of us see as relevant; they tend to focus on the needs of the organization. Whose preparedness definition should we then accept? To answer this question, let us take advantage of a unique field study that was done in Israel but has extreme relevance to the issue of preparedness.

ANSWERS FROM THE FIELD

The debate of who determines preparedness was solved in a novel way; both groups were asked. This included a focus group panel of Israel's Home Front Command officials—the disaster management experts—and the potential disaster victims, who were interviewed in a longitudinal field study.[1] Surveys of this kind have been going on in different forms in Israel since the Gulf War (Kirschenbaum 2001a). This field survey was unique, as it was founded on the real-time behavior and attitudes of the Israeli public toward its preparation for a variety of disasters, including nonconventional biochemical attacks. The initiative for the study was the realistic assessment by Israeli policy makers that the "next" war would be primarily against the civilian population. This assessment was borne out in the Gulf War and in the Palestinian use of homicide terror against civilian populations.

Along with the field study was a focus group panel composed of top-ranking officials in the Home Front Command. This organization is Israel's official disaster management agency. It was originally established (under a different name) in 1949, and is organized along the lines of the Israeli defense forces. It is a national organization manned primarily by military personnel whose specific goals are designed to protect the civilian population from natural, technological, or war- or terrorist-related acts. Its stated goals are clearly defined in law. Since its inception in 1993 it has undergone several stages of reorganization, with the latest making it the prime service supplier of plans, products, equipment, and social–psychological services to the civilian population in case of disasters and emergencies. It is a highly visible and transparent organization, as it has had to deal with a constant flow of emergencies and war- or terrorist-related acts over the last fifty years. This visibility has intensified since the Gulf War, opening up the Home Front Command to public scrutiny and criticism. Its core members are obligatory army service recruits as well as short-term reservists. In accordance with its military command approach, training and real-time simulations include the participation of the civilian population and coordination with a broad range of other emergency organizations. Unlike local municipal disaster management agencies, the Home Front Command is mandated by law as the overall national command organization in cases of national emergencies. As such, it is responsible for preparation and mitigation as well as actual recovery after disasters.

Comparing the Israel Home Front Command with other public sector disaster agencies in terms of its organizational structure and mission shows it to be very similar to other such agencies all over the world. A glance at such organizations in most of the European countries, China, Southeast Asia, and the United States shows them to be quite similar in structure and goals. Some of these disaster agencies are more complex and formalistic than others, reflecting a distinct military chain of command. Some are more responsive to their stakeholders, while others are more politically oriented. Despite these differences, however, they all share a common administrative structure typical to bureaucratic organizations in the public sector. It is for this reason that the Israel Home Front Command can easily be employed as a good example of public sector disaster organization.

SOURCES OF A DEFINITION

If preparedness meant so many things to so many persons, it was clear that to establish at least *face validity* of the concept it was absolutely necessary to make use of what disaster managers as well as the potential disaster victims think about the concept. Face validity is a technical term that says on the whole that a concept must have a consensual meaning among various individuals for it to be useful tool. This being the case, both of these groups' (expert disaster managers and general population) responses could then be utilized to provide a comprehensive theoretical list of preparedness meaning-measures. As part of this approach, I sought the official definitions of disaster agencies so that all in all there was a inclusive list from the research literature, disaster agencies, and disaster manager experts. In its most generalized form, *preparedness was nominally defined as intent by an individual, the community, or the disaster agency to minimize death, injury, and economic loss.* On the other side of the coin were the potential victims of a disaster event. How they defined preparedness will be examined in more detail in a moment. First let us concentrate on what the scientific literature has to say and then on how both the disaster agencies and managers conceive of appropriate definitions of preparedness. (See Figure 2.)

The first stage in seeking face validity of preparedness was based on a review of the disaster literature. The *research literature* stressed either a psychological or sociological approach (Larsson and Enander 1997) that emphasized either individual "mental states" (e.g., personal meaningfulness, societal commitment) or community-level social group collective behaviors (Buckland and Rahman 1999). The third approach in this trilogy of potential definitions was found at Web sites of disaster management *organizations.* Here the concept of preparedness was dominated by definitions aligned to their organizational needs as public sector agencies involved in disaster management [such as Federal Emergency Management Agency (FEMA) and

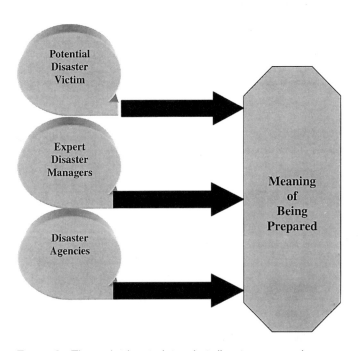

FIGURE 2 The major inputs into what disaster preparedness means.

Swedish Emergency Management Agency (SEMA)]. As I have already pointed out, most disaster management agency definitions showed preparedness to mean lists of what to do or what to have available if an emergency occurred. Emphasis in the lists seemed to match the types and frequency of disasters prevalent under the auspices of each organization. This observation was extremely interesting, as it pointed out the local orientation of these agencies toward what they thought to be important components of preparedness. A cursory analysis of these lists showed them to be heavily weighted in terms of physical protective items, with some lists including planning and family activities. Such definitions are actually double-edged, as they also reflect organizational as well as client needs (Kirschenbaum 2002).

EXPERTS' VIEWPOINTS

A second avenue used to obtain a consistent face value definition of preparedness was sought through a focus group panel of disaster management experts. Utilizing a sample (of forty) of Israel's national Home Front Command officer corps who are directly involved in the planning and operation of emergency and disaster management, a series of focus group panels were conducted. These officers are equivalent to vice presidents in private sector organizations and are responsible for the planning, operation, and implementation of the Home Front Command goals. Given their intimate knowledge and practitioner perspective of disaster management, they were chosen as experts on the subject of preparedness. As experts, they were provided an open-ended question asking each to define preparedness. A second round of questionnaires focused on the actions that civilians should take to be prepared. Both were analyzed by content analysis techniques.

The results of the content analysis of the Home Front Command officers to the open question of *their* definition of preparedness resulted in a mix emphasis. On the one hand, there was the nominal "state-of-mind" definition suggested by psychologists (Asgary and Willis 1997), and on the other, the practical organizational emphasis on protective assets as described by disaster agencies (Lalo 2000; Rubin 1985). The results revealed that close to half (48%) of the forty disaster manager officers defined preparedness in terms of its mental and emotional content. Two-fifths (43%) independently listed having proper equipment and other means to protect oneself and one's family. Less than a third (28%) named having useful information and appropriate skills, a quarter (25%) cited a strong belief in government actions and decisions, another quarter (23%) referred to an awareness of risk and an ability to cope, and only a small number (13%) remarked about the link between preparedness and the government's ability to protect its citizens.

When asked about what citizens should do to prepare themselves—an indirect means of ascertaining preparedness—the results reflected Israel's major concerns in light of the Gulf War, when thirty-nine intercontinental missiles with potential biochemical warheads struck civilian targets. In a sense, these responses reflect some of their own personal understanding of what preparedness is, but mainly their practitioner's viewpoint of what is necessary to save lives and property. More important, as I will talk about in Chapter 5, these responses really reflected how they assessed the risks of different disasters actually occurring.

As a first step, the disaster managers were given an open statement to note down what the population should do to be prepared. Adding these responses up, I saw that what was most noted was that families had a well-maintained and operational (bomb, security) shelter (73% noted this) and access to a radio or television (73%). In addition, the civilian population should have available means to counteract biochemical agents if attacked and access to other means of communications, such as a telephone (68% and 65% ranked extremely important). Less important was the need to prepare a "survival kit" (50%), a family emergency action plan (45%), ways of being updated on the situation (45%), knowledge of the warning systems (43%), a plan in case the family splits up (40%), and an evacuation plan (28%). As these disaster managers say, having a strong shelter and access to communications are key to survival.

The second step was to ask them to then *rank* these items in terms of their importance (Table 1). The results in Table 1 give a much more refined

TABLE 1 Response of Disaster Managers in Ranking by Most Important "What Actions Civilians Should Take in Preparing for Emergency Situations"

Suggested action	Percent
Have protective mask kit available	73%
Seek knowledge and awareness of situation	38%
Have and maintain an equipped shelter	33%
Be mentally prepared	20%
Have family emergency kit	18%
Have a family emergency plan	18%
Participate in neighborhood exercises	8%
Follow orders of home front officers	8%
Keep emergency telephone numbers	5%
Have family practice emergency plan	3%

Note: N = 40.

and definitive view of what they think the population should do to be prepared. The most important ranked item was to be prepared for an unconventional biochemical attack. Seventy-three percent ranked having a gas mask kit available as extremely important! Half this amount felt that keeping up to date with the situation and abreast of new protective equipment (38%) was extremely important. What we were told by these managers about this issue was that they saw keeping abreast of new and better protective equipment against biochemical warfare as important. Again they emphasized the risks of an unconventional attack. Maintaining a bomb shelter in good working order (33%) and being "mentally" prepared came next in importance. A list of specific practical items such as keeping emergency numbers at hand followed this. These rankings reflect what kinds of disasters these experts expect to happen, otherwise why would they suggest that the population be especially prepared for them? What is crucial to understand is that this pattern of responses reflects personal feelings mixed in with those dictated by their organizational affiliation.

A MASTER LIST

These responses as well as those from disaster agencies and the research literature provided the raw material to generate a master list of alternative meaning-measures of preparedness. As a first step to eliminate redundant measures, a set of general guidelines was followed. In a case in which there was an overlap in the objectives, the measures were aggregated (e.g., flashlight batteries and radio batteries), and certain measures were eliminated that were either overly specialized (e.g., have available a satellite dish or barometer) or too general (e.g., try to keep assessed of potential threats). This reduced number of proposed meaning-measures of preparedness was then presented to another smaller group of independent disaster experts (three) to have them re-evaluate the items as an additional assurance of this reduced list's face validity. The final list contained thirty items, reflecting general preparedness of *households* as well as more specific measures appropriate to Israeli concern for unconventional warfare. (See Figure 3.)

These thirty items of alternative meaning-measures of preparedness fell into seven general categories. These included a general preparedness set of items, involving mainly the family, especially family-based discussions of what to do in case of an emergency. The second category focused on the availability of protective gear. In the case at hand, given Israel's experience with ballistic missiles with potential biochemical warheads, this meant gas mask kits. The third and fourth categories referred to having access both to items related to protective bomb-resistant shelters (either public or private)

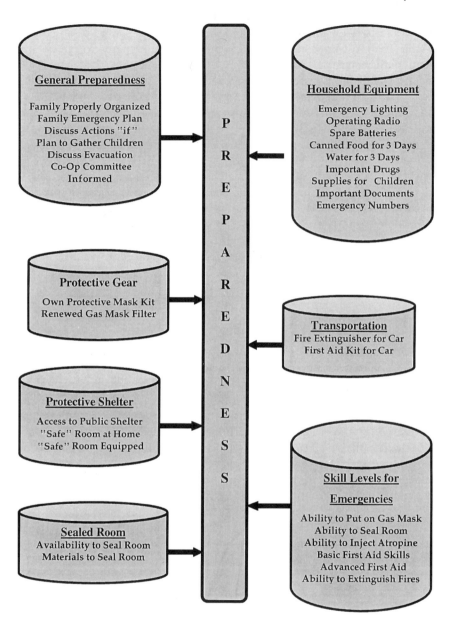

Figure 3 Preparedness measures based on disaster agency and disaster manager judgments.

and to a sealed room in case of a gas or biological attack. To this can be added a long list of household equipment, including enough water for three days, extra batteries, food, and even drugs. An interesting separate category consisted of two items associated with automobile transportation (most likely relevant in case of evacuation) and finally with skill levels in case of emergencies. This last category of what preparedness means is interesting, as it stresses immediate types of actions that can be taken before and after something happens. Again we see that concern for biochemical and conventional attacks are the key items.

The list attests to a broad range of meanings. It became clear from a reading of this set of preparedness measures that differences in emphasis would likely occur if utilizing a panel of disaster managers or public sector agencies (federal or local) whose concerns were, for example, earthquakes, floods, or tornados. Despite these potential differences, an underlying theme is *family unit preparedness*. Concern for family has long been recognized in disaster research as a core social unit involved in decisions affecting evacuation (Drabek 1986), risk assessment (Kirschenbaum 1996) and postdisaster recovery (Oliver-Smith 1986). It also appears to be of significance in preparedness. For example, a full third of the items are directly related to family safety, with another third indirectly related, by specifying either the family unit or physical items related to the household. Only a third focus on individual preparedness, primarily by identifying levels of individual knowledge or ability. These measures also suggest that preparedness may have its epistemology woven into the social fabric of the family unit. Several recent studies of the link between gender and disasters, especially among women, seem to confirm how important the family is in affecting disaster behaviors (Fordham 1999).

With thirty different definitions of preparedness and each one having its zealous proponents, how is it possible to come to a consensus about its meaning? In fact, the original argument that due to its multiple meaning-measures the general construct of preparedness may in fact be masking a series of independent subcategories that reflect its pluralistic nature can now be explored. Simply put, preparedness may be nothing more than a number of separate measures that in combination form its overall meaning.

WHEREIN LIES THE TRUTH?

To test the assertion that preparedness is composed of more than one meaning, a representative sample of Israeli households was interviewed and asked what they did about all these meaning-measures of preparedness.[2] Each household was given the list of thirty consensus items of preparedness generated by the experts, agencies, and literature and asked to indicate if they had performed some type of action related to them. For example, if they had emergency water and food at home, if they had a plan in case the family had to evacuate, or if their sealed room or bomb shelter was in working order. By responding to these questions, it was possible to judge their actual behavior related to preparedness and to what degree they were prepared for a disaster. Each of the items was given a score (ranging from very prepared to not prepared), and these scores were used to see if groups of these items tended to coalesce. The idea behind this was to decipher clusters of items that were seen by the potential victims of disasters as personally relevant.

To assess this possibility, we entered the responses to the thirty meaning-measures of preparedness into a factor analysis. Such an analysis is a statistical means to see if there is an underlying association among the different items and if so, to collect them together into separate "factors" or clusters. The results of the factor analysis clearly demonstrated that four distinctive configurations (or factors) appeared among the thirty items.[3] (See Figure 4.)

These components reflect how different people view and define preparedness. The clustering of items into four distinct groups also allows us the opportunity to see what it is that each group has in common. Examining each of the groups closely shows that one factor can be labeled *provisions*, as it contains a list of physical items (e.g., spare battery, radio, water, food) essential for nearly every type of potential disaster under the assumption that basic services will be disrupted. For the second factor, it makes sense to call it *skill level*, as it reflects a meaning of preparedness closely linked to individual knowledge and skills that are aimed at either saving lives or tending those hurt (e.g., first aid, fire control, and proper use of a gas mask). The third factor, which I call *planning*, reflects a meaning of preparedness from a point of view of family organizing. Included here are measures

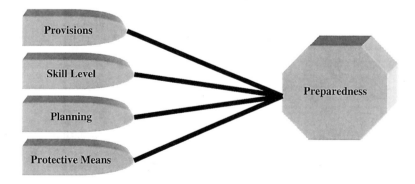

FIGURE 4 Primary factor components of preparedness.

concerning family discussions about operational emergency and evacuation plans. The last clustering of items can be seen in terms of *protection*, as it reflects the existence of physical means to safeguard individuals and family members from an external threat. In the context of Israel, this factor represents the availability of a gas mask, an accessible bomb shelter, and a specially designed (sealed) safe room. In other regions it might be represented by fire hydrants, tornado cellars, snow shelters, earthquake-resistant homes, and so on.

What does this all mean? Taken together, the extensive list of what preparedness is supposed to be compiled by those who are intimately involved with disasters and emergencies turns out to be completely different from what one expected. There is no one overall definition! The potential victims in fact relate to four basic preparedness activities: having provisions, gaining skills, planning for the worst, and providing themselves with adequate protection. What this means is that to use preparedness in its generalized form does not reflect the reality of either those who provide disaster management services or those who are receiving these services. The consequences of these results have a direct impact on the decisions of disaster managers, who decide how to allocate resources to enhance preparedness. If they choose to view preparedness on the basis of their own particular biases, there is the very real possibility that there will be negative consequences leading to unnecessary suffering and loss of life and property.

HOW TO EXPLAIN PREPAREDNESS

It now seems that preparedness is too imposing and amorphous a concept to use when it comes to preparing plans for a worst-case scenario; disaster managers must dig much deeper into their bag of magic tricks to find a suitable set of solutions, and as I have just shown, there is *another* way to approach how we can define preparedness—namely using empirically based definitions rather than "gut" feelings or organizational imperatives. This alternative approach has demonstrated that there are different characteristics, different boundaries, and different meanings to preparedness. With this empirically substantiated, it is now possible to begin to explore the determinants of each of its distinctive characteristics. The idea behind this approach is fairly straightforward; by understanding what it is that affects how people define different types of preparedness, it becomes possible to understand the conditions under which it can be enhanced. By knowing this, plans for a worst-case scenario can be formulated with greater accuracy and sensitivity and ultimately save lives.

As there is, theoretically speaking, an extremely long list of possible variables that could be associated with preparedness, a sensible (and practicable) search procedure would be to first look at a review of the disaster research literature. Here we can find some potent and empirically substantiated clues of what types of explanatory variables to look for. What has been found so far can be categorized into a series of conceptual blocks.

What We Are

The first are *sociodemographic* variables. These variables reflect clear-cut statuses of the individual. Included here are age, marital status, health status, family size, gender, educational level, income, religion, self-reported religiosity, nationality, native or immigrant status, and homeowner status (Fothergill et al. 1999; Morrow 1999). All of these provide a glimpse into normative behaviors that are associated with each status, so, for example, older men or married women might view the preparedness components differently than younger men or single women. Another case would be that the more educated individuals might be more knowledgeable of the impact of certain disasters and thereby be more prepared than those who are less educated. All these possibilities can be formulated into testable propositions.

Whom We Meet

A second set of alternative explanations relates to the impact of our social networks on how we perceive preparedness. Interacting with people creates social networks. The frequency and intensity of these social relationships—be they with family, friends, or neighbors—influence our attitudes and impressions of what is happening around us. No doubt for this reason social networking patterns have relevance to disaster behaviors (Kirschenbaum 1992; Bland et al. 1997; Kaniasty and Norris 2001). A hypothetical example would be that persons who are strongly involved in their communities and who have strong ties to their family or friends as opposed to "loners," would be more aware and sensitive to their family and community disaster needs and therefore be more prepared.

Our Experiences

There is little doubt in most individuals' minds that our experiences affect what we do when faced with a similar event. This also applies to the area of disasters. What was done here was to look at the cumulative experiences of the respondents who had experienced both major and minor disasters. This included having been in road or other accidents involving injuries or fires. In the case of Israel, I also included experiences with terror incidents, missile or Katusha attacks, war, and evacuations (voluntary or forced), as well as having past military experience and going through the process of obtaining a gas mask (Kirschenbaum 2001a; Briere and Elliott 2000; Norris et al. 1999).

The basic proposition that could be offered was that those persons who had experienced emergency and/or disaster incidents were more likely to be better prepared in those areas of greatest relevance to them.

How We Acted

What better way to predict a person's behavior than to see what he or she had already done. This approach, focusing on the actions of persons, has gained momentum in the research of social behavior and to some degree disaster-related behavior. Translating this in terms of explaining preparedness meant looking at actions taken either during or after the Gulf War. For this reason, the representative sample of Israelis was asked about their past actions in preparing and sealing security rooms, actually using the sealed rooms during attacks, and obtaining gas masks and finally putting them on during attacks (Shavit et al. 1994; Palm and Hodgson 1991).

How We See Risks

A final block of explanatory variables concerns the impact of how individuals perceive the risks of a disaster (or unconventional war or terror attack) on their preparedness behavior. The broad literature on risk perceptions basically says that our behavior is dependent on how we evaluate the probability of something (bad or good) happening. The intensity of that risk would prompt people into action (i.e., being prepared), but there are different levels of risk perception and it was for this reason that the study looked at personal, family, and national levels of war-related risk. Accordingly, respondents were asked to evaluate the nation's (military) ability to cope or neutralize unconventional attacks along with a cumulative risk composed of a series of measures asking about the chances of being injured from war, terror attacks, natural disasters, and accidents (Rogers 1997; Jacobs and Worthley 1999; Weichselgartner 2001).

WHAT MAKES US PREPARE?

Before beginning to answer the question of what influences us to prepare for disasters, it is extremely important to reiterate that the general concept of preparedness has been *empirically* found to be a composite of four separate categories of actions. These actions relate to: (1) provisions-those items that are crucial for basic survival if a disaster strikes, (2) skill level—a form of potential behavior based on the ability and knowledge to act to reduce injury and death, (3) planning, mainly family coordinated and cooperative readiness to act as a unit in the face of a disaster, and (4) protection—the availability of physical means to reduce, ameliorate, or neutralize the effects of a disaster.

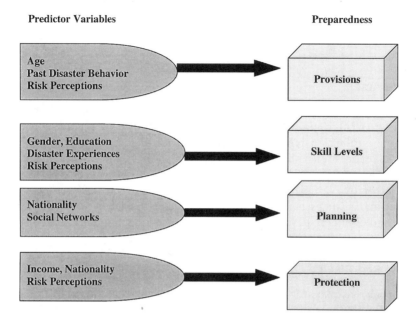

Predictor Variables   Preparedness

Age
Past Disaster Behavior
Risk Perceptions   Provisions

Gender, Education
Disaster Experiences
Risk Perceptions   Skill Levels

Nationality
Social Networks   Planning

Income, Nationality
Risk Perceptions   Protection

FIGURE 5   Summary of significant predictor variables of preparedness.

These four components of general preparedness can now be examined in greater detail in order to discover what makes us be prepared.

The way I will go about this is by utilizing a certain statistical procedure known as a regression model. What it does is check the importance of those independent explanatory variables that I (and other researchers) have argued are sensible explanations of preparedness. The selection process is based on a mathematical procedure that determines whether or not a variable (in competition with others) can significantly explain why it is that certain people are more prepared than others. By doing this for each of the four types of preparedness constructs (provisions, skill level, planning, and protection), we gain a better idea of what leads to being better prepared. More important, we can discover if indeed the different types of preparedness actions depend on different circumstances, for if they do, disaster managers must take this into account when setting their priorities. (See Figure 5.)

KEEPING STOCKED

The results of the first regression model concentrating on "provisions" provide the following picture. Overall, it appears that the focal explanation for being prepared by stocking survival provisions has to do with how we acted during past disasters. This was distinguished in several ways. Being older, for example, proved an asset to being stocked with survival provisions. This may have to do with the lifelong experiences of the elderly with occasional shortages or disruptions during emergency situations, making them more wary and sensitive to the need for stocking provisions. Indeed, persons who actually experienced the Gulf War, having utilized their sealed room and taken a gas mask when distributed, were found to have more of the basic provisions to survive a similar disaster than those who did not. In the case of voluntarily evacuating their homes during the Gulf War, those who left were less well stocked than those who decided to remain. Apparently, people who chose to leave viewed this as an alternative to stocking up on survival provisions. In addition, the perception of risk also played a significant role in that those who felt that the overall risk of another war was high were better provided. This was particularly apparent among those who felt the military would not be able to cope with the situation.

KNOWING WHAT TO DO

The second component of preparedness that emerged from the analysis was related to skill level, the degree of individual knowledge and skills that can be used to either save lives or tend those who are injured. Here the regression model generated a mixed bag of significant factors, but with a common theme relating to access in gaining these critical skills. For this reason gender, educational level, and army experience played a significant role in explaining why some have greater skill levels than others. Women, for example, reported themselves to be less knowledgeable or skilled in these disaster skills than men. This may be related to the fact that most of Israel's male population goes through some form of army service in which these skills are part of basic training. It also explains the finding that having had army experience contributed positively toward having the necessary skills to handle injuries in disaster events. Independent of these two interrelated factors was the fact that persons with greater levels of education also displayed greater skill levels associated with this type of preparedness. Here again we see it is the access to the knowledge related to these medical skills that directly affects the ability to use them.

EMERGENCY PLANNING

The *planning* component of preparedness has an underlying assumption that individuals both understand and recognize the need to plan ahead "just in case." Of course planning ahead is much easier in highly stable cultures in which change is relatively slow and comes in small doses. In a highly dynamic society such as Israel, which is inundated by immigrants, experiences rapid economic transitions, and is under the constant threat of war and terror, planning is to some extent a short-term proposition that has turned into a necessity for survival rather than a leisure-time activity. It is perhaps for this reason that among all the variables that could explain this component of preparedness that nationality emerges as a significant predictor. Also, it appears, that planning is significantly more evident among Israeli Jews than Israeli Arabs. One could speculate that this is a religious–cultural phenomenon and probably be right. In addition to nationality, the regression model also points toward a social networking factor, involvement in their co-op committee as another significant predictor of planning. In Israel, most residential configurations are of a condominium type, which requires cooperation among the residents on just about every issue, especially preparedness for both conventional and unconventional wars. The reason for this is that by law each building must have a shelter. What the data show is the large degree of interdependence between familial ethnocentricity and group cooperation among the Israeli population in terms of planning. Those who are involved in their condominium's committee machinations, however, while likely to prepare general emergency plans, are less likely to do so for their own families.

PHYSICALLY PROTECTING OURSELVES

This fourth component of preparedness provides some answers about what it is that leads individuals to raise the level of protection for themselves and their families. The analysis indicates that three apparently independent variables significantly contribute to understanding this type of preparedness. They include income, nationality, and risk perception. It should be understood that protection is a combination of having a sealed security room or a bomb shelter, or acquiring a gas mask kit. Under Israeli law, residential units must have access to or contain a bomb shelter, and more recently must have a sealed security room. Gas mask kits are distributed free to everyone. It comes as little surprise, then, that those households with greater incomes are more likely to have more physical means of household protection available. The analysis again points out that Israeli Jews make more effort to be better protected than Israeli Arabs; again perhaps a religious–cultural difference (as in planning preparedness) that is linked to priorities in how income is disposed. Finally, the regression points out that the greater the doubt that the military (substitute government, local authorities) can neutralize an unconventional attack, the more individuals have invested in means of protection.

WHAT CAN BE LEARNED

A Rigorous Approach

What has all this told us? For one, preparedness as a core concept in disaster research and management has been badly mistreated. It has been so clouded by diverse meanings and alternative measures as to confound critical thinking about very practical issues that concern disaster managers' decisions and consequent organizational actions (Pidgeon and O'Leary 2000). Such critical thinking can affect the lives of individuals who are put at physical, emotional, and economic risk because of both natural and technological disasters. By better understanding the concept of preparedness, disaster managers will be able to allocate resources to increase their organizations' ability to reduce these risks and save lives. Before they can do so, however, they have to know what preparedness is all about, and rather than trust intuition or what seems reasonable, it is a sounder strategy to seek out the empirical basis of preparedness by employing scientifically tested methods. This approach, while extremely demanding, sometimes stands in stark contrast to answers derived solely from convenience. When a rigorous scientific approach is actually pursued, however, as was done here, an empirically grounded testable and consensual meaning of preparedness can be generated.

Misguided Agencies

It is from the results of the analysis that a claim can be made that the impact of the internal bureaucratic organizational processes seems to have led disaster managers to a restricted and bureaucratic self-fulfilling definition of pre-paredness. Ignoring other dimensions of preparedness that emerged from the analysis may be one of many reasons why they seem to have faltered in their mission. Let me expand on this point.

The categories of disaster-related behavior that were found to be associated with preparedness cover a much broader range of actions than those put forward by disaster management agencies. The result is that they have only touched on one narrow area of its meanings—namely lists of physical items—yet there are at least four major categories of preparedness that were found in the analysis; namely provisions, skill level, planning, and protection. By focusing on one of these types of preparedness, other relevant aspects are abandoned. Take, for instance, the realistic case in which disaster managers have just allocated their organizations' resources to inform the public that they should have provisions stocked in their homes in case of a disaster. But what if an evacuation is necessary, or if the event requires a sealed security room due to a biochemical terror attack? What if first aid skills might be needed? What these managers have done is squandered their resources on preparedness items that are focused on only one set of potential disaster scenarios. Why do this? Again the answer may lie in the organizational structure that is concerned with its own internal agenda rather than with the potential victims. At the end of the day, the wonderful detailed plans for worst-case scenarios may prove inadequate if not outright disastrous. The narrow definition propagated by the disaster organizations without consideration of other preparedness components will seriously depreciate the plan's effectiveness.

Even more critical is that public sector disaster agencies have forsaken the fact that besides being inadequate, the relevance of their preparedness lists differs for different population groups and situational factors. As the analysis has poignantly stressed, what helps explain preparedness evolves from a complex and diverse set of factors; stocking up on provisions stems from how individuals acted in previous disaster situations, knowing the survival skills needed in emergencies was explained by accessibility to this knowledge, planning for emergencies was related to religious–cultural attitudes, and exhibiting protective behavior was correlated to amounts of disposable income, nationality, and risk perceptions. For disaster management agencies to ignore these relevant sources of preparedness would seriously hinder their efforts in saving lives. Even more damaging is the very fact that the potential victims of a disaster view preparedness differently from the public disaster management agencies; what the bureaucracy defines as preparedness does not match how the public defines it.

Universal Application

The analysis of the data, which originated in Israel, should reflect universal preparedness concepts applicable to most disaster situations. For example, the derivative of protection measures may be substituted according to the predominant disaster in a specific area. For Israel, sealed rooms and bomb shelters form the basic measures. Substitute tornado cellars, flood-resistant homes, fire sprinkler systems, or earthquake/hurricane-resistant structures in accordance with the prevalent types of disasters. The result is a more locally appropriate measure of the same concept of protection. In addition, the original master list was derived from a wealth of international sources, including experts in disaster management. The people who were asked about preparedness had lived through and survived the Gulf War under a missile attack and the threat of a biochemical war. This was not a "theoretical" tabletop simulation game but a reflection of reality.

This same universal application to the meaning of preparedness can be applied to those factors that explain how preparedness arose. The set of explanatory variables used here can certainly be expanded to express diversity of culture and geographic area. As greater knowledge accumulates about disaster behavior, more variables can be introduced into the model employed to understand preparedness. For example, religion and nationality can be made to reflect local conditions and subtle but critical diversity even among the same religious or nationality groups. Experiences with past disasters might include war situations, but also floods, earthquakes, and landslides—or even pollution. This rule of thumb is easily applicable, as there is no hard and fast rule that biases one type of situation or factor over another. What is important is that social and cultural diversity be taken into account.

ARE WE REALLY PREPARED?

Overall this chapter expands on the problematic nature of disaster management as it is presently situated in public sector bureaucratic agencies. It has done so by stressing how the basic conceptual basis of disaster management, preparedness, has had little scientific grounding and is plagued by conflicting interpretations, all of which suit organizational demands rather than the potential victims' needs. It is a concept that has been distorted to reflect how well an organization is prepared rather than how well it serves the potential victims of disasters. The result is that when this concept is utilized for the public's preparedness, it usually provides virtually nothing that the potential victims do not already know. The implications are that the present use of the concept of preparedness by disaster managers may actually be doing more harm than good.

To prove these points, an empirical analysis was conducted based on seeking definitions of preparedness through the research literature, asking disaster experts, and looking at definitions by disaster agencies. When a comprehensive list was finally formulated and empirically analyzed, four basic independent subcategories of preparedness were discovered. They included (1) provisions, (2) skill level, (3) planning, and (4) protection. Each reflected a specific and different type of preparedness behavior that, as I have shown, has broad application and can be universally utilized. The next step was to ask the potential victims of disasters, all of whom had been through the harrowing experience of the Gulf War in Israel, what they thought about. Their responses led to the conclusion that each type of preparedness behavior depended on different circumstances and at times different characteristics of the responders.

What became crystal clear from this analysis is that preparedness can be understood either from an organizational or a victim's perspective. When the focus is on the organization, as it is today, the potential victims of disasters find themselves at even greater risk. What is even more disturbing is that there appears to be little linkage between what the organizations do to prepare themselves and their effectiveness. This point I will take up in the next chapter, but as I pointed out, the way disaster management organizations operate, putting all the eggs in one preparedness basket or dividing them incorrectly has only led to diminishing preparedness levels. It also has direct implications on what aspect of preparedness disaster managers feel necessary to prop up or strengthen and which types of catalysts to employ to optimize being prepared. As disaster management is an emergent field, and where organization behavioral constraints can have direct impact on how preparedness plans for the worst-case scenario are developed, a more sound empirically based understanding of preparedness is an absolute must. It will aid managers in fulfilling their public trust. It will also reduce deaths, injuries, and economic loss to the victims of disasters. More important, it might shift the emphasis from the organization to the potential victim.

NOTES

1. In the summer of 1999, a national representative household survey of the Israeli adult urban population residing in areas of 10,000 or more was used to gauge the level of the population's preparedness. A total of 814 household head interviews in 150 urban areas were conducted over a two-week period with sample size based on each urban area's proportional population size as recorded in the 1999 Israel census. The survey employed a random digital dial, computer-assisted telephone survey of each household head based on interviews that lasted about 20 to 25 minutes. Only residential household units were included in the population from which the sample was drawn. The only constraint imposed on the sampling design was that the gender of the adult household head be equally distributed (rotated) regardless of marital status. The actual telephone interview relied on a closed-ended structured question-naire that included, among other questions, the list of preparedness constructs. Given the subject matter and sponsor (Israel Defense Force Home Front Command), refusals were extremely rare. Only 11 households refused to be interviewed, with alternatives randomly selected. Included in this survey were questions covering a broad range of areas and variables theoretically linked to preparedness. The final sample matched census data on the basic characteristics of the Israeli population living in urban areas. Most of the household sample are married (80%), have 2 to 3 children (52%), are highly educated with a college or more education (44%), live in dual income households (60%), are in good health (72%), are between 40

to 60 years of age (47%), are native born (51%), are in the labor force (54%), are Jews (87%), and are evenly distributed for above and below average income.

2. For a detailed description of the study see above. The background for the study comes as a result of the threat of another gulf-style war. The vast majority of the sample had experienced the Iraqi ballistic missile strike against Israel during the Gulf War (93%) as well as continuous threats as late as 1998 of another attack. As for the sample, Israel is culturally homogeneous but ethnically pluralistic, composed overwhelmingly of Jews (82%) of various ethnic origins from Asia (15%), Europe/Americas (15%), Africa (20%), and native born (50%).

3. These were nominally called provisions, skill levels, and planning, each having substantial levels of commonality (alpha Cronbach 0.72–0.74). The fourth factor, protection, has a very low alpha (0.20) but was kept (rather than diluted by variable removing to increase the alpha), as it reflected an important local aspect of preparedness in Israel. The total cumulative variance explained reaches 37.4%.

3

Are Disaster Agencies Effective?

LOOKING FROM OUTSIDE IN

In the previous chapters I was extremely critical of how public sector disaster agencies are beset by dilemmas that are inherent in their bureaucratic organizational structure. These include a long list of conflicting goals and organizational behaviors that obstruct the agencies from optimally fulfilling their goals. The uniqueness of disaster management agencies is that their goals are directly related to preventing the loss of life and property, an objective most service organizations do not entertain. It is for this reason that a great deal of attention must be paid to such organizations, as their success or failure has a direct impact on our survival. Until now, I have argued that enough evidence is at hand to suggest that typical behavioral patterns of formal disaster organizations and those who manage them has had a minimal bearing on attaining their goals.

Does this mean that all disaster agencies cannot fulfill their role adequately, or can changes be made to enable them to be truly effective? In the last chapter it became clear that one of the more complex issues involved in their success stems from the lack of a clear definition of core concepts in disaster behavior; muddled and confusing concepts lead to ineffective disaster management. Now I will discuss another crucial aspect of the problem; namely, examining how to measure these organizations' effectiveness. We have seen that even with the increase in the number of disaster management agencies there has not been a decrease in the number or severity of disasters. Is this an artificial artifact of bureaucratic redefinitions of disasters or are they actually becoming less effective?

Let us therefore try to look at disaster management agencies from the outside in. Rather than focusing on how the organization functions with all its idiosyncrasies, the emphasis will be on its clients. As a public human service provider, disaster agencies must answer to their clients, the potential victims of disasters. The reason for this is fairly simple—it is the public who legitimizes and financially subsidizes these organizations. We, the public, are in fact its major stakeholders—its clients.

For a long time, disaster agencies were judged successful by standards that their managers or political mentors dictated. The problem with these standards was that they reflected internal performance criteria based on organizational needs. For example, effectiveness was based on criteria that judged if proper communications channels were used, correct forms were filled out, interdepartmental coordination was in place, and so on. A glaring omission is an external independent measure that looks at the organization's objectives and goals and seeks to measure to what degree they had been attained. By external I mean the clients or customers of the services. The bottom line of this perspective is that effectiveness will depend on if we are provided with what we need in order to be prepared for disasters. It's all well and good that we are told that rescue teams will be available or that information will be distributed about biochemical terrorist activities, but the proof of the pudding is in its "provision!" This perspective turns the tables on internal auditing and seeks effectiveness measures outside, primarily by the final judges (and potential victims) of disaster management agency performance. How well it performs is an important benchmark of its effectiveness.

WHAT IS EFFECTIVENESS?

Disaster management organizations face issues of measuring effectiveness that are similar to those of other organizations. In fact, organizational theorists have struggled for many decades over the thorny issue of how to gauge organizational effectiveness (Campbell 1977; Bedeian 1994; Hall 1996). Like most amorphous concepts, the measures have varied in name, focus, and ideological underpinnings (Scott 1995). Most of the effort in measuring effectiveness has been associated with profit-based organizations, leaving effectiveness measures in the public service sector up to one's imagination, yet a consistent component of organizational effectiveness has been based on performance, which in many ways has been equated with success (Hall 1996; Etzioni 1964).[1] Performance in this respect did not mean individual output, but performance by the combined efforts of all those in the organization. Given this history, human service organizational effectiveness has traditionally meant focusing on internal performance measures affecting output (production) of services, and to a lesser extent its quality (Julnes and Holzer 2001).

In the private sector, cost was a major part of this formula, but only against actual revenues. In the case of public service organizations, however, cost was irrelevant in measuring effectiveness, as it was a "given"—always there from the public pocket. If a public agency was running a budget deficit, the easiest solution was either the transfer of other public funds to it or getting the public to pay through increased taxes. From the perspective of a public servant running a bureaucracy, increasing costs would bring greater demands for greater slices of the public budget. Greater budgets would then be translated in formal organizational terms into more manpower and greater political power and prestige. If we add to this the complexity of deciding which of the competing preferences to use to measure effectiveness and the more practical need to succeed in a noncompetitive market, it is no wonder that the "bottom line" for public services was seen as irrelevant. In the case of both private and public sector human service organizations, the emphasis thus was rarely if ever put on measuring organizational effectiveness by such external measures as client evaluations (Njoh 1994). In both cases, the bottom line counted—either a profit or a balanced budget.

PERFORMANCE

The pros and cons of how to measure organizational effectiveness led to the development of what we today call alternative strategies. On the whole, they were academic in nature, but they did strike at the basic structural essence of both production and service organizations. One of the most important distinctions made was between efficiency and effectiveness. Being efficient did not automatically mean that the organization was effective. For example, moving information around the organization efficiently at the speed of light might help, but what if the information was faulty, misdirected, or selectively filtered? On this basis, researchers understood that effectiveness had to be linked to actual performance. Given this agreement, performance-effectiveness measures have for the most part been framed by a combination of three major theoretical approaches, the (1) goal, (2) resource, and (3) internal process approaches (Daft 1998).

For the most part, these approaches have looked inward; they approached measuring effectiveness on the basis of internal organizational processes. The question that was raised was primarily what to look at. One assumption that was agreed upon was that organizations are dominated by one overriding goal. A second assumption was that actual performance (and not intentions) was the only criterion from which to measure effectiveness, so for example, the *goal* approach stressed actual performance against goals; goals became the benchmark from which to judge whether or not an organization met them. The degree to which they were met determined how effective the organization was. The *resource* approach focused on how well the organization used its resources to provide services. Here again the emphasis was on internal elements of the organization and the way they were exploited to attain goals. Effectiveness was based on a measure of the optimal use of the organization's resources—both material and manpower. The third approach stressed *internal processes*, but focused primarily on internal (managerial) performance criteria. From this approach emerged many of the studies on managerial style and what today is appropriately called human resource management. Without exception, all saw the organization—and all that happened within it—as the basis for measuring its effectiveness.

SHIFTING ALLEGIANCES

The focus on these three approaches to measuring effectiveness began to change with the growth of service industries and a concomitant trend toward viewing human service organizations as consumer service providers (Hasenfeld 1992). The emphasis on consumers put a new twist on measuring effectiveness. Until this point most approaches focused primarily on internal organizational criteria of effectiveness, criteria decided upon and endorsed by the organization's members. It takes little imagination to recognize that such criteria had built-in safety devices to protect the organizational members from criticism as well as enhance successes. The force of the marketplace and the growing militancy of consumers, however, started to influence even the most diehard researchers into rethinking how to measure effectiveness. Only a few daring researchers actually went beyond the organization's boundaries by viewing consumer-clients as a critical component in measuring organizational effectiveness. These few pioneers led to the emergence of what today is called the multiple constituency approach (Julnes and Holzen 2001; Tsui 1990; Connolly et al. 1980; Zammanto 1984; Jobson and Schneck 1982; Fried and Worthington 1995). (See Figure 1.)

MULTIPLE CONSTITUENCY APPROACH

This approach focuses primarily on a simple assumption that there are a multiplicity of stakeholders in (and outside) an organization who evaluate the success of an organization in attaining its goal(s). As each constituency or stakeholder may have a different set of standards by which to gauge their

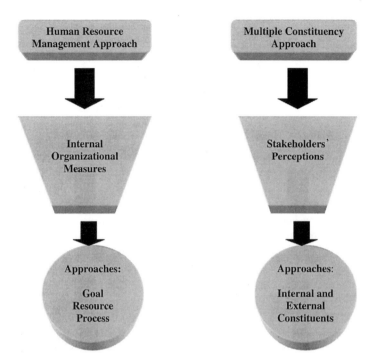

FIGURE 1   Perspectives for measuring the effectiveness of organizations.

organization's effectiveness (Alvarez and Brehm 1998), specific constituencies may have widely different evaluations of the same organizational objectives (Kanter and Summers 1987). On the one hand, this is a major constraint on its utilization, as there is not a single effectiveness score. For example, different effectiveness scores appear when comparing how managers evaluate their organization's goals to those of their clients (Gowdy et al. 1993). Not surprisingly, managers tend to give higher scores than clients. Variations likewise appear when asking practitioner-experts who are familiar with the ins and outs of their organization with other nonexpert stakeholders (Herman and Renz 1997). In this case, familiarity does indeed breed contempt, as the experts tend to be more critical of how work processes are done. On the other hand, however, looking at evaluations of various constituencies broadens the base upon which an effectiveness measure can be built, as it considers the multiple goals inherent in organizations. This is an important point, as organizations, especially human service ones, have multiple goals. This recognition of a multiplicity of goals represented a major breakthrough in how researchers approached organizational effectiveness, but more significant was the view that organizations are made up of stakeholders. As the name implies, the organization is made up of groups of individuals who have a stake in the successful running of the organization.

STAKEHOLDERS

From this perspective, stakeholders are any group of individuals who have a direct interest in the success of the organization. Employing the jargon of politics, stakeholders have been described by some as "constituencies" or "interest groups" that reside both within and outside the organization. Interestingly, it is from this reference to constituencies that researchers have labeled this perspective the multiple constituency approach. It should be made clear at this point that having such an interest in the success of an organization does not necessarily mean only a monetary interest. What characterizes such constituencies are their similar interests or positions within the organization, thus if we take a cross section of an organization, we can distinguish between groups based on their occupational skills, organizational positions, managerial levels, and even career paths. These categories represent those stakeholders *within* the organization.

There is also a large constituency *outside* the organization, however. In a sense, this constituency is similar to firms whose stockholders—albeit distanced from everyday firm activity—can still leverage the policy directives of the CEO. They can also approve or disapprove of mergers, or through their proxies affect company policy. Constituencies go beyond just stockholders, however. For example, they can also be a football or baseball club's ardent fans, whose attendance at games contributes both directly and indirectly to the club's financial stability and league standing, or the customers of a mail order company, cable television addicts, or even computer freaks who will decide whether to purchase or utilize services or goods being offered based on the perceived quality of the service provided. The ability to purchase goods in a competitive market makes them an external but very important constituency.

For public sector human service organizations, the primary stakeholder is the public. In our case of disaster management agencies, the external stakeholders are those who receive an organization's services. There are, however, other stakeholders in public agencies, such as politicians, bureaucrats, and suppliers. The largest and most consequential are the external stakeholders whose evaluations as customer-clients are the most relevant for the successful running of the organization, because customers can make or break a service company, even a public agency financed by public money. This is because when services are evaluated as inferior or when the goods provided do not meet the needs of the customers, the private market usually takes up the slack and becomes an alternative provider. To some extent this has already occurred in the United States in such areas as correctional facilities, private police and security.* In many cases these alternative providers are nongovernmental or voluntary organizations. When this happens, the public sector comes under scrutiny and faces the threat of reduced budgets and manpower. In many cases, this power of the public stakeholder can stimulate internal changes that lead to better, more appropriate, and higher-quality services or goods.

The fact that public sector organizations depend upon their clients also means that they have a complex relationship with them (Hasenfeld 1983). Anyone familiar with or having the experience of trying to obtain a social service can easily recognizes this. The basic and underlying philosophy is somewhat paranoiac. On the one hand there are the rules, forms, and criteria—assuming that everyone trying to take the public money does not deserve it and must meet stringent and always changing criteria. On the other hand, there is *protekzia*, knowing someone who knows somebody to expedite requests, smooth things over and get things approved. This duality of the formal and informal systems spills over in human service organizations to create a symbiotic relationship with their clients, making clients into stake-holders, along with other types of stakeholders, an integral component in this symbiotic relationship. Being an essential part of these organizations makes the client-stakeholder a critical cog in the measure of their effectiveness. No longer do the managers and other employees have the final say of their effectiveness; now the recipients of these services also can express their opinions of the organization's effectiveness. This approach has a direct and extremely important effect on how we can now evaluate the effectiveness of disaster management agencies.

WHO COUNTS?

The innovation of the external stakeholder approach is that it assumes that differing constituencies within and outside the organization may have differ-ent standards and perceptions for measuring effectiveness. On a more practical level, this means that bureaucratic civil servants within public sector organizations see things and evaluate them differently from the way their clients do. These perceptions are directly associated with the specific goals that these individuals or groups are expected to attain. In some cases, the flip-flop of goals and means has led civil servants to see providing their clients (the public!) with their rightful services as a tiresome nuisance. This is typified by

---

* I will discuss the issue of privatization of public sector service organizations and especially disaster management agencies in greater detail in Chapter 8.

the horror stories that employees use to justify negative attitudes toward those applying for social services. Client-stakeholders use these same horror stories, but they typify the uncaring and nasty bureaucrat. Above and beyond these stories lies an underlying difference in how these two constituencies, the suppliers and receivers of services, perceive of the organization's effectiveness.

Take this typical example. A local emergency management unit is asked to evaluate its effectiveness in getting vital information about potential hazards to its local population. The manager rates the department's effectiveness as very high due to the fact that he or she and his or her employees created a comprehensive data pool of key potential recipients and mailed the information directly to their homes. When asked how they, the clients, evaluated the effectiveness of the emergency unit, many of the recipients gave a very low score. Residents complained they did not receive the material, others could not understand what was wanted of them, some did not understand English, and most just saw the material as another piece of junk mail and threw it into the garbage. The upshot of the story is that for the civil servant the organization is highly effective while for the client it is not. This poses a problem of how to measure effectiveness. As the saying goes, there are two sides to every coin; the organization–client gap can be resolved by taking into account both the organization's concerns—its goals—and those of its major stakeholder—the client.

GOALS AND TRANSPARENCY

The discrepancy between providers' and receivers' perception of success can be potentially understood employing the goal model. In this respect, the goal model for measuring effectiveness seems the most appropriate to examine. In the case of the goal model approach, it specifies that effectiveness depends on whether or not the organization attains its stated goals (Etzioni 1964). These goals can be either ideological or material and represent standards by which members of the organization can judge their performance (Daft 1998). This means that goals extend beyond bottom line profits to such other amorphous things as providing quality service, or as in the case of disaster management agencies, saving lives. In general, when applied to these goal standards, an organization's performance, internal decision-making processes, leadership qualities, and external social networks have an impact on its effectiveness (Hall 1996). For this to happen, however, these goals must be clear, final, consensual, measurable, and consistent (Robbins 1983). This ideal situation, however, rarely if ever occurs in reality. Only in a military-type chain of command or in highly formalistic bureaucratic organizations—and to some extent in manufacturing units—do we come close to this ideal. The reality of the competitive demands of the market—even in the public sector—is a major constraint on knowing the exact nature of an organization's stated goals. In many cases additional goals are added and others dropped. Here is a good example of a public agency trying to get a piece of the terrorism action by broadening its goals.

> EPA Seeks Cabinet-Level Talks To Resolve Administration-Wide Chemical Security Dispute: Environmental Protection Authority officials are trying to schedule a cabinet-level meeting to resolve a governmentwide dispute over whether the agency has the authority to finalize a new initiative establishing mandatory security requirements for chemical and other industrial facilities. The agency is expected to argue that the Clean Air Act allows EPA to establish requirements calling on industry to reduce the likelihood of intentional sabotage by criminals or terrorists, in addition to preventing accidental releases (Inside Washington Publishers August 29, 2002).

Typically, this example of adaptation of goals as a mechanism for organizational survival and growth does not provide consistent goal standards by which to measure effectiveness over time (Harvey 1996), particularly when what is expected from employees is always changing (Schneider et al. 1980). This is exceptionally acute in human service organizations, whose goals may be affected by the vagaries of political rather than market conditions (Glampson et al. 1977; Gilbert and Parhizgari 2000). Can you imagine the time and effort spent on setting new priorities and goals every time a new election comes up or a new "social crisis" erupts? Despite the potential for changing goal priorities, however, at any given time the stated goals of a human service organization are in the main *transparent and stable* to both its members and its clients. This is because such services are highly visible in the public realm and regulated in the political arena (Grandjean and Vaughn 1981). Unlike a private business firm, a public agency is much more open to criticism and public debate, and because of this its stated goals are an open secret and extremely difficult to change. It must be said that for the most part changes in basic organizational goals in public administrations rarely go beyond marginal issues. In most cases the basic stated goals remain in place. Just ask yourself if welfare agencies or more recently disaster management agencies have made any radical changes in their goals of providing welfare and safety to their clients.

THE CONSTITUENTS

This transparency of goals in public sector human service organizations is the potent link to the constituency approach. The core idea of this approach in measuring organizational effectiveness is that an organization must satisfactorily fulfill the minimum requirements of its stakeholders. In a large sense, this approach is both political and economic in nature (D'Aunno 1992). If such an organization does not provide what its stakeholders want, it jeopardizes its political existence and leaves the market open to private competitors. More important, the major stakeholders in human service organizations, particularly nonprofit ones, are likely to be those who are also the major consumers of its services and who wield the greatest power over the survival of the organization (D'Aunno 1992). It is the stakeholder-client who can purchase these public services, ignore them, or find alternative private market sources. These abilities make client-stakeholders a powerful group. The degree of their power as a constituency in the private market is legendary but has been more or less ignored in the public market. There have been some exceptions in the public sector, such as lobbying by the elderly or HIV victims, but these are not the general rule. The power of constituencies should not be underrated, however. Just take the media as an example; ratings (by customers) can influence the types of products and services provided as well as "make or break" programs and entertainers. This sensitivity to the client-stakeholder has yet to trickle down into the area of public services.

The exception to this rule occurs when there are alternative private market alternatives. An excellent example of this occurred in Israel when a voluntary organization was formed to provided an easy and convenient way to obtain needed medical equipment on a temporary basis. The client just had to deposit a symbolic sum that he or she received back when they returned the equipment. Until this organization was established, the only alternative was to go through the Ministry of Health, which like most monopoly public agencies, made the client fill out the requisite forms, face numerous committees, obtain official documentation, and then wait for an official approval. Many times the equipment was not on the list of approved medical devices. At other times additional documentation was required. In some cases, by the time the needy client received the device he or she did not require it any longer or died before having it available. Within a short time, newspapers and other media started to criticize the Ministry of Health, which found itself without customers to justify the manpower and budget it obtained to operate this service. This was because when the public was faced with an alternative, most chose the voluntary organization, branches of which seemed to spring up everywhere throughout Israel. The result of this competition led the Ministry of Health to streamline the procedures, reduce the bureaucracy involved, and provide more varied medical devices. Despite these changes, the Ministry of Health could still not keep up with the more dynamic nature of the voluntary organization, which continued to find better ways to serve its potential customers. Due to competition from the private market, it has slowly started to adjust its goals (as best it could) to take into account the client-stakeholder's lack of interest in its services.

The above example also provides another important point. A constituency exercising its client-stakeholder rights assumes that first and foremost there is knowledge and awareness of the service being provided. This is a fundamental condition in measuring organizational effectiveness. Only by confronting the service organization's goals against its client's awareness of them can some sort of effectiveness measure emerge. This is not an offhand statement for several reasons. A public agency may have on its books a service (e.g., providing minority students preferential scholarships) that is all well and good only if those who can benefit by it know of its existence. Not being aware of the service means it cannot be evaluated. Not being aware of it also means that the service agency has not been very effective in attaining one of its stated goals. The goals may thus exist but are worthless if clients are not aware of them. (See Figure 2).

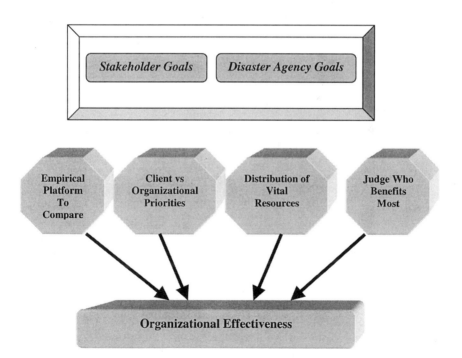

FIGURE 2   Primary reasons why comparing organizational goals and stakeholders' goals can help measure effectiveness.

WHY GOALS?

Now the question arises, Why focus on goals among the possible options to measure effectiveness? If my argument is correct that disaster agencies are not doing a very good job at preventing or ameliorating disasters, what will knowing about their goals tell me? Does it really matter if these organizations' major stakeholders don't see eye to eye with the experts? Let me answer these questions simply.

First of all, goals will provide an empirical basis or platform from which to actually evaluate whether or not such organizations are effective and if not, where have they failed. Until now, this problem has been avoided, as it raises embarrassing questions for disaster managers and politicians!

Second, by delving into the heart of disaster management organizations, namely their goals, a clear benchmark can be formulated to judge if the priorities they set are what we want.

Third, perhaps these organizations have missed their mark by being ethnocentric—by creating goals for their own benefit and not for those whom they are mandated to protect.

Finally, there may be a serous mismatch between what the public thinks the disaster agency goals should be so that vital resources are being squandered on what the stakeholders consider as being marginal or outright useless.

AN EFFECTIVENESS MODEL

To ascertain the relevance of these arguments, a working model was generated to provide a framework to evaluate organizational effectiveness. This model, shown in Figure 3, argues that in order to evaluate the effectiveness of a public sector disaster management agency (or another other type of human service organization), it is crucial to focus on how client-stakeholders perceive of the organization's stated goals. These perceptions are in part dependent on how well the organization gets its goal "message" across. It also depends on how the message is received.

What this model suggests is that stakeholders' goal perceptions are influenced by a number of selective variables. These variables were not picked out of a hat but represent the results of other research in both organizations and disasters. As Figure 3 illustrates, our perceptions do not exist in a vacuum. They can be influenced by, among many other things, our backgrounds, fears, and experiences. On the basis of this assumption, I will determine which one(s) are important and the extent to which each of these factors affects how goal perceptions are developed. For example, all of us have fears and have gone through many kinds of experiences—both good and bad—with events that we

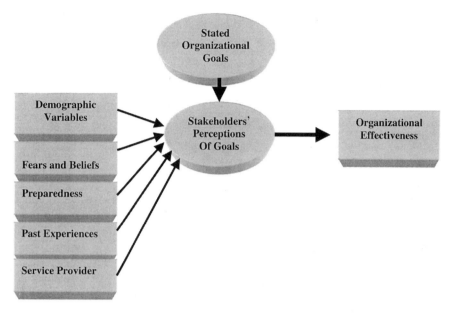

FIGURE 3 Schematic model of stakeholders' perception of a disaster management organizations' stated goals and its impact on effectiveness.

call disasters. It may have been a car or industrial accident, a natural disaster such as a tornado or hurricane, or a terrorist incident, but who can say with certainty which of these has made a more powerful impression on the way we perceive the effectiveness of disaster management organizations?

A second implication of the model is how you and I interpret what we are told are the goals of the disaster agency. Do disaster management agencies abide by "truth in advertising?" As I mentioned earlier, there is a possibility that what is officially advertised as the organization's goals may not be recognized as such by its clients.

To come up with a measure of effectiveness thus requires not only trusting what we are told by disaster managers, but what we—its clients— perceive as their goals. It's like the traveling salesman who gives his pitch about all the things a particular item can do but when you try it out it never seems to live up to your expectations! When a match is close and when what managers claim to be its goals are agreed upon, then it is possible to focus only on the organization's goals as a benchmark from which to measure effectiveness. If there is no match or if a gap between what is stated and what is perceived exists, a major problem arises, for then the situation becomes complicated and we must ask ourselves whose goals we use as a benchmark; the organizations or the client-stakeholders.

This dilemma will be resolved in the analysis that follows, but it should be noted that even though I am using the Israel Home Front Command (HFC),[2] the measure of its effectiveness is applicable to other agencies found throughout the world. Hopefully, both the method that I will now demonstrate and the results themselves will provide a rich source of information to extrapolate for other types of public sector human service organizations.

GOAL MEASURES

On the basis of my arguments, a strategy was devised to ascertain the organizational goals of Israel's national disaster management agency, the HFC. This provided a first step in measuring its effectiveness. To determine its goals, both the explicit stated goals of the HFC as well as those expressed by senior-ranking officeholders were employed. The fact that the HFC is obliged by law to provide emergency services to the entire Israeli population makes these clients its major stakeholder and essential in evaluating its effectiveness. For this reason, a national survey, which included alternative client perceptions of HFC goals along with other disaster-related information, was constructed.

Organizational goals were measured in two complimentary ways: stated goals of the HFC and perceived goals as expressed by the organization's senior managers. Stated goals were obtained from public documents published by the HFC, which included statements from official public records as well as various public information publications. These stated goals are based on both law and military regulations that officially mandate the HFC as solely responsible "to prepare the civilian population for emergency situations." Emergency situations originally related to wartime activities, but were expanded over time to also include natural, technological, and non-war-related disasters.

Stated Goals

Taking what the HFC stated were its goals provided empirical evidence of the multiple goals under which this agency was burdened. A total of fifteen goals was discovered. Of the fifteen specific goals were ten that dealt with providing direct and indirect services to the civilian population. Five were directed internally toward its own organizational functioning. This distinction is important, as it provided fresh evidence of how much of an organization's own resources (in this case one-third of its declared goals) are reinvested in its own running. The stated goals relevant for *internal organizational purposes* include (1) providing organizational protocols and guidelines, (2) plans for intraorganizational coordination, (3) rules for coordination with other relevant public emergency agencies, (4) creation of regional and urban preparedness guidelines, and (5) clear issues of population behavior during emergencies to assist internal policy decisions. As can be seen, these goals alone provided fertile ground to keep most of the HFC employees busy. (See Table 1.)

Those *goals directed outward* and directly relevant to the well-being of the civilian population include: (1) informing the civilian population of potential emergencies, (2) providing instructions to emergency organizations about how to deal with civilian populations, (3) controlling and managing hazardous materials and coordinating organizations to maximize civilian safety, (4) providing, maintaining, and informing the population about warning systems, (5) preparing and responding to biochemical and atomic threats through the distribution of gas mask kits and shelters, as well as maintaining them, (6) exercising authority over civilian population, including evacuations and postdisaster rehabilitation, (7) recruiting civilian manpower during emergencies, (8) coordinating civilian logistic and supply organizations, (9) preparing civilian emergency health and medical facilities, and (10) having the authority over the requisition of all types of civilian emergency equipment. These ten goals are the direct link between the HFC and its client-stakeholder. How the stakeholder evaluates these stated goals are the crux of the measure of the HFC's effectiveness.

TABLE 1 Disaster Organizations' Client-Directed and Internal Organizational Stated Goals

Stated organizational goals
Client-directed goals
Information to population of potential disasters
Instruction to other agencies about population behavior
Civilian safety management coordination for hazmat
Provision warning systems
Preparation for nonconventional attacks
Authority over civilian population in evacuations
Recruitment of civilian manpower in emergencies
Coordinating logistic and supply organizations
Preparation of civilian health facilities
Authority for requisition of emergency equipment
Internal organizational goals
Organization protocols and guidelines
Plans for intraorganizational coordination
Rules for coordination with other agencies
Preparation guidelines for regional units
Internal policy decisions based on population behavior

The duality of having both externally and internally oriented goals is nothing new in the study of organizations. What is new is that a fairly large number of the goals are self-fulfilling, aimed at increasing internal efficiency rather than directed toward the client. To some extent these internal goals (e.g., coordinating and providing instructions to various emergency organizations, or managing technical control of emergency equipment) have consequences for its cliental, the civilian population. How much, however, is highly debatable. More important, the end result—the service actually provided—is what can be judged. For this reason, only those goals that were externally and directly relevant to its major client-stakeholders were incorporated into the effectiveness measure. (See Figure 4.)

Managers' Goals

To allay concern that the stated goals were only window dressing and did not reflect the real objectives of the HFC, its senior managers—those who literally ran the agency—were interviewed. To this end, an open-ended questionnaire was distributed to forty senior-ranking officials (equivalent to departmental vice presidents) in the HFC. The responses were collated and underwent a content analysis. Asked to delineate their organizations' goals and rank their priority, it was found that the basic stated goals of the organization and the perceived goals of its managers were very similar. This was not surprising, due to the strong sense of identity and commitment of the staff. In some cases, the goals of coordination with other specific disaster agencies were not explicitly stated but could be inferred from their responses. Differences were found, however, in how they ranked what they felt should be the operational priority of the goals. For example, some managers felt it more important to put

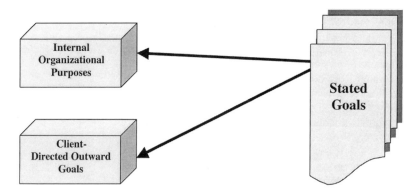

FIGURE 4   Internal and external stated goals of the disaster management agency.

additional effort into distributing gas masks than into technical educational training of the population. Overall, however, the stated goals of the HFC were reflected in the eyes of their own managers. This meant that stated goals were actual goals being implemented by the organization.

GAUGING EFFECTIVENESS

The next issue in my effort to measure organizational effectiveness requires finding a way to gauge effectiveness. To do so meant walking a fine line between the organization's multiple goals and its clients' perception of these goals. The guiding principle was to seek a clear-cut measure that acknowledged the *actuality and delivery of stated goals*. Having stated their goals, organizations still need to provide them as a precondition for client-stakeholders to evaluate their effectiveness. For example, an organization can declare that it provides specific services to its clients in line with its stated goals, but these services may or may not have been supplied or have reached the intended clients. There is also the possibility that along the way the intended end users may not be aware of the existence of these services. In addition, the client may misinterpret the meaning of the goal objectives (Grandjean and Vaughn 1981).

To take these possibilities into account, alternative measures of the perceived goal services were introduced into the survey.[3] Focusing on the ten stated client service goals, questions were formulated to measure if each of these service goals was perceived as being provided by the HFC or not. The key to the questions was not so much if they "thought" the service was or was not provided but if they actually received it, knew where to get it, or were eligible for it. We refrained from measuring perceived satisfaction with the services, as this measure is highly suspect and intercorrelated with a host of intervening variables,[4] therefore emphasis was put on client perception of the actual supply of the service, an unequivocal measure of the organization's ability to attain its stated goals.

The gap between what the HFC says its service goals are and how individuals perceive the degree of its actual (or potential) delivery became the measure of organizational effectiveness. The rationale for this approach assumes that the first crucial step in an assessment of an organization's effectiveness is if the organization delivers what it promises. It is the cognitive recognition that services are actually supplied that sets the stage to evaluate organizational effectiveness. This means that organizational effectiveness differs from measures of quality of services, placing them on two different sides of the organizational coin. Organizational effectiveness is based on the client (stakeholder) perception that stated goals are being delivered, while quality of service depends on the relative (usually peer-related) value judgments of a service already provided. Simply put, stated goals exist if client-stakeholders perceived them to be so (as potentially or already delivered services or goods) and form the basis for a measure of organizational effectiveness. If quality of services is sought, it can only be evaluated when the stated goals are transcribed into actual service delivery.

EYES OF THE BEHOLDER

The next question that arose is: How do you measure the delivery of services or goods that are promised in the stated goals of the organization? The answer comes in two parts. The first is that we must look toward the client-stakeholder, who is the primary recipient of these services. The second is that we must only consider actual delivery of those services and goods. What was done, therefore, was to compare the HFC-stated goals with its client's perceptions of them. This led to the formulation of a series of possible measures asking the client-stakeholder population if it received the HFC service or if it knew a specific service goal was supposed to be provided by the HFC.[5] For example, respondents were asked if during emergency situations the HFC coordinates fire and rescue services. The response ostensibly measured the clients' perception of the HFC role in directing and coordinating these services, but more important provided evidence of the degree to which a primary stated goal is perceived as linked directly to the HFC. If it was not, this could be interpreted as either a failure of the HFC to inform its clients of this goal or a failure to fulfill it. It may also have meant that another organization, and not the HFC, provides this service. In all cases, a negative response indicated that the HFC-stated goals were not being met, as far as its customers were concerned. This same type of measure was employed for other stated goals, such as providing the technical, financial, and logistical services to provide the civilian population with bomb shelters, guidelines, and instructions for sealed rooms, and supplying an amount an ample of basic survival goods (food and electrcity), as well as identifying and coordinating the neutralization of hazmat materials and distributing protective gear against unconventional attacks.

GOALS CONFLICT?

We have on the one hand what the HFC says are its goals, yet on the other hand we have what the client-stakeholders perceive them to be. The question that will be asked next is if the goals that the HFC says are operative are actually perceived to be so by its client-stakeholders. The first step is to see the degree to which the HFC-stated goals are similar to those perceived by its clients. Conceptually, publicly stated goals by the HFC fall into three basic categories: (1) goals directed toward prevention and response, (2) those that

FIGURE 5   Stated goals of disaster management agency.

aimed at a direct service, and (3) those related to preparation through information, training, guidelines, and advice. (See Figure 5.)

A factor analysis was generated to empirically substantiate if this conceptual categorization is similar to that perceived by the disaster agencies' clients. In the case of the client-stakeholder, goals were derived by how the clients saw them; did they exist and if so, to what degree. All the stated goals were put before the sample population and asked if they recognized them as the HFC goals. Their responses were fed into the statistical analysis, which grouped together the different goals in terms of their commonalities. Not surprisingly, the conceptual and empirical categories turned out to be similar. Of the questions that were employed to measure the perceptions of the ten external customer-directed HFC-stated goals, three factors emerged. The results (see Figure 6) reflect this differentiation in goal direction. For example, prevention-response goals focus on handling hazardous materials (factor 1, Hazmat) and the service-oriented goals describe the distribution and maintenance of gas masks (factor 2, Gas Masks), while goals related to preparation and mitigation focus on the basic emergency providers (factor 3, Authority). What these results showed was that the potential victims of a disaster recognized the major areas of activity of the HFC but *not* its specific organizational goals.

HOW EFFECTIVE

Refining the analysis provided a glimpse into what the client-stakeholders thought of HFC-stated goals. What was asked was if what clients perceived as the HFC goals were actually supplied by that organization. This approach provided the basis for measuring the effectiveness of the disaster agency. No longer did this measure rely on the organization's employees (who are partial in their criteria and evaluations), but on its clients. Did the HFC deliver on its word? Did what it said its goals were conform to what they were perceived to be by the potential recipients of its services? These questions formed the basis of a measure of effectiveness, and it was this type of information that was introduced into the analysis. The results are fairly straightforward; they rely on comparing the proportion of positive responses client-stakeholders made

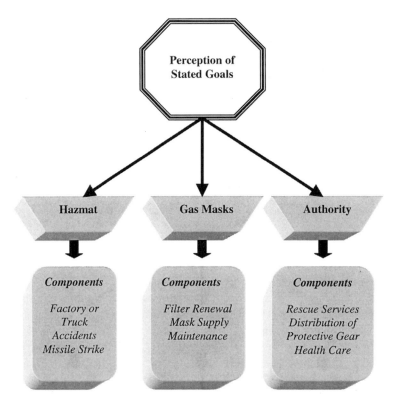

FIGURE 6 Summary of factor analysis based on stakeholders' perception of disaster agency stated goals.

of their perceived goals of the HFC. Each person in the sample of client-stakeholders rated each of what he or she saw as the HFC's goals in terms of its actual delivery of goods or services as promised. (See Table 2.)

A first examination of the results in Table 1 found that the client-stakeholders did indeed rate the organizational goals differently as to their effectiveness. It is important to reiterate that they did not look at the entire disaster organization, only the specific goals they perceived as relevant. What was also found was that when looking into each of the conceptual goals (factors), differences appeared within them as well. (See Table 2.) For example, perceived effectiveness was highest for those goals related to gas masks (88%)—service-oriented goals describing the distribution and maintenance of gas masks. Effectiveness was also high for authority (85%), reflecting the ability of basic emergency providers to prepare and mitigate disasters. On the low end of effectiveness are those stated goals dealing with hazmat items (31%), reflecting prevention-response goals dealing with handling hazardous

TABLE 2   Degree of Organizational Effectiveness Based on
Stakeholders' Perception "If Stated Goals Are Actually
Provided"

Perceived goals	Organizational effectiveness
Hazardous materials	31%
Factory	24%
Truck accident	26%
Ballistic missile	59%
Gas masks	88%
Renew gas mask kit	84%
Supply of gas masks	87%
Maintain gas masks	83%
Authority	85%
Rescue teams	76%
Distribution centers	91%
Health services	81%

materials. At first glance we see that the HFC seems to be fairly effective—except for hazmat goals—from the point of view of its client-stakeholders. These effectiveness scores may be seem to be somewhat deceiving, however when a closer look is taken of the variability within each of the goal categories.

Doing this revealed other interesting results. It should be remembered that each of the global goal categories as perceived by the client-stakeholder is composed of its component parts. When calculating the effectiveness scores for each of these specific subcategories, wide differences appear. For example, those grouped in the hazmat category range from very low effectiveness scores of 24 and 26 to a medium range of 59. This means that the potential victims of these disasters do not see the HCF as fulfilling its stated goals of preventing or responding to hazmat disasters that are associated with toxic materials in factories or to traffic accidents. In the case of the relatively high effectiveness scores associated with authority, here too the range is not consistent. Perceived stated goals linked to rescuer services (76%) are seen as inferior to those involving health services (81%), and even more so services associated with the organizational distribution of gas masks (91%). Only in the case of the gas mask goal category is the effectiveness score fairly high and consistent, ranging from 83% approval to 87%.

Overall, these scores give us a clear picture of how client-stakeholders—the potential victims of disasters—assess the effectiveness of the disaster management agency's ability to fulfill its organizational promises. What can also be gleaned from this is that there is apparently no ubiquitous overall organizational goal that can be assigned the role of godfather to measure effectiveness. Such complex public sector organizations have multiple goals that appear to affect different people in different ways. What appears to be the case is that individuals are extremely local in their perceptions of organizational effectiveness, choosing to direct their attention to distinct and specific subgoals. As I have shown, these goals do not necessarily match what the organization states them to be; they are what the client-stakeholders perceive them to be and are evaluated in these terms.

WHAT AFFECTS PERCEPTIONS?

This distinction made by stakeholders in evaluating organizational goal effectiveness begs a further question as to how and under what condition such effectiveness scores develop. The adage that people see and hear what they want to see and hear may be applicable in this case. Certain types of persons may be more "into" biochemical threats, others flooding or earthquakes, making them more sensitive to certain disaster agency goals than others. Being so may trigger them to be more cognizant and thereby more critical or lenient of the organization's effectiveness. This sensitivity on the part of the client-stakeholders to what is happening around them, especially in their social and political environment, is a potent clue as to how effectiveness is gauged. In our case, the situation revolved around the Gulf War, but it certainly is not the only potential explanation.

Taking both situational and core disaster behaviors as a starting point, the question was asked as to what among these possible variables would help explain the variations in effectiveness scores. To uncover the most likely explanatory variables affecting variations in the effectiveness scores, a search was made in the research literature for core disaster behaviors that would be helpful (Schneider 1995), thus such basic sociodemographic characteristics as age, education, gender, marital status, and religion are included. Along with these are preparation variables (e.g., have equipment, plans and knowledge; past activities), "belief" (e.g., that defense forces can eliminate or cope with threat), "fear" items (i.e., fear of a disaster or hearing the warning); satisfaction with disaster-related services, understanding of and compliance with disaster instructions, and as I mentioned before, Gulf War experience and concerns. Taken together, these situational variables reflected what could best be described as the framework within which client-stakeholders develop their awareness to the services provided by the HFC. (See Figure 7.)

SOURCES OF AWARENESS

Why is it that certain perceived goals of the HFC were seen to be more effectively carried out than others? What led people to perceive of these goals rather than others? What led them to evaluate the disaster management

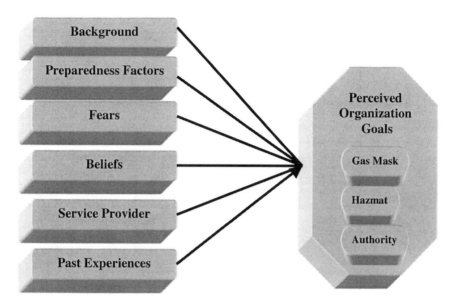

FIGURE 7 Predictors of perceived organizational goals.

agency effectiveness in terms of actual implementation? To obtain an answer required that I look more carefully at each of the separate perceived goals defined by client-stakeholders.

To begin to answer these questions led to the following analysis. In practical terms, it meant looking at the hazmat, gas mask, and authority goal categories in order to determine what variables could best explain how the potential victims of disasters came to their conclusions. As in the case of how I examined preparedness in the previous chapter, I will take advantage of a similar set of statistical tools to seek an answer here. To do so required a statistical procedure that involved separately regressing these potential explanatory variables against each goal factor. As Figure 7 shows, each of the organization goals that the client-stakeholder perceived as relevant to him or her was dissected to discover what best explained each. Without this type of analysis, your guess as to why, for example, an individual's past or character led him or her to decide if hazmat goals were important or not is as good as mine. In more technical terms, the regression procedure seeks to determine what variables among the many that I have proposed best explain the development of perceived organizational goals.

DIFFERENT GOALS

The results of the analysis show that awareness of each organizational goal is developed through different sets of variables. In other words, there is no omnipotent *single* variable that can by itself help us explain how we go about deciding which goals are important; nor are these variables always alike. It all depends on the goal. Again, it should be recalled that by determining which of the goals of the disaster agency are important to him or her, the client-stakeholder utilizes them as a way to devise disaster behaviors. What the analysis did find was that each of the primary perceived organizational goals does have at least one significant catalyst that directly affects how it is perceived. Let me now present the results of the analysis. A summary is presented below that briefly looks at each of the organizational goals separately.

First and foremost, the perceived choice of the *hazmat* goal as to what the disaster agency should provide to decrease vulnerability is primarily dependent on the level of preparedness of the client-stakeholder. When individuals are more knowledgeable of the danger of hazardous materials and they take actions to avoid them, sensitivity to this goal increases. An additional demographic component, religious affiliation (Jew/Muslim Arab), also affects its perception. (See Figure 8.)

Sensitivity to goals related to *gas masks*, which reflects the service-provider arm of the HFC, shows a combination of variables as significant. In general, these variables reflect the degree to which the client-stakeholder is satisfied with the general service provided by the disaster agency, a strong belief that the military can cope with the threat of an unconventional war, and the availability of equipment (a gas mask kit). Ethnic background also plays a hand here.

The perception of the *authority* goal, reflecting the HFC disaster preparation and mitigation service goal, appears to coalesce as the result of well-founded fears, past war-related experiences, and religious affiliation. The regression model indicates that fears of another war-related disaster, of again hearing the warning sirens indicating imminent incoming ballistic missiles, concerns after the Gulf War of another conflagration, and religious affiliation (beliefs), are all significant variables predicting greater sensitivity to this goal.

Taken together, the analysis strongly points toward a complex relationship between the client-stakeholder and the disaster management agency. The disaster organization states it goals, but the stakeholders perceive them differently. Disaster organizations set priorities, but the stakeholders have their own. *Most important, the stakeholder develops both priorities and perceptions of what the disaster organization should provide in a manner primarily outside the organization's framework.*

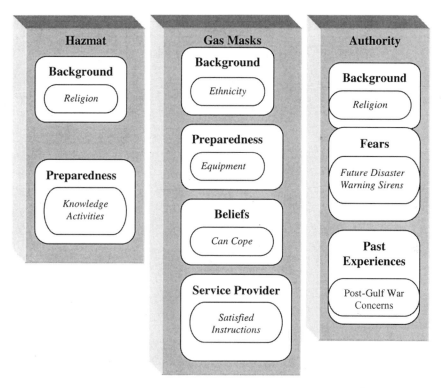

FIGURE 8 Variables that contribute to explaining the development of disaster management goals among client-stakeholders.

ARE DISASTER AGENCIES EFFECTIVE?

Where has all this gotten us and what have we learned? First of all, the HFC's own client-stakeholders recognized only *three* of the ten client-targeted organizational goals.[6] What about the seven other lofty goals that are supposed to save us in case of disasters? In addition, effectiveness as measured by how people evaluated the actual delivery of services varied both among the three goals (hazmat, gas masks, authority) and among its specific components. In the case of two of the perceived goals, the stakeholders gave a fairly high grade for organizational effectiveness. In the third (hazmat), the scores were very low, but again, what would be the scores for the missing seven stated goals? As they were not even recognized as goals, their score would have to be zero!

It is difficult to avoid facing the reality that for all the good will and honorable intentions the majority of the disaster organization's stated goals (as expressed by its own expert employees) are not even recognized as such by its client-stakeholders. This should make us pause to reconsider what it is that leads to the effectiveness of these public sector disaster agencies. It is obviously only marginally dependent on their stated goals. It is certainly more dependent on perceptions of their client-stakeholders. This gap can have devastating consequences, for to be effective these organizations must make a reality check with those whom they are mandated to help. When these organizations become goal- and not client-driven, what they have to offer may be too little and too late.

SUMMARY

This chapter has focused primarily on the problematic nature of public sector disaster management organizations. I have done so by critically looking at these organizations from *four* reference points. The *first* has been as usurpers of community-based disaster survival behavior. The underlying theme of this perspective has been that we have learned and inculcated into our institutional social life hard-learned lessons from the past about surviving disasters. These latent behavioral norms have served us well for thousands of years, and they are continually being "updated" with the threats of different types of disasters that, through the process of urbanization and industrializing, we now face. The process of modernization, however, has also been a time in which public sector administrations supported by the state have replaced community-based disaster management. The establishment of public sector disaster management agencies within the formal bureaucratic apparatus of public administrations has not only deprived local communities of their long-standing knowledge of disaster behaviors, but actually imposes on them a narrow organizational perspective of what to do and how to do it in the face of disasters.

The *second* point relates to the structure of disaster management organizations. The imposition on us by public sector disaster management is basically organizational in nature. Despite its dominance, it has not been very successful in reducing the number and intensity of disasters. One reason maybe inconsistencies within the organization itself. Such organizations are characterized by their formal bureaucratic structures. As such, they inevitably are confounded by a set of built-in conflicts that severely constrain policy making, internal activities, and actual operations. These conflicts emanate primarily because of the informal social structures present in them. The clashes that are typical are based on such irational considerations as internal departmental competition, political rivalries, jealousies, and interests. These built-in conflicts are a guarantee that resources will not be optimally used.

Adding to this, the structure as it now stands puts misplaced emphasis on nonessential goals. As disaster management organizations are relatively new to the world of public administration, there is a continual need for legitimization. Part of the organizational process to gain such legitimization comes through redefining disasters. More disasters mean the need for more budgets, more manpower, and eventually more recognition. The relatively simple task of administratively redefining disasters can by default triple the workload. While floods were formerly part of nature and taken in stride, now they are disasters. Terrorism and various forms of biochemical attacks are now defined as disasters. Disasters are now "discovered" through the use of satellite surveys and instant communications, so instead of focusing on preparing or mitigating disasters, time is put into internal administrative efforts to "create" more disasters.

In addition to this is the process of self-aggrandizement endemic to most bureaucratic organizations. This again means diverting time and effort to gaining power, prestige, and especially larger budgets. In this case, primary goals related to helping potential disaster victims are subverted so that the disaster agency comes first. To this end, many of the goals are sidelined, being replaced by transforming the administrative means into legitimate goals. For example, committees are formed and task groups created to study problems or create plans, all at the expense of using these same resources for the organization's primary goals of saving human lives. The implications are that such clear-cut disaster-prevention goals as mitigation are given low priority. Finally, the organizational structure contains the essence of all public sector organizations; namely, it is permeated by political considerations. Goal priorities and resource distribution are not likely to follow along totally rational lines as long as these service organizations are linked to clients who can vote. (See Figure 9.)

A *third* argument for the poor performance of public sector disaster management organizations is tied up in the confusion over core concepts that are used to guide disaster management. This confusion is compounded by the possibility that different definitions will lead disaster managers to view, evaluate, and execute their responsibilities differently. Just imagine the potential internal organizational disruption when discussions begin of what preparedness is! Each type would require different policy and resource allocation. In fact, focusing on preparedness, a core disaster concept that as it turned out had dozens of meanings, showed this problematic situation to be the case. Preparation was actually made up of four basic components, provisions, skills, planning, and protection. What was discovered was that disaster managers had one set of views on the definition of preparedness while the general public had another. Even more revealing was that each of the preparedness components was determined by different characteristics of the beholder. This confusion could certainly be cited as contributing to why disaster management organizations have been lax in their effectiveness.

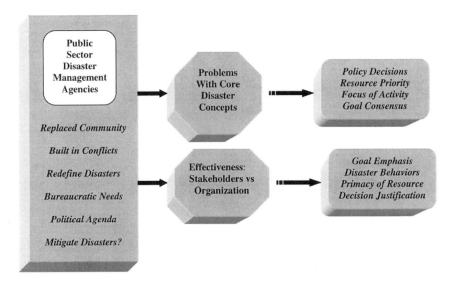

FIGURE 9 Summary of basic problem areas in disaster management.

The *fourth* point of reference in trying to explain why disaster management organizations have not met our expectations goes to the very heart of measuring effectiveness. As public sector service organizations, disaster management agencies are mandated to provide services to the public. By taking the point of view that performance measures of organizational effectiveness are more appropriate for private sector firms than disaster management agencies, a constituency approach was chosen. The constituency in this case is the potential disaster victim. By evaluating the disaster agencies' goals and the actual services provided, client-stakeholders provided a clear picture of effectiveness. For one thing, don't believe what you are told! As a benchmark for measuring effectiveness, disaster management agencies' goals may be misleading, as they may not be recognized as such by their recipients. Second, a number of the factors that impinge on how stakeholder's goal perceptions develop have little to do with the organizational goals themselves. What this implies is that if we evaluate the effectiveness of a disaster management agency on the basis of its client-stakeholders, a large number of them would probably fail. It also means that a warning signal has been raised to revise how we think about disaster management organizations' effectiveness. What is clear from all this is that the present internal organizational measures of effectiveness may be misleading and at worst harmful. Perhaps a more appropriate way to manage disasters, as is strongly suggested from the analysis, would be to incorporate the client-stakeholder into the blueprint.

WHAT'S NEXT?

Taken together, I have argued that public sector disaster management organizations are for a number of good reasons not the appropriate organizational form to take care of us as potential disaster victims. As I showed in Chapter 1, disasters and management agencies mandated to do something about them seem to run in parallel. What is even more disturbing is that disaster management organizations were created to provide us, their stakeholders, with what has already existed in our communities—the ability to utilize behaviors that have stood us in good stead for thousands of years! All is not lost, however. In the following chapters I will look at the victims' side of the story. In this next section I will reinforce the notion that there is still a great deal of latent disaster behavior that can be tapped outside formal organizations. Traditional sources for disaster role modeling are still alive and well, perceived risks still form a potent part of the ways in which we prepare, and finally, the family unit and its gatekeepers sustain us in the survival game.

NOTES

1. There is ample and sometimes confusing literature arguing the advantages and disadvantages among each of three sometimes interchangeable concepts of organizational success, performance, and effectiveness. For a more detailed exposition see Hall (1996).

2. The Israel Home Front was described in detail in Chapter 2, along with the methodology involved in the national sampling procedures and focus group interviews.

3. A fuller explanation of the survey is found in Chapter 2.

4. There has long been a debate about the usefulness of a "satisfaction" clause in questionnaires concerning the effectiveness of programs, marketing, and in general-prediction of actual behavior. Empirical evidence is scant but has shown that satisfaction is a very poor predictor of actual behavior. This holds true in evaluating programs and marketing strategies, but in a more complex way. In our case here, satisfaction questions about the provision of services are confounded by the fact that they focuses on individual tastes and preferences rather than on the organization's goals. Satisfaction thus may be linked to the "kindness" of the clerk where a person received a product or even the excess queuing time to get a service. The inability to decipher which satisfaction we are measuring makes its use very problematic.

5. Given the constraints of the telephone survey, most of the measures of perceived effectiveness were based on a 3–4 point Likert-type

scale. As each of the nine stated goals included at least three separate measures of their effectiveness, the average of the responses was employed as the score of perceived effectiveness. To further refine this average score, each set of responses was categorized in terms of the proportion of positive (yes, provide a service) or negative (no, does not provide or do not know) reactions to each of the service-goal questions. Positive responses reflect an evaluation by the client-stakeholder that the organization is indeed effective, for its goals are recognized as such and its service products are either provided for or can be obtained. Negative responses reflect their absence. This scale ranged from extremely positive to completely negative.

6. One small word about why Israel's HFC can be used as an example of how to measure organizational effectiveness; it is very much like other such agencies that are structured on the command model organization. Perhaps the HCF is a bit more formal than most other disaster management agencies, as it is closely structured long the lines of the military, yet like other public sector bureaucratic disaster management agencies, it has clearly delineated stated goals and operational procedures. Also like other such disaster agencies, it provides a human service to its clients, the potential victims of disasters. All in all, the example of Israel's HFC can thus be seen as a case study with realistic implications for other such disaster agencies.

4

The Power of Tradition

NOT SEEING EYE TO EYE

What my analysis of disaster management organizations has shown us is that disaster managers and their client-stakeholders don't see eye to eye on a number of critical issues. This has surfaced in a number of ways. The *first* and most basic is that public sector organizations have attempted to dilute the community of its ability to prepare, mitigate, and recover from disasters. This has stripped the community of a wealth of hard-learned lessons in critical disaster behaviors that have sustained it over time. What was once the province of organic community organizing in response to disasters has been transferred to noncommunity bureaucrats. A recent example of this was a study in a Midwestern metropolitan area that looked at how disaster organizations and local community service organizations tackled the issues of volunteerism and resource sharing (Zakour and Gillespie 1998). The critical use of volunteers to quickly help communities recover from disasters and in bringing needed materials to victims has long been part of traditional disaster behaviors (Rosse 1993). The researchers concluded, however, that emergency management organizations had a very limited service range, tended to block the distribution of vitally needed resources, and limited volunteer participation of community members in helping their neighbors. In other words, the community was actually being deprived of many of its vital social resources to cope with disasters.

An ethnographic study of the Northridge earthquake in California in 1994 reinforces how the exclusion of community-based help by formal bureaucratic disaster management actually leaves large gaps in community disaster needs (Bolin and Stanford 1998). Even as far away as Peru, a nation that experienced a major earthquake in 1990, the official relief agencies failed in their mission to provide basic goods to the victims because they were unfamiliar with local community conditions (Schilderman 1993). The result was a mismatch between what the authorities were trying to give to the victims and what they actually needed. Unlike the Peruvians, it seems that the lack of public sector intervention may have actually been a boon for those Japanese who experienced the great Hanshin earthquake. In the immediate aftermath of the earthquake, neighborhood associations or *chonai-kair* were extremely active in dealing with the physical destruction and welfare needs of their neighbors (Iwasaki 2000). Along with local gangs, they were in fact the first responders and providers of necessities for those affected by the earthquake's destructiveness. Only much later did the local and national government emergency agencies start to function. What these studies have shown is that the intervention of official public sector disaster agencies may be misplaced and at times ill-advised. More distressing is that it may leave communities even more vulnerable.

A HELPING HAND

A *second* area of confrontation is generated from within the very organizations responsible for disaster prevention; namely, how preparedness, a core concept in disaster management, is defined. As I discovered in the previous section, preparedness definitions are primarily created to serve the internal needs of the organization and *not* its clients. A good example of this occurred in Zambia during a major flood in Lusaka in 1990 that left thousands of squatters homeless (Mulwanda 1992). The "authorities" independently decided on a suitable package of services to prepare and afterward help the flood victims. This "package of services" completely ignored the potential victims' input and understanding of what had to be done. Luckily for those who knew firsthand what was happening they used their own wits and muscle to prevent their homes from being completely washed away. This case illustrates what happens when disaster managers consider preparedness from a point of view (a sterile service package) that does not match that of community members.

Things turn out much differently when managers see preparedness from a community's perspective. Take the case in which "officials" from the Society of National Integration Through Rural Development approached the problem of preparedness by not only asking the people of a fishing village in the Prakasam district in India what they thought would be the best way to prepare for floods and monsoon rains but also prompted them to take things into their own hands (Newport and Jawahar 1998). The result was less death, injury, and destruction of property.

A GOOD JOB

A third area of potential contention dealt with assessing the effectiveness of disaster management organizations. Apparently such measures neglect to take into account client-stakeholders and rely primarily on internal organizational measures. As goals are a benchmark to measure effectiveness, disagreement can easily arise between disaster managers and the organization's stakeholders—the potential victims of disasters—as to what disaster management agencies are supposed to do and how well they do it. Many studies have indirectly tried to look at the effectiveness of disaster agencies but almost never take up this issue directly. One such study of the 1993 Midwest floods in the United States actually attempted to compare why certain rural communities fared better than others by taking a closer look at community survival from the point of view of the client-stakeholder and focusing on community goals (Sherraden and Fox 1997). This case study is important in what it does *not* say! To begin with each of the five communities examined had equal access to aid from both public and private sources but with recovery success varying. According to the authors, one crucial factor that led to successful recovery was the community's consensus on what it perceived as its goals for recovery and the ability to activate local leaders and organizations to attain them. The implication is that if a community (client-stakeholder) had its goals defined and the provider disaster agency does not impose its own agenda (it just provided money for recovery), successful community recovery was probable. What would happen, however, when the disaster agencies' goals and agenda differed from a community's idea of what was best for it? The result would be a gap between the goals expressed by disaster managers and those whom they are supposed to serve. This gap led to diminished community recovery. It also exposed disaster agencies to harsh criticism by community members for not providing what its clients needed. The result creates friction and contention between the suppliers of disaster services and those who are its customers.

UNDERLYING TENSIONS

These conclusions expose an underlying tension between the organizational format for disaster management and survival activities based on traditional community-based behaviors. A recent study (Perez 2001) of a flood in Puerto Rico traced both the event and the efforts of the disaster management agencies to deal with it and concluded that the formal agency–media–information sequence was ineffective. The assumption was that this formalized way of providing information would create an awareness of potential disasters and therefore prompt people to be more prepared. The reason why this organizational format failed was because it neglected to take into account community leaders and others in community-based institutions that could have potentially affected people's sensitivity to mitigation and preparedness. In a way these agencies were trying to force upon the public a message that was not market-friendly and was devised not to persuade but to artificially educate (Bay Area 1985).

These and other examples raise the delicate question of why the congenital conflict between disaster organizations and the public that they serve. Tensions have been exacerbated to such an extent that the U.S. Department of Environmental Protection even commissioned a detailed manual for disaster agency managers on how to reduce their frustrations in dealing with communities that do not listen to their advise or focus on the "wrong" risks (Hance et al. 1988). The question still remains as to why this clash occurs. One plausible explanation stems from a long-standing clash that has evolved in the transition from a traditional to modern society, from community-based disaster behaviors to formal bureaucratic organizations, but as I have pointed out, not everything modern is for the best. As I said before, the sad fact is that despite more public agencies to deal with disasters, their number and intensity continues to grow. Faced by this troublesome fact, perhaps there is an alternative way to approach disaster management.

We have seen the relevance of these differences in the last chapter, where client stakeholders—the potential victims of disaster management—disagreed with what others thought was good for them. There may indeed be something more in the behavior and responses of the potential victims of disasters. This will now be explored even further by focusing on what the potential victims of disasters see as disasters, their belief and trust in public agencies, and especially the best way to survive both disasters and the disaster agencies! In doing so, we will once more see the clashing perspectives of how chaos is organized. On the one hand are the official formal organizations that are mandated to deal with disasters. On the other are the citizens who are the potential victims of disasters but who have at their disposal a rich history of successful disaster behaviors. As we have seen, the two perspectives of disaster behavior don't mix very well.

PRIMORDIAL CHOICES

In attempting to find the root cause of disaster behaviors it makes a lot of sense to look back over thousands of years of societal development. Stone-age man barely survived. Bronze-age man built on these survival skills and incorporated them into his religious and social life. Time and experience accumulated. Cultures developed around the abundance of food, leading nations such as ancient China and Egypt to develop even more sophisticated mechanisms to both avoid and cope with natural disasters. Problems of water and food distribution led to more structured organizational societies that formalized these disaster behaviors as normative imperatives. No longer was disaster survival just a "hit-and-miss" situation constantly being relearned with every new generation, but institutionalized and set in place to be built upon and expanded. Throughout all these centuries, sets of normative disaster-related behaviors have taken hold, and like most institutional norms, have been adapting to the changing environment.

Today we have the flagship of modern public administrative organizations as the stewards of disaster management, yet despite the emergence of formal disaster organizations, the deeply embedded institutionalized norms defining disaster behaviors remain intact. This point has been emphasized over and over again in the hundreds of case studies of disasters that have documented how individuals, families, and communities have acted in the face of disasters (Natural Hazards Center 2002). Like many other kinds of traditional forms of social relationships, the potency of these disaster behaviors cannot be easily dismissed. Because of this, as I will now show, traditional forms of disaster behavior continue to play an extremely important role in societal survival.

ADAPTATION

What a disaster is depends on whose disaster it is! Its meaning has changed over time and is inextricably linked to either the victim or those whose task it is to deal with it (Dombrowsky 1998). In short, how disasters are defined depends on the eye of the beholder. This definitional problem is further complicated by polarized and sometimes very emotional claims that disasters should be seen as generic social constructs and *not* the output of organizational machinations (Hewitt 1995). As I pointed out earlier, the core operative construct preparedness was devised in the halls of bureaucratic organizations, while our definitions have been inherited from our ancestors. To a great extent, the nearly total monopoly of public sector disaster management organizations has created a playing field on which practitioners are pitted against theoreticians and stakeholders against bureaucrats. On the one hand, the argument that disasters are indeed social constructs makes a great deal of sense (Quarantelli 1998). For thousands of years, we as a species have honed social mechanisms to assure survival. The result has been the development of a large number of behavioral patterns adapted to various forms of disasters (Oliver-Smith 1986). On the other hand has been the transformation of societies into what has been aptly called the "modern state," in which public administration has taken over the basic survival functions through interlocking, complex bureaucratic organizations. What we may be seeing in the clash between these "organic community" and "bureaucrat mechanical" social forms of disaster management is another stage of adaptation of organizations in the face of tenaciously held traditional social forms of disaster behavior. What I can only hope for is that this adaptation process will make public administration more user-friendly.

To put this adaptation process into wider perspective, for example, take the absurdity of the fact that disasters of today were simply natural phenomenon of yesterday. Fires, floods, volcanic eruptions, earthquakes, and droughts were all part of everyday life and followed the natural course of nature; they were not considered disasters. Social groups developed ways to deal with them so as to assure survival and minimum physical and social damage. For the most part they relied on the intricate social networks made up of family, friends, and community. *Disaster behavior was simply another form of normal social group behavior found in communities.* A recent example of this occurred after the 1976 Tangshan earthquake in China, in which over 3000 women were left widowed (Chen et al. 1992). Despite the negative attitudes toward remarriage as a violation of traditional norms, remarriage was seen as an appropriate behavioral response to the devastating economic effects and family disruption of the earthquake. Earthquakes had happened in the past and would continue to occur, and adapting to them was a form of community survival.

Not so today. For example, examine what happened when disaster management agencies massively entered the scene as part of public sector administrations just over fifty years ago. Suddenly nature was thought to be just another annoying issue that with enough money, ingenuity, and will could be manipulated, modified, and conquered. Disasters were seen as an intrusion into this ability to control nature. It was expanded to included newly generated man-made, nonnatural technological and environmental disasters (Crouch and Kroll-Smith 1991). The original social construction of disasters thus met head-on with the formalized definitions and managerial techniques created within the convolution of bureaucratic organizations. The question to be raised now is not who the winners or losers are but to what degree disaster behavior has remained outside formal organizations in its traditional format. Just as the Chinese widows remarried despite its traditional violation as a means of community survival, have we continued to favor "folk wisdom" over disaster agencies "wisdom?"

TRADITIONAL WAYS

It is important at this point to set the ground rules of what is traditional disaster behavior. I believe the best way to understand this concept is to recognize that any type of normative behavior initiated by individuals and associated with disasters falls into this category. The reason why is that these types of social behaviors did not spontaneously generate. On the contrary, they have a long history behind them. They are part of the cultural baggage that is embedded in any particular society, and to a large degree are the direct reaction to the environmental situations that exist. A study of the impact of intervention into severe droughts in rural Australia brings this out very clearly (Gray et al. 1998). When the Australian government initiated special policies to ameliorate the drought situation, one unexpected side effect was a disruption in the traditional way of life in the rural community. The drought, it seems, was a catalyst for maintaining community solidarity. As a traditional cultural symbol of a collective threat, it acted to promote communal bonding, at times even leading to concerted collective action to help neighboring communities. It was only when outside intervention appeared that these long-held traditional forms of social behavior became more apparent. In more severe environmental situations, we see people falling back on traditional survival mechanisms. Take the case of Tengani villagers in Malawi who also suffered from a severe drought during the period from 1990 to 1992 and found themselves among 60,000 Mozambican refugees (Chilimampunga 1997). To say the least, there was an acute shortage of basic commodities. To survive, traditional behaviors that were successful during past droughts emerged, with households sharing their resources with neighbors and family, people changing eating habits, some migrating to other areas, and others seeking alternative means to generate income. Most survived and almost certainly passed on this knowledge to future generations.

These types of "helping" behaviors during and after disasters, along with the social transfer of vital disaster-related information among rural Australians and Malawi refugees, is a typical case of long-surviving disaster behaviors. They include what to expect, how to act, and whom to rely on. The natural social link between individuals and the consequent intensity of their interactions provides the incentives for collective group and community disaster behavior. Here, too, norms are generated about how to organize and act in the face of disasters. As I have already pointed out, organizing seems to be the best way to increase our chances for survival. Outside the framework of actual behavior is a whole range of attitudes and values that contribute to normative behavioral patterns. In many cases these attitudes influence how we act before and after disasters. These attitudes set the stage for us to assess, for example, risks of a disaster occurring or on whom to rely for accurate information about how to prepare for a disaster. (See Figure 1.)

MODERN TRADITION

The concept of traditional disaster behavior therefore rests on normative disaster behaviors that occur outside formal organizations. They relate

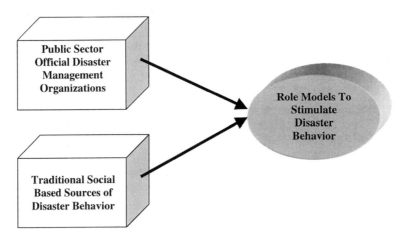

FIGURE 1   Theoretical framework to assess the impact of "official" and "traditional" sources of information on role modeling for disaster behavior.

primarily to the predisaster management era, when surviving disasters was the job of the group and community and when what to do and how to do it rested on the lessons learned by our ancestors. Information was socially generated and passed along through social networks. This particular point was touched upon in an analysis comparing disaster behaviors in floods that occurred in the Po River Valley of 1994 in Italy and the Mississippi–Missouri River flood of 1993 (Marincioni 2001). What was found clearly showed that cultural backgrounds and social–institutional differences were key in explaining the differences in how people reacted to each of the floods—especially traditions related to organizational behaviors, community integration, and perceptions of the environment. In short, traditional disaster behavior has its origins in and is based on a "people-to-people" scenario.

The extent of the power of tradition is evident even today when the world is facing global terrorism. Here are just two examples of community and individual disaster behaviors that are embedded in our society. The first talks about group behaviors, and the second about community norms.

The events of Sept. 11 confirmed 50 years of research showing that disasters rarely produce group panic and self-interested hysteria, but rather that people are more likely to risk their own lives to save others, a Rutgers University sociologist reports (Lou, 2002, United Press International).
...to help local communities deal with terrorism. Most of these groups already had deep roots in their communities and this seem

like effective barriers against panic (David, 2002, Newhouse News Service).

WHO TO RELY ON?

If, as I have argued, traditional disaster behavior is still in our midst, it does not prove either that it is applicable or an accepted way of behavior. There is, as you will recall, competition for such "homemade remedies" in the form of public sector administration disaster management agencies. One of the ways to learn if formal bureaucratic disaster management agencies have actually won the hearts and minds of their constituents is to ask the potential disaster victims whom they rely upon in case of an emergency or disaster. While not a perfect measure of which type of disaster behavior is favored, it does put to the test the degree to which traditional forms of disaster survival behavior are still with us. Put simply, whom do we trust and rely on? Is blood still thicker than water or have we transferred our sense of survival from the organic community to the formal disaster management organization?

This seemingly innocuous question has rarely been directly asked in the research literature. There are a few studies, however, that have by implication indirectly touched on it, and mainly through the issue of hazard risks. One example was a review of the Chernobyl nuclear accident that utilized data from countries directly affected by the radioactive fallout—Sweden, Ukraine, Belarus, Poland, and Russia (Drottz and Britt 2000). The conclusion was that trusting the information being pumped out by official spokespersons on the possible health effects of the radiation was evaluated in terms of social trust. Could you believe people who probably want to cover up something? In former communist nations, this was probably the norm. In Sweden it was not. The bottom line was that when individuals trusted the source of the information, they usually acted upon it. When they did not, they ignored it and did what they thought was appropriate. This was also the case after an earthquake in the town of Erzincan in eastern Anatolia, Turkey (Ruestemli and Karanci 1999). One of the predictors of preparedness for the earthquake was based on the perceived control of the government and trust in officials. In both Russia and Turkey, when official information is questioned, problematic disaster behaviors appear (Horlick 1995). For example, the "sensational" Love Canal toxic contamination incident near Niagara Falls in upper New York State led researchers to conclude that one of the problems in both the cleanup and relocation of the area and its residents had to do with trust (Fowlkes and Miller 1983). The long-drawn-out process and consequent health problems generated by the toxic pollution led the residents to view public officials as incompetent and untrustworthy or as having special interests in protecting private corporations from massive lawsuits. The result was a protracted series of litigations, extensive coverage by the media, and unfortunately a lot of sick people.

A TESTING GROUND

This question of "trusting the message" finds a fertile testing ground in Israel. On the one hand is the Israel Home Front Command, a typical public sector disaster management organization that asks you to believe what officials tell you. Then there is the traditional culture-religious society, which provides disaster remedies emergent from the immediate social milieu of friends and family or neighbors. These competing sources for optimizing survival-type disaster behaviors are built into the history and social fabric of Israel, providing a viable choice for its citizens. To understand this choice it should be recalled that in the last half century Israelis have experienced an astounding number of "disasters" emanating primarily from their neighbors' ambitions to destroy their country. Besides out and out wars, including the ballistic missile Gulf War attacks on civilians, there has been a continuous reign of terror, and more recently homicide bombings, so while blessed with few major natural disasters (except for a minor earthquakes, occasional forest fires, and drought), man-made disasters are plentiful. Since its inception, Israel has found it necessary to create a home front command to provide all forms of help to the civilian population in times of national emergencies, including natural and man-made disasters. In the eyes of most Israelis, this organization has been perceived as a poor relation to the Israel Defense Forces on which it was modeled. As I pointed out in Chapter 3 the Home Front Command is modeled after the typical chain-of-command centralized bureaucratic military organization. It has monopolized disaster management, however, and is the final word (by law) on disaster management.

The alternative to seeking trustworthy information from the Home Front Command emanates from the rich networks of information generated by the social networks that make up the backbone of the society. Israel is a country in which religious and cultural traditions are core to its social structure. Demographically, it is a fairly homogeneous nation built on immigration by Jews from all over the world that by tradition have sets of common norms and values. As an immigrant nation, survival skills have been sharpened over the centuries because of the immigrants' former minority status and persecution, creating an extraordinary reliance on family and community for survival. The last half century of continuous wars and terror have tended to strengthen this bond with family and community. These characteristics would foster a great deal of trust in these social institutions.

There has thus been in place for over a half a century the usual bureaucratic public sector disaster management agency typical of the kind found in most parts of the world. Simultaneously we have at our disposal a society having a rich tradition of reliance on traditionally derived disaster behaviors that are available from families and community for its survival needs. This contrast forms a wonderful research framework in which to explore the tensions between them. It is here that the question of trust is important. The underlying assumption is that trust in the source of disaster information will affect consequent disaster behaviors. By tapping into where people seek or the extent to which they use information to increase their survival chances, we will be able to decipher how much trust they put in traditional or official sources for disaster role modeling. It will also provide a glimpse at the degree to which traditional or official disaster management systems hold sway. The choice of their family, friends, neighbors, or other community members will point toward traditional disaster sources. These are the sources that have been traditionally used over the millenniums. If, on the other hand, people choose official sources that emanate from disaster management organizations, we can conclude that such organizations have replaced these traditional means of disaster behavior. The data from the Israeli field study supply the empirical evidence to document these differences.

ALIVE AND WELL

Israel is not only an in vitro laboratory in which to discern the power of both traditional and organizational information sources to role model disaster behaviors but also a battlefield of disasters. Given the disaster history of Israel, it is no wonder that close to *one-third* of the urban household population (in 2000, just before the recent terror reign of Palestinian suicide bombers and mortar attacks on settlements) reported having been involved in emergency situations in which someone was injured or killed. The range of these incidents extends from everyday small-scale events to those of societywide disasters. They included accidents (car and others), fire, terror, evacuations, bombings, and war. Two-thirds of those who have experienced or who have been caught up in any kind of disaster-type event (which accounted for a third of the total population!) reported being involved in only one emergency (64%), with the remaining third having been involved in two or more incidents.

When those involved in such emergencies were questioned about whose instructions they followed during or just after the incident, it began to emerge that reliance on the Home Front Command was far from absolute. In fact, except for cases of extreme emergencies, such as the attack by ballistic missiles or Katusha rockets and actual war, a large proportion (43%) of the sample indicated that they simply relied on themselves, their neighbors, passersby,

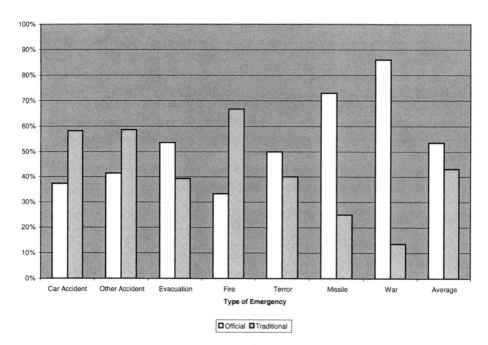

CHART 1 During an emergency, to whom do you turn for advice?

and even their own knowledge, but *not* official disaster management agencies. This proportion varied by the type of disaster event, ranging from a low of 13% in cases of war to a high of 67% in situations involving fire-related emergencies. (See Chart 1.)

What the data show through these responses is that traditional social forms of disaster behavior are alive and well. When we look for information-based role models about how to act or what to do a large number of us revert back to tried-and-true forms of disaster behavior accumulated through historical experiences. Even in cases of extreme disaster-type situations such as missile attacks, which have no reference in past disaster history, a fairly large proportion of the respondents continue to rely on traditional socially based means of disaster behavior.

TRUSTING BEHAVIOR

To confirm the viability of traditional socially based disaster behavior also requires confirmation that such behavior is not due to default; that is, avoiding the poor service or lack of trust in public sector disaster agencies. As a start, those who were involved in emergency incidents and in actual contact with emergency service units were asked how much they trusted these agencies. As can be seen in Chart 2, the proportion of the sample population who had actual dealings with these disaster management agencies was rather small, ranging from 10 to 20% of the population sample, yet their degree of faith or trust in these disaster agencies after such experiences was extremely favorable. It was highest for the Israel Defense Forces (IDF; 93%) and lower for the local authorities (67%), with the police, fire, and medical services all receiving high levels of trust (80% +). This was confirmed when the household sample was asked in the national survey, "Whom they trusted for their safety in case of a conventional and non-conventional war." Over 80% indicated they put their trust in the IDF.

When asked about chemical, biological, or other types of unconventional attacks, this proportion continued to remain at these levels. As part of the IDF, it was also not surprising to see that satisfaction with the Home Front Command was also high (85%). What these reactions demonstrate is that there is a high level of reliance and trust in Israel's public sector disaster management, yet despite this trust, individuals still choose traditional socially based disaster behaviors, not because of faulty services of public disaster agencies, but apparently on the basis of their social utility in providing both information and role modeling to survive disasters.

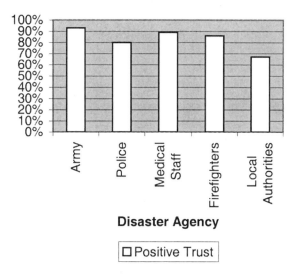

CHART 2   Trust of disaster agency after being involved in emergency.

HOW DO YOU KNOW WHAT TO DO?

Taking this line of thinking one step further led me to ask how individuals knew what to do during the emergencies. Were these behaviors "instincts," socially acquired, or dictated by circumstance? More specifically, where did individuals acquire the knowledge about what to do in potential emergencies? In answer to this question, it was surprising to find out that most of the respondents could *not* pinpoint a specific source from which they felt they could obtain adequate information about what to do in emergencies. Close to two-thirds (63%) could not cite a specific source. Of those that did, most cited the "media," including TV, radio, the Internet, and even the phone book (which contains a special section on emergency behavior in the Yellow Pages). An even smaller number cited various organizations (including driving schools) as well as the army, in which emergency medicine and first aid are mandatory. It should be reiterated, however, that most of the respondents could not cite any particular source that provided them with an information-based disaster behavior role model to imitate. This vague response of 70% of the sample was puzzling. What it did suggest was that their reactions to emergencies and disaster were instinctive, embedded in the very social networks that have traditionally given birth to what seem to be "natural" reactions during crisis. (See Table 1.)

To further clarify this argument, the question was refined to ask "from whom to whom" (and not *where*) you would seek information about how to act during a disaster. Here the emphasis was on concrete human sources that could be identified and associated with certain types of organizations or professions. Suddenly, just about everyone knew of someone or someplace they would go to for information. This, as it turns out, was also related to the

TABLE 1   How Do You Know How to Behave During an Emergency?

Source of knowledge	Percent
No particular source	62.9
Various media	17.5
Organizations	8.1
Social networks	2.9
Home front command	1.0
Army	5.5
Other	2.1
Total	100.0

degree to which they put their trust in the various sources. The main sources to which the respondents turned were nearly equally divided between official formal sources and socially based traditional sources. Just over half (57%) sought out information sources that were identified with experts and reliable information (e.g., official publications, TV, and newspapers). This *did not* include the Home Front Command, even though it is the legally authorized and sole source of authentic disaster information in Israel. (See Chart 3.)

The second group of the respondents (43%) continued to rely on various informal social networks from which to obtain information about what to do and how to act in case of a disaster. More specifically, they cited their family, friends, or just acquaintances, all of which played a prominent role in their choices of disaster behavior. When asked if they went to or contacted official emergency organizations for advice, close to 60% responded they *never* did, with an additional 30% saying they rarely did. This pattern of behavior of seeking information from social sources is even more striking when supported by the fact that over 80% of the sample respondents were convinced that most of their neighbors would help them in an emergency. Again we see a duality in how potential victims of disasters behave. True, expert information provided by official public sources such as the media are sought after, but there continues to be a determined outpouring of seeking information and role models through traditional socially based sources of disaster behaviors when facing an emergency or disaster. (See Chart 4.)

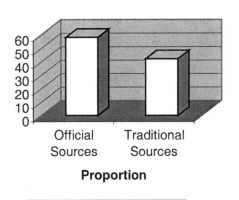

Proportion

☐ Percentage Responding

CHART 3 To whom do you turn for information about emergencies and disasters?

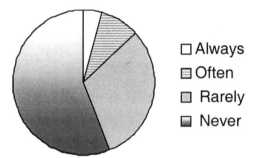

□ Always
▤ Often
▥ Rarely
▨ Never

CHART 4   How often do you seek advice from official emergency agencies?

TRADITIONAL VERSUS OFFICIAL BEHAVIOR

This persistence among a sizeable proportion of the sample population to seek out traditionally based social sources of information about disaster behavior will now be examined more closely. It should be clear that seeking out information of this type implies that the sources are more likely to be trusted (or believed), making the information more valuable, accepted, and adhered to. Who, though, are those individuals who purposefully choose a traditional information source when official knowledge is probably more readily available and perhaps more up to date and reliable?

To answer this question requires two tasks: to discover who it is that chooses each information option and observe if the type of emergency or disaster involved affects that choice. Taking this into account, the analysis sought to see if some key characteristics of individuals influenced their choice of traditional or official sources to rely on. The idea behind this approach was the assumption that the sociodemographic characteristics of individuals are empirical reflections of normative behaviors. To make this more pragmatic, let us take the example of when someone tells us "to act our age." Age is the empirical demographic characteristic (how long you have lived since birth), which goes hand in hand with how we act, or our normative behavior. We are expected to behave in tandem with our age. The same link applies for gender, education, or marital status, which not only prescribes, but also funnels our behaviors in certain directions.

Let us propose a set of possible testable hypotheses. Because of their traditional role as family protectors, married women with children may seek out the best information wherever available. Single women may be satisfied with official statements; mothers may not. Men might choose official sources while women utilize their social networks. Similarly, more educated persons may know how to exact information from multiple official sources while those less educated may rely primarily on their friends and family. Income may also play a part here, as it usually is correlated with education. Religion and immigrant status are additional key normative characteristics, as they reflect cultural distinctions in both belief systems (fate vs. control) and acculturation processes. Based on this assumption, the more traditional and less acculturated will seek out social rather than official sources of information. Are these hypotheses correct, or is there some flaw in my thinking?

Choices to Mimic

To empirically determine if significant differences exist in the way people choose between traditional or official information sources for their disaster behavior, a Pearson chi square test was performed. This statistical test basically asks if the choices made by individuals fall within or outside normal random limits, based on comparing real choices against probable expected choices. If there is something special about the choices that cannot be explained by simple chance, then we can also say that there is something special about the character of those making the choice. Unlike coins, people do not have just a fifty–fifty chance of being heads or tails. They can choose, making the randomness test an excellent way to judge if their choices are linked to their characteristics. The results of the analysis (see Figure 2 reinforce the notion that choices are indeed linked to the character of the chooser and by the type of emergency or disaster they had been involved in.

The first thing that strikes the eye is that seeking out traditional or official sources of information is not a random or haphazard exercise; individuals take such choices very seriously. Indeed, one's gender, age, education level, religion, and native status do affect the choice. Only marital status and income level have no significant effect on the choice of information. More important, the individual's characteristics that affect a choice tend to relate to specific types of disaster situations. For example, *gender* is only important in cases of being involved in general types of accidents and outright war. Here, men tend to choose official sources of information concerning what to do and how to behave more than women, who seek out more socially based traditional sources of disaster behavior information (64% vs. 51%). In all other kinds of emergencies or disasters, men and women make similar choices. *Age* differences are even more limited, only being significant in the case of general accidents. In this specific case only, older people prefer official to traditional disaster behavior sources. Again we see that the type of accident has very little affect on which age group will select traditional or official information sources.

Education, religion, and especially immigrant-native status, however, have a far more important role to play in the choice of traditional or official sources of disaster behavior. *Educational* level is a significant behavioral filter

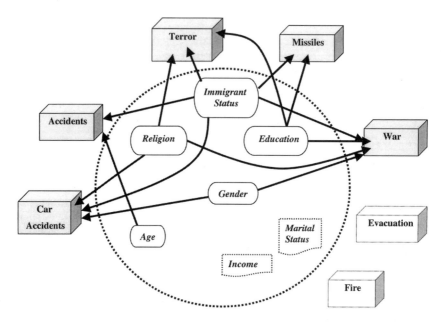

FIGURE 2 An individual's characteristics that make a significant difference in choosing a traditional or official source for role modeling disaster behavior by type of disaster encountered.

in making a choice among disasters that involve terror, a missile attack, and actual war. In general, as educational levels increase so does the reliance on official sources of how to behave in disasters. This applies to those involved in incidents of terror ($p < 0.01$), missile attacks ($p < 0.05$), and war ($p < 0.01$). Apparently being more educated may increase sensitivity to the "not too pleasant" outcomes of these types of disasters (especially if they involve un-conventional weapons), driving individuals to seek more informed sources through official channels.

CULTURAL INTERVENTION

Religious-ethnic background also plays a role in selecting where we obtain information about disaster behavior. The assumption that religious-cultural distinctions would affect a choice became a reality when dividing the sample population into two categories, Jew and Arab. In Israel, Arabs are predom-inantly Muslim and self-segregated residentially and occupationally. This combination is a self-sustaining formula to maintain traditional clan social structures. Jews, on the other hand, are urban with a long history of adaptation to modernization and change. These differences are apparent when the two groups choose their source of disaster role models. In fact, the significant differences between these groups' choices of information appear in a wide variety of disasters, including general accidents, terror, and war. Overall, whereas the Jewish households mainly sought official sources of information (60%), a similar proportion (63%) of Arab heads of households sught disaster information from traditional socially based sources. This opposing trend among Jews and Arabs in both low-key as well as horrific types of disasters is a first but clear indication of how religious-cultural factors can have an impact on disaster behaviors.

In light of this finding, the analysis went another step forward to scrutinize another characteristic of culture by focusing on the immigrant status of the respondent. When examining how a *native-immigrant status* affected an information choice, there was only a slight difference between native and immigrant Israelis in their choice of official and traditional sources of disaster behavior. Most sought official over traditional sources (60% to 40%). When taking into account that there are only a small number of immigrants among the Arab population, however, this picture has to be substantially revised. It is here that we can see the significance of these cultural differences more sharply. For one thing, native-born Israeli Arabs overwhelmingly choose official over traditional sources of disaster behavior (70% vs. 30%). Non-native-born Israeli Arabs completely reverse this pattern by choosing traditional ways for gathering disaster information (75% vs. 25%). Jews, on the other hand, continue to choose official sources in the same proportions despite their native or immigrant status (60% for official vs. 40% for traditional). What is also remarkable is that the choice by immigrants and natives to seek official or traditional sources of disaster behaviors significantly differs if the information they are seeking concerns emergencies related to car or general accidents, a terror incident, a missile attack, or outright war. The only exceptions are for evacuations and fires. Here again we obtain support for the cultural argument and reinforcement for how ethnic-religious background can affect the types of information sources we seek to augment disaster behaviors.

WHY A TRADITIONAL CHOICE?

Why is it that individuals continue to choose traditional sources of disaster information? Why do they look to their neighbors, friends, family, and community instead of official public sector sources? In partial answer to these questions, I have argued that such behaviors are embedded in our social structure, the result of thousands of years of trial and error. This argument presents the rationale for what has slowly been emerging from the data. True, people do look toward the official government-accredited sources of infor-

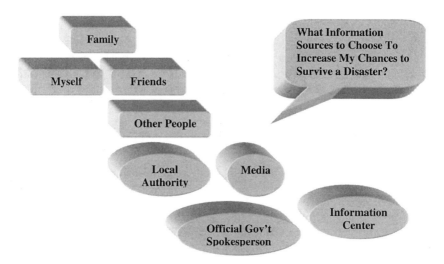

FIGURE 3 Types of choices available: from whom would you seek information concerning how to act during an emergency?

mation about how to act in disasters, but a sizeable number do not! This leads me to another stage in the analysis: to not only know that people want traditionally based information about disaster behavior, but being able to know how this choice comes about. (See Figure 3.)

I will now explore the difficult area of predicting why some people and not others choose traditional sources as a blueprint for disaster behavior. We have said that such choices are not simple dichotomous "yes–no" responses. Choices are not made in a vacuum, but in relationship to the social and political environment in which they occur. As we are examining individuals who have gone through the harrowing experience of the Gulf War, including thirty-nine potential biochemical missiles attacks, the environmental impact is not hypothetical but very realistic. In addition, these individuals are immersed in a "culturally traditional" society alongside a centralized public sector disaster management agency. Incorporating the wide range of "lesser" emergencies and disasters with the experience of the Gulf War and terrorism creates a contrasting environment in which potential choices and behaviors in varied emergency and disaster situations can be evaluated.

ALTERNATIVE CHOICE MODEL

To perform such an evaluation first requires devising a theoretical model. This may sound dramatic, but it is essential in creating a series of potential

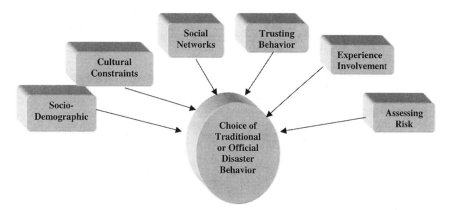

FIGURE 4   Significant factors affecting the choice of traditional or official sources of disaster behavior information.

hypotheses that can then be tested empirically. The model, seen in Figure 4, provides a visual outline of the *dependent* variable we are seeking to explain. This variable, the choice of traditional or official information sources from which to gauge disaster behavior, is operationally measured by a question posed to the Israeli household sample, namely *"From whom would you seek information concerning how to act during an emergency event?"* (translated from the Hebrew)! [1]The alternative responses included friends, family, official information from the defense forces, interpreted information provided by the media, telephone information centers, one's own experience with emergencies, no one, and anyone who would supply this information. These responses fell into two basic categories: those that focused on official sources and those that focused on traditional social sources. Traditional social sources included responses that indicate seeking information from family, friends, one's own experience, and other people. These sources, which have emerged from community group living, have been the backbone of disaster behavior over the centuries. The second category, official sources included all those sources originating from various formal organizations, including the media.

Sociodemographic Explanations

To determine what contributes to seeking disaster behavior role models in a traditional or official manner, a series of key independent explanatory variables are introduced into the model. These explanatory variables have been gleaned from the research literature. The purpose of these variables is to create possible propositional links between them and the dependent variable and set a framework to empirically evaluate their viability. These include basic *sociodemographic* characteristics of the sample, representing the usual basket of such variables as age, sex, education, marital status, and family size. As each of these demographic variables is mirrored by a distinct set of normative behaviors, together they represent a possible explanation of the choice of a traditional or official role model to emulate. For example, we often associate age stages with different degrees of conservative behaviors. Older people seem to be more "set in their ways" than younger individuals. If this is the case, we could expect older persons to seek out more traditional sources of information about disaster behaviors. On the other hand, age is accompanied by greater life experience, which may prompt older people to seek out what they consider more reliable information through official means. This same pattern may be true by gender. Women have been found to be much more "sociable" than men both inside and outside the workplace, making them more likely to seek advice and information through a social medium than through formal contacts. Again, knowing that the value of such social information depends on the degree to which it may be tainted by misinformation, women may alternatively seek official sources for proper disaster behavior models.

These types of dual alternative explanations also apply to the remainder of the sociodemographic variables. For example, simply out of sheer convenience or respect, married persons may seek information about disaster behaviors from close relatives rather than anonymous government officials, or because of their concerns for their family might seek information from what they perceive to be the most reliable official sources. A similar possibility applies to the impact of education on a choice of information. For example, individuals who have greater levels of education may seek more detailed information outside the official channels by approaching informed friends or relatives. On the other hand, they may trust official information sources over family or friends, as the disaster experts are likely to have access to knowledge not available to the general public.

Cultural Constraints

In addition, the analysis will include *ethnic-religious* variables that reflect cultural differences affecting choices by distinguishing the sample's nationality (Jews, Arabs), degree of Jewish religiosity, and immigrant-native status. These variables have already proven themselves to be of significance, but it remains to be seen if they can actually predict behavioral choices. To complicate matters, there still remain alternative possibilities. For example, even though the native-born significantly prefer official sources of information, the religious among them—Jews and Arabs alike—still tend to choose traditional sources of information that they feel will help them in coping with disasters. These facts, however, do not mean that each or all are good predictors of that choice. This is an important point to remember, as what is sought here is finding out which variables can *predict* the choice and not just that they are chosen nonrandomly by one group over another.

Social Networking

A third set of independent variables, those associated with *social networking*, evolved from the knowledge that decisions involving other disaster situations, particularly evacuations, are related to asking advise from close neighbors or family (Kirschenbaum 1992). This possibility suggested that seeking a traditional rather than official information source may be due to the intensity to which individuals are immersed in such networks. For example, there is the physical component that reflects not only how close but also how frequently family members and/or friends get together or talk on the telephone. There is also involvement in neighborhood activities, volunteering, and neighborliness. Logic dictates that the intensity of these interactions in the wide variety of social networks mentioned should be able to predict which source is chosen, but as in all good research, what may seem obvious may not be correct! Strong close social ties, for example, may provide the individual with the impression that his or her family or friends have inadequate or misleading information about what to do in an emergency. This would push him or her to seek the alternative official sources. Weaker ties may have the opposite effect. Only the empirical analysis can resolve this dilemma.

Experience and Involvement

Looking at the past, especially experiences relating to disasters and emergencies, broadens the picture of possible determinants of a traditional choice of role model during disasters. The adage "burnt once, twice cautious" probably makes us wary of negative experiences, influencing from whom and what types of information we would seek in the future. In the study here, I evoked these experiences based on the individuals' *past experiences and actual involvement* in the realities of a disasters. The sample, for example, was asked if their own or nearby neighbors' homes were damaged during the Gulf War. Also included was something peculiar to Israel but extremely significant— Israeli Army experience. Having military experience (which is required of both Jewish men and women) has become an integral part of everyday life in Israel. The army provides both basic survival skills (medical, organizational, leadership, etc.) and familiarity with battle situations, both of which create a solid platform of diverse experiences that should influence where reliable sources of disaster information sources will be attained. Added to these past experiences are measures of *actual involvement* in emergencies and disaster, from car accidents to missile attack and war. Involvement here is not vicarious, but more direct and bona fide. Hearing someone you know tell you or seeing the results of an emergency or disaster is not the same as actually going through it yourself. This is why actual disaster behaviors such as putting on a gas mask or entering a sealed room or bomb shelter are also incorporated in this set of determinants. The assumption is that those persons who have experienced emergencies and disasters, especially first-hand, will likely seek out others like themselves (i.e., traditional sources) for support in their decision of what to do.

Assessing Risk

Finally, there is the *risk* factor. How you evaluate the risk level of a future emergency or disaster should affect the degree to which you will invest time and effort in seeking out information, and as we have seen in the chapter on preparedness, in actually preparing for a disaster. There is, of course, the scenario of "it won't happen to me," but such optimistic behavior does not last long for most of us in the face of reality. As the most convenient sources of how to behave are those closest and accessible, namely friends and relatives, it would make sense to use them in times in which the risk of disaster is perceived to be high and reassurance is needed. There is also the contrary possibility that when disaster risk is great, people will seek out official sources rather than their social relations in the hope of attaining more reliable and up-to-date information, especially when facing unconventional war. To say the least, risk is a complicated concept. Because of this it will be explored in much more detail in the next chapter. At this point, its measure will be global, incorporating eight different types of potential disasters into a single determinant. These include assessing both personal risk and risk to the nation as a whole due to various natural and technological disasters.

Trusting Behavior

One of the most compelling but least examined aspects in the choice of selecting sources of knowledge from which to guide disaster behavior has been trust. I have previously touched on these aspects in this chapter but have not really gone into depth about their significance. Some work has been done on belief systems and their impact on disaster behavior (Schmuck 2000). The results strongly argue that belief systems (fate or free choice, e.g.) can play a decisive role in what we do in disasters. Little if anything, however, has been empirically examined in the case of trust.* No doubt a deep-seated universal human response that has been tied to many of our behaviors stems from the simple notion of trust. In the case of what to do in situations involving disasters, trust can lead to decisions of paramount importance. It may, in fact, save lives. As I have already shown, trust leads us to selectively seek out information to increase survival chances, but more important, as a universal character of mankind, it links the past to the present. Trust is built on reinforced past behaviors, and it is this past–present duality that makes it possible to start distinguishing who those persons are who seek out traditional forms of disaster behavior information from those who prefer official sources. I have already shown that there is a great deal of trust in the established disaster managment agencies and their operational departments in Israel. That being the case, it would be expected that in seeking information about what to do and how to act during emergencies a very large proportion of the population would turn to these institutions, and yet they do not. Trust is being examined by looking at two of its measures: (1) whom to trust when you want to know what to do and (2) whom to trust to ensure that what is planned is the best thing.

A PARSIMONIOUS MODEL

The variables that I have just outlined reflect the major but not the only factors enveloping a disaster environment that may affect how individuals choose their information sources on how to act. They are obviously not exhaustive of all possible variables. They do incorporate what is presently available in the research literature about disaster behavior, however (Lindell and Perry 1992). Each can be reasonably justified as a predictor of disaster behaviors and therefore has the potential to help in understanding who and why traditional disaster behaviors are still so heavily chosen over official sources. Seeking to find out which of these independent variables best explains (and therefore predicts) traditional (vs. official) disaster behaviors led to the use of a logistic regression procedure. [2] This type of statistical analysis allows the introduction of a number of possible independent explanatory variables to enter simultaneously into a regression model and measures if each one can explain (beyond simple randomness) the choice of a traditional or official source of disaster behavior. The variables that appear significant are then used to evaluate if the model itself can be relied upon.

The stages of the analysis included entering separate conceptual blocks in the regression model and observing the results. Cautiously, those variables

---

* The area of trust will be taken up in greater detail in the next chapter, which deals with risk.

that did not appear to be of any significance were dropped from the model. Eventually, a parsimonious model was fashioned. This model contained the optimal number of the predictors for making a choice between traditional or official information sources affecting a disaster behavior. This was confirmed by the fact that the model itself was significant ($p = 0.00$). In fact, it was able to correctly predict 88% of the official choices and 29% of the traditional choices. This can be interpreted to mean that by taking just the parsimonious model variables alone I could predict with various degrees of accuracy what each individual would choose. In the case of selecting official sources of information, my accuracy would reach close to 90%. In cases of traditional choices this accuracy would be much lower, only correctly predicting about 30% of the time. In each case, having access to a minimum number of variables, in this case five, I would know how each affects the choice.

PREDICTING A CHOICE

The results of the parsimonious model (see Figure 5) clearly demonstrate that of the original thirty-four individual variables composing the seven categories of independent variables, five emerged as significant. These include three basic

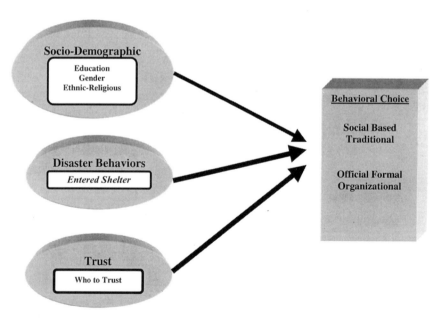

FIGURE 5 Parsimonious model predicting choice of traditional or official information sources determining disaster behavior.

socio-demographic variables, namely, levels of education, gender, and ethnic-religious differences. Also in the model is a single variable reflecting actual disaster behavior (entering a bomb shelter) and trust (whom you trusted). What is interesting about these reults is that they are heavily weighted in favor of basic characteristics of the respondents. This preponderance toward predicting whether or not an individual will make use of traditional or official information sources to increase chances of survival is very telling. The sex, educational level, and Jewish–Arab ethnic character of the potential victims are the key components in predicting such behavioral choices.

The point that should be stressed here is that singly or in combination these three characteristics of the potential disaster victim allow us to delve more deeply into the staying power of tradition-based disaster behaviors. For example, women more than men decide how to behave during an emergency or disaster on the basis of role models sought through family, friends, or neighbors and *not* from official channels. In sharp contrast to Arabs, Jews choose official sources much more often than relying on traditional models exemplified by family, friends, or neighbors. This same probability pattern of behavior appears for the more educated, who view official information sources as their best bet for surviving disasters.

SOCIAL IMPERATIVES

The sophisticated statistical analysis has now winnowed out the best predictors for choosing a traditional source for disaster role models, but it still remains to be asked what is behind these choices. My best guess is that they stem from deep-rooted, normative types of behaviors. Being male or female, being historically associated with an ethnic group, or having information or values imparted to you by your parents or peer group are characteristics that permeate into and impart important qualifying constraints on normative behaviors. To make this more realistic, just take some everyday admonitions, such as "Stop acting like a sissy" (gender), "Remember your forefathers" (ethnic), or "Don't be stupid" (education). Each saying has an underlying motive that sanctions, promotes, or disqualifies certain types of behaviors. This may also be the case here with seeking role models of disaster behavior. Gender reflects the historical development and changes in family- and sex-related role model behavior. Ethnic origin—in our case being a Jew or an Arab—has its normative roots in historical events. Education reflects not only intellectual abilities or opportunities but also the narrow or broad perspectives it harbors, affecting our lifestyles, openness to ideas, and social class values. These three sociodemographic predictors of disaster behavior choices thus open up the door as to why traditional forms of disaster role models have survived and to some extent flourished. They also provide some very strong clues as to why they will likely continue. Before talking about these issues, however, let us not forget the other two predictors; whether or not the person went into a shelter when the warning signal went off and his or her degree of trust of the information being distributed.

TRUSTING YOUR SOURCES

Two additional predictors of disaster role behaviors using traditional sources are an actual behavior during a disaster and an attitudinal trust question. On the surface they do not appear to be in any way similar. Placing these measures in the context of the Gulf War, however, with all the uncertainty and conflicting information dispensed by the media and through rumors, both have a common base: namely, a form of trusting behavior. In the case of entering a shelter when hearing the warning siren,[3] the results showed that people were more apt to enter the shelters when their information came from traditional sources. The siren was a cue, but trust in friends and neighbors led to actual behaviors. While the specific question does not delve into the actual process of gathering this information, other studies in Israel (Kirschenbaum 1992) have shown that individuals primarily depend on their neighbors to affirm taking such actions; they simply trusted their neighbors more than the official warning siren of an impending attack.

This same type of trusting behavior is more obvious in the specific question that asks (again during the Gulf War) "In order to know what to do, who did you trust the most?" Again the responses were dichotomized into "people-oriented" versus "organization-oriented" categories. The results were just the same. *Those whom you trust are those whom you will emulate.* As persons felt they could trust the established organizations more than those around them, they sought out official information agencies as models for disaster behavior. In contrast, not trusting the establishment led to seeking such role model information from such traditional sources as friends and neighbors.

Overall, the utilization of the parsimonious model to test the veracity of official and traditional sources of information affecting disaster behaviors has proven extremely beneficial. We can now point out that such choices rarely appear spontaneously, but are imbedded in our social histories. These histories apparently focused on two areas of our lives. The first are behaviors, which have evolved into norms expressed in our gender identification, ethnic character, and worldly perspectives related to our educational accomplishments. These norms create the framework for both expectations and actual behaviors that are essential in seeking a role model for disaster behavior. The second has emerged through the more intimate social discourses that form the social world around us, namely whom we trust. This is a particularly sensitive issue, as we are dealing with life-and-death situations. Whom we trust in potentially dangerous situations is also a disaster role model source. It is also a potent influence on how, when, and if we will implement survival behaviors at all. Taken together, we can now point to traditional sources of disaster behaviors as a substantial source of the way we accommodate ourselves to potentially dangerous situations.

THE END GAME

After the step-by-step analysis I have presented, the basic assumption that disaster management belongs exclusively to public sector administrative agencies is no longer self-evident. The historical development and staying power of traditional social sources of disaster behavior cannot be dismissed. Modernization has brought with it different forms of organization, but it has not changed the basic social processes that have been devised to ensure our survival. The most remarkable part of the analysis has been that even when there is by law only one absolute disaster management agency, such as the Home Front Command in Israel, over 40% of the population continues to rely on and use multiple social sources as the primary mechanism to deal with disasters. They do not do so by default, for the official agencies are generally trusted and have been given high grades by those persons who have been involved in disasters and seen these agencies in action, yet traditional social sources for disaster role modeling remain. This very fact again challenges the utility, not to mention effectiveness, of public sector disaster management.

The picture that unravels is at times quite astonishing. One is the fact that when asked about where they obtained information about how to act in disasters, close to two-thirds (63%) could not pinpoint any particular source. Is this because what to do is part of the self-evident embedded normative disaster behaviors that we have passed down from generation to generation, or that when seeking disaster role models from traditional sources we predominantly do so on the basis of disasters and emergencies that have been part of our historical experiences and survival repertoire? For accidents and fires, we overwhelmingly turn to traditional sources of information about how to act. For war, evacuations, terror, and missile attacks, we need to seek new sources, as they have not yet become part of our historical social baggage. Even here, however, initiating a search for appropriate disaster behaviors apparently goes against our historical grain. Close to 90% of the sample in the field study rarely or never sought official agencies' advice. What this leaves us with is nothing less than another large, bold question mark as to the relevance of public disaster management organizations in the ongoing struggle to survive disasters.

In my attempt to isolate who chooses a traditional or official information source to role model[4] disaster behavior, seven categories of possible alternative situations were carefully examined. In one way or another, all kept pointing backward toward basic social phenomenon as key predictors of that choice. Gender roles, links to a cultural past, educational horizon, and trusting behavior all heavily contributed to a choice between traditional and official role model sources. If you think about these key prediction variables, they are really socially embedded catalysts that prompt us to emulate certain disaster role modeling. This is the way of the world and our adaptive process to survive.

Who is the winner? The answer, I suggest, is that traditional and official sources for disaster role behavior are constantly being integrated into our survival repertoire. With modernization have come new forms of disasters, primarily man-made and technological in nature. They have only an indistinct connection to our past, but have become a common part of the present disaster vocabulary. What is seen as today's official source of disaster role modeling will, if effective and given enough time, be perceived as accepted and traditional sources for surviving disasters. It will become embedded into our social conscience and revert to a historical traditional form of disaster behavior, so the only winners are the survivors, and a large part of surviving rests squarely on the shoulders of traditional disaster behaviors that have shown their resilience and adaptability over time.

NOTES

1. These questions were the result of a series of field pretests that included alternative measures and open-ended responses.
2. A linear logistic regression is computed in this part of the analysis due to the fact that the dependent variable, the type of disaster behavior, is a dichotomous variable coded as "traditional" or "official." It measures the log of the odds of a case falling into either a traditional or official choice. The logit distribution takes on the appearance of a log linear form of the probability of success. This method allows us to see which of the independent variables are the best predictors of the two possible disaster behavior choices.
3. Later on during the war the radio was used in conjunction with the neighborhood siren system. As ballistic missiles took only a few minutes to land in Israel from their origin in Iraq, the regular siren systems did not allow enough warning time to get into a shelter or sealed room. In addition, the fear of an attack during the night prevented many from getting proper sleep. This led to the recommendation that mass media be used, especially the radio. Radios

were left on to certain "silent" channels during the night, with a warning signal given only in case of an attack.

4. The concept of role model is indigenous to both sociology and psychology and has been loosely used here to represent how a combination of both personal example (the role model) and/or information (the inanimate but behavioral model) can bring about disaster behaviors.

5

The Odds of Being a Victim

AN ENDANGERED SPECIES

Disaster managers are under serious threat of becoming redundant. Their monopoly over disaster management is being confronted by a persistence among potential victims to role model their disaster behavior by unofficial traditional means. From the perspective of managers in these organizations, this choice on the part of the public does not make sense, even bordering on madness. What could be more rational and logical than accepting well thought out information that provides people in danger with instructions about what to do? Ignoring these instructions increases their risk of injury and death, but the fact is that a large proportion of individuals seek alternative nonorganizational forms of disaster information. Does this indicate madness? I think not! As we already discussed in the previous chapter, one important reason individuals revert to traditional forms of disaster behavior is that information garnered from friends and family is felt to be trustworthy, and even when the experts were ignored, such a choice did not lower their levels of preparedness or increase their exposure to harm. This raises a problem for the disaster manager. Perhaps something is wrong with what is offered by official sources. Perhaps they are not even needed! As is heard very often, "You can take a horse to water but you can't make it drink"; perhaps what is being marketed by disaster management agencies reflects what they and not the consumer consider to be good products.

We have already seen that the goals of the disaster management organizations are not perceived in the same way by the potential disaster victims. Why does this gap exist? One reason, which will be explored in this chapter, has to do with perceptions of risk. In public sector disaster management organizations, rational decisions are buttressed by administrative edict, making risk assessment a highly formalized and informed process. The assumption is that disaster managers are privy to information that we, the potential victims, are not. On these bases, internal organizational assessment, however faulty, comes to influence various decisions concerning preparedness and mitigation guidelines. These guidelines are then passed down to us as official writ. For disaster managers, these organizational processes rarely apply to us as individuals. As I have argued, they are created under the constraints of organizational needs and internal conflict. The inputs into "risk" assessment therefore rarely take into account how individuals perceive of these risks.

One example of this type of misinterpretation was discovered in an analysis of the Guadeloupe Dunes oil field spill (the largest in U.S. history). What was found to influence the residents' perception of risks had nothing to do with calculated responses to the hazard and its health consequence by official disaster experts; it had to do with the breach of trust on the part of the corporate and government institutions that tried to cover up the incident (Beamish 2001). There has even been some research suggesting that compulsory risk analysis through legislation may actually boomerang, as public discussion of uncertainty (at least in health risk assessment) actually tends to increase perceived risk (Johnson and Slovic 1994). Indeed, when by some luck such inputs do include possible reactions on our part, they are more likely to be based on reports that turn out to be discredited disaster myths (Fisher 1998) than actual behavior. These include the infamous "panic" or "looting" behaviors that rarely take place but are introduced into disaster managers' assessment for predicting risk. Take the following typical scenario as an example: "When word is spread that gas masks will be distributed, the population will 'panic', make a rush on the distribution centers, ignore orders, grab or steal masks. Disturbances and perhaps riots will break out. Police and the army will have to be called in to restore order. Inadequate supplies will set in motion a black market and lead to unscrupulous dealers and price gauging."

In the only recent actual case of gas mask distribution among civilians (in Israel just before the Gulf War), none of these "expected" behaviors occurred (Kirschenbaum 2001a). This was accomplished by using premarketing media marketing techniques, localized distribution methods based on the logistic syntax of military operations, and short-term hands-on training instruction courses during mask distribution. Comparing those entering the centers with those leaving after being processed showed a remarkable degree of civility. Most of the people felt that the whole operation was orderly, that the instructions were clearly presented, and that they felt more confident and safe afterward.

In fact, in most disasters these panic myths do not appear. When disaster organizations do incorporate these myths about how the victims are supposed to behave into their organizational risk assessments, however, a self-fulfilling prophecy emerges that generally exacerbates the seriousness of the disasters. It also puts the victims at a great disadvantage as being "adversaries" rather than helpers! The results can actually increase damage to lives and property. Not only will valuable and scarce resources be misdirected toward mitigating the disaster, but also such action will hinder people from doing what they "naturally" would do; namely, being first responders. These behaviors were prevalent, for example, during the earthquakes in Mexico City and Turkey, in which local people actually saved countless lives even before the "professional emergency workers" arrived. Imagine for a moment your feelings when you are trying to extract a family member from under the rubble of a collapsed house and an emergency worker forces you away because you are "disrupting" the professional emergency work!

A by-product of such misdirected risk assessment in which the victims are viewed as adversaries has another consequence; namely, it is likely create a negative image of public disaster services. This type of reaction was clearly implied in a study of the low compliance of communities in the United States to mandated emergency preparedness committees for highly hazardous materials (Lindell 1994). In effect, what the people of these communities were saying was that forcing us to make emergency management committees on the basis of "your" (government) risk assessments is not in tune with what we know about our communities.

DISCOUNT THE VICTIM

Some of the more glaring examples of organizational-based risk assessment simply discount us completely. This makes a lot of sense for those working within the walls of formalistic public sector bureaucratic organizations. What counts are the experts. They can act in a rational, logical framework without the emotional baggage that ordinary people carry with them in assessing risk.

The events of September 11 have substantially enhanced this perspective in the United States by not only creating another bureaucratic disaster agency (Department of Homeland Security), but by pouring billions of dollars into related organizational and technical means to confront "threats" and increase the numbers of first responders (i.e., disaster agency members, such as police and fire) (U.S. Government 2002). The new Department of Homeland Security approved by the U.S. Congress will combine twenty-two agencies and 170,000 employees, and will be run with a budget of approximately $38 billion. Like its predecessors, this mind-boggling organization will most probably opt for this rational approach to risk assessment.

As part of the trend to dehumanize and make the *art* of disaster management more scientific, experts create lists then manipulate and simulate them to come up with an "objective" measure of risk. Take, for example, the risk assessment of a fire breaking out. The risk of urban fires has traditionally (until the advent of terrorism) been calculated primarily by a check-list series (FEMA 2002), which includes building codes, availability of fire stations, trained manpower, technical equipment, circuit breakers, extinguishing points, fire doors, and exits. If all these items are present, the risk of a devastating fire is substantially reduced. Of course, this program of assessment does not account for noncompliance with building codes, deliberate arson, or failure to obtain insurance payments, nor does it take into account remembering to keep fire doors closed, smoke alarms in working order, applying various building codes, or matches away from children. It seems incomprehensible with laws, a national fire code, inspectors, and a pool of lawyers on its side, that the United States has had 1.7 million fires annually, 4000 dead, and 22,000 injured (FEMA 2002) at an estimated cost of $11 billion. More important, have these risk assessments deterred persons from entering or residing in "high-risk" fire-prone buildings, from living in residential areas in which wildfires are always a present threat, or choosing to live near highly flammable or toxic industries? In short, fire experts catalog items they feel can either raise or lower the chances of a fire and then artificially calculate risks. Ordinary people like you and me simply make do by assessing risks on the basis of common sense, taking into account what is important to us, and adapting to the constraints of the immediate situation. Of course, a lot of our "calculations" may contain a host of irrational elements related to our own personal likes and dislikes.

Take evacuations. The risk assessment formula on outflow from buildings is based on simplicity itself: the number and width of exit doors, size of individuals (with or without clothes), and number of stairs and stories. For evacuations from neighborhoods or cities it is basically the same, but with the added factor of road systems and transportation facilities. Does it also account, however, for behavior that may lead to rushing and jamming exits, locking emergency exits, going back to find family members, accounting for persons in wheelchairs, or simply having someone trip? Transportation experts are in the same dilemma. How do they evacuate large populations in the face an impending disaster such as a flood or hurricane? Just look at what happens on the highways during normal rush hour; a minor accident occurs and there is a traffic jam for twenty miles and five hours. Numerous case studies of area evacuations due to hurricanes or flooding stress the same predicament in trying to dehumanize a very human process. Human behavior simply cannot match the rational number crunching of simulated models that flow from disaster organizations. This has been repeatedly pointed out, especially in evacuations, by the varying perspectives of officials and evacuees over a whole range of issues, from assessing the risks to leaving to the advisability of returning (Stallings 1991).

The point here is that assessing the risks of something "bad" happening as an organizational concern is by necessity calculated on a different basis than by the individual, family, or community. Conceivably there may be something in our historical past that triggers how we identify and assess the risks of disasters and how to cope with them. This might be akin to our sensitivity to certain smells that aromatically inform us of "bad" food that will harm us. Institutionalized normative behavior providing the clues of an impending disaster may be invisible to us, but nevertheless are in place. If this is true and we act upon them, are we, as the disaster managers claim, putting ourselves in harm's way, or by following our historical "instincts" are we increasing our chances for survival? To begin to answer these fateful questions requires first examining the concept of risk and then assessing its impact on preparedness.

EVERYTHING IS RISKY

Over the centuries our perception of the world has changed remarkably, but nevertheless has been consistent in the way norms helping us survive disasters have been institutionalized. Shifts in environmental conditions have stimulated us to see the world around us differently, particularly in the assessment of what, where, and when risks arise. There are those of us to whom the assessment of risk is a forgone conclusion, as it is "determined" by fate, the gods, or singular cause and effect events. To a great extent most of the world continues to perceive what happens in these terms. Today, there is the strong notion or belief that risk is nothing more than "chance," based on the rationalistic concept of statistical probability. The creation of a statistical infinity, for example, means that when I thrown a ball into the air, there is a chance it will continue into outer space, or I will get a straight flush when playing poker, or a disaster will occur. This does not mean that these perspectives are exclusive and totally independent of each other, as in the same breath, people can assess a situation by calling on fate and chance simultaneously. One often hears, for example, "it might have been his fate to die but why did he take such a chance by not buckling up when he drove!" Despite the recent upsurge of science and its rationality, it should thus be remembered that a large part of the word continues to hold that fate is the prima facie mover and explanation of all action.

Despite fate, however, when you look carefully at the behavior of individuals during disasters, you see there is still a large element of rational risk assessment involved. We may call upon fate to explain some event, but we continue to act fairly rationally. The saying "Praise the Lord and pass the ammunition" reflects this nicely. In a sense, everything is risky because everything can potentially have negative consequences. For example, we eat to survive, but eating too much increases our risk of heart disease. The irony is with the reduction of early death by infectious disease and cardiovascular aberrations have come sport, road, and work accidents, which are a leading cause of injury and death in the Western industrial world (WHO 2002). *This point is extremely critical in understanding risk, as by reducing the risk of something happening, you increase the risk of another related event occurring!* For example, creating backup systems in a nuclear plant reduces the risk of a leak due to technical problems. At the same time it increases the risk of human error!

In addition, each culture has its key risk questions. For Icelanders, it is "What are the chances the volcano will erupt?" For Indians, it is "Will the monsoon floods be extensive?" These larger culturally related risks also find their way into our ordinary lives. If you think about it, we are constantly making risk assessments (calling it chance) that relate to our daily activities: driving cars, crossing streets, buying food, health insurance, making investments, to name but a few. The fact that we are mortal enhances these ordinary assessments, as they can either separately or cumulatively lead to our injury or death.

The difference between these assessments and those related to emergencies and disaster lies in the enormity of the event and its potential cumulative effect on societal survival. As I pointed out, organizing has been the prime means of enhancing our survival. In modern times, formalistic bureaucratic organizations are dominant and built around a singular confidence in both rational predictability and the control of behavior and nature. The formal bureaucratic organizational structure is a prime example of this thinking. Risk assessments emergent from such organizations therefore cannot help but be organizational in concept and spirit. This type of risk assessment differs, however, from how we as individuals, groups, and communities assess it. In fact, there is a basic discordance between what organizations consider risk and how the potential victims perceive such organizational assessments. Risk assessment in organizations is determined by an organization's structural environment, while for individuals it is determined by their social environment. To understand this difference, I will review some of the ideas related to risk.

SOCIAL RATIONALITY

In an imperfect world, everything could be considered to be either risky or not, depending on how we evaluate each situation (Ewald 1991). The implication is that we are in a constant state of evaluating risks as we negotiate our way from one situation to another. Take the following everyday sequence of driving to work, finding a parking place, crossing the street to enter a building, lining up at an elevator, getting out on the fiftieth floor, and so on. All these situations put you at risk in the worst-case scenario of being injured or killed. Do we carry around a laptop computer crammed full of information about events that took place at each of these places to evaluate these risks? Obviously not! We have another set of data that combine our own experiences and those of others and that cue us about the level of risk involved in each situation. This is what is called "perceived risk." Such perceptions of risk are not at all random, but based on social rationality that we sometimes like to call common sense. It's a combination of cognitive, social, and cultural imperatives that leads us to make a risk assessment of different situations, based on how we socially construct experience and what we learn from it. When seeing a driver weaving down the road, for example, we come to the conclusion that the driver is probably drunk and keep a safe distance away. This type of social rationality helps keep us safe.

To make my point, let me emphasize those everyday sequences of behavior that we take for granted. For example, as we are about the cross the street, we prefer to go in groups and when the light is green. When waiting at the elevator, it feels less safe when we are the only one aboard. Seeing others on the fiftieth floor going about their business reassures us. We evaluate all these situations outside a rational organizational framework of actuarial cost-benefit risk assessment. It is based on social rationality, which combines our own personal experiences with that of others. The "others" are in fact the historical institutionalized and normative behaviors that have served us and those around us well in the past. We make assessments of disaster risks primarily on the basis of historical social events that have been passed down to us. Since disasters are socially transmitted constructs, the perceived risks associated with them have passed the test of time. In a Darwinian framework, the social context for disaster survival emerge through the filter of cultural and environmental conditions. Changing conditions may lead to new forms of survival behavior, and as we have seen, the advent of bureaucratic disaster management agencies is such a change. They have not completely dominated disaster behaviors, however. Apparently, there remains a large reservoir of traditional sources of disaster behavior that utilizes existing belief and trust systems of our social past and incorporates them into adapting to present conditions. Such behaviors are witness to the extraordinary flexibility and persistence of social rationality in assessing risks.

PERCEPTIONS OF RISK

By assuming that our behavior, especially during emergencies and disasters, is guided by social rationality, it makes a lot of sense to look at the concept of risk as a socially based phenomenon. For this reason, researchers have seriously considered risk based on its perceptions (Lupton 1999). Simply put different persons may perceive the same event differently. A study of emotional reactions to a flood that occurred in Phoenix, Arizona, in 1978 is one of a number of such studies that looked at the relative perceptions of risks. Here the researchers found that the fears that another flood would occur had practically nothing to do with how close these individuals lived to the actual flooding areas. In fact, those whose perceived fears were greatest lived no closer to the flood area than those with low or moderate fears of flooding (Shippee et al. 1982). One good reason for this is that individuals and groups are characterized by various and diverse backgrounds. Such diversity influences both how we perceive of events and our reactions to them (Fothergill et al. 1999; Dominitz and Manski 1997; Rosa et al. 194; Perry and Lindell 1991).

Examples of how this type of diversity affects risk perceptions are not hard to find. An Israeli traveling on a bus in the United States would react differently from an American if both saw a package left on the bus without its owner. Given past experiences, the Israeli would perceive of the packages as a potential bomb while the American would view it as a discarded package. This example represents only the tip of the iceberg of the sometimes subtle individual and cultural differences that have an impact on how we perceive of risks. Eskimos know the subtle differences in snow color and their consequences for hunting, fishing, and danger. Bedouin travel and survive the desert by traditional knowledge of water sources; New Yorkers learn how to avoid risky neighborhoods and exhibit nonconfrontational behavior on subways. We can also see the same pattern of diversity in disaster behavior. Here the social definitions of disasters—which affect how risk is assessed—are the key to behavioral patterns (Kirschenbaum 2001a; Fothergill 1996; Fordham 1999). For Indians living along the Indian Ocean monsoon path, an Englishman's estimation of a flood is a joke. Drought for a New Yorker who has to cut down watering his or her garden pales in the face of those persons living at the edge of the Sahara Desert. What these examples tell us is that not only is there a diversity of perceptions of disaster risks, but that they can have different behavioral consequences. (See Figure 1.)

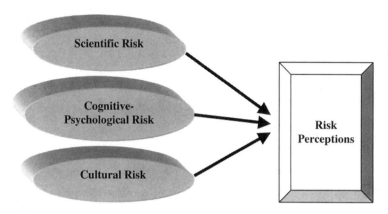

FIGURE 1   Different theoretical approaches to risk perceptions.

SCIENTIFIC RISK

The research literature has provided a rich inventory of how risk perceptions have been viewed and examined. (Weyman and Kelly 2000). From the perspective of the social sciences, this has included incorporating into its definition a broad number of social and cultural values (Pidgeon et al. 1997; Slovik 1987). The most dominant and accepted has been on scientific-rational analysis, focusing on the likelihood and strength of risks to occur. For disaster managers, this created a "scientific" platform from which to preach their message. The clarion call was based on the fears and anxieties associated with the likelihood of a disaster and the resulting damage (Bradbury 1989). This perspective reflected an ideological convergence in engineering, statistics, economics, and actuarial accounting, with an emphasis on correctly identifying the type of risk and the chances of it occurring.

Like all good rational systems, inaccurate predictions or difficulty in quantification are usually blamed on the habit of individuals to rely on such unscientific facts as their intuition or hunches (Lupton 1999). This "problem" was overcome to some extent by introducing stochastic disaster models based on the person's "belief." Belief thus became an "objective" component that could be introduced into probabilistic models. This allowed the substance of the rational models to remain intact but with a new twist; incremental belief could now, like other more objective factors, lead to a change in the probabilities of risk. This can occur as a two-stage process. In the case of disasters, individuals who believe (and eventually see) that improving preparedness leads to better coping and greater self-efficacy will believe that such behavior decreases the risk of disaster. By doing so it will lead them to increase preparedness behavior and change the original probabilities of risk (Russel et al. 1995). It is important to recognize that assessing disaster risks by employing this kind of 1970s health belief model is still being utilized today (Russell et al. 1995). More important, it reflects an approach that says that risks can affect behavior as a type of iteration process where the original risk assessments' affect on behavior brings about a new evaluation of the risks.

COGNITIVE–PSYCHOLOGICAL RISK

This approach emphasizes the development of perceived risks as part of the cognitive learning structure involved in decision making. It also seeks to explain inconsistencies and bias in such risk estimations. During the 1970s and 1980s, a consensus grew that what was sought was some trade-off measure between "objective" and "subjective" risks (Weyman and Kelly 2000). Objective risks, as measured by experts, could then be compared to those subjectively expressed by the general public. Focusing on the individual, however, and assuming a rational decision process as the foundation for this approach, researchers discarded exogenous social and cultural-environmental factors (Lupton 1999). They threw away the proverbial baby—in this case the social context of risk—with the bathwater by assuming that all things are equal, which as we all know is never the case. One of the major problems that advocates faced in attempting this perspective of risk was in trying to understand why nonexperts made such bad evaluations of risks (Slovic 1987; 1999). For example, a recent study I did clearly showed that the perceived risks of being harmed depended on one's physical proximity to the disaster. Believe it or not, the relationship was contrary to common sense. Those physically farther away from the disaster (in this case a gas storage farm fire) perceived the risk of being harmed as much greater than among those persons right across the street from the fire and explosions (Kirschenbaum 1992). Alternative explanations have emerged to account for this seemingly odd but empirically consistent behavioral response to risk perception; among them the "familiarity breeds contempt" argument (Douglas 1986), in which the expected consequences of familiar disasters create an aura of predictability, thereby lowering perceived risks. Another explanation argues that unexpected and spontaneous types of disasters are perceived as more dangerous than natural cycle disasters (Lupton 1995). In the case of the gas farm fire, nearly everyone expected such a disaster to happen. In contrast, the perceived risks of an unexpected meltdown in a nuclear plant would significantly differ from the risks derived from the weatherman telling us of an impending hurricane somewhere out in the ocean. A third explanation stresses the unclear meanings we attach to risk that differentiate common day-to-day risks to those associated with catastrophes (Maris et al. 1996). Crossing the street is risky, but with the collapse of the Twin Towers due to suicide terrorists, working in tall skyscrapers may be seen as exponentially even more so.

CULTURAL RISK

The inconsistencies between experts and ordinary people of how risks are perceived has led certain researchers to suggest that the answer to this gap lies in our diversity of worldviews and cultural imperatives (Slovic 1987). The basis for this is the assumption that risk is the product of our social environment, created through what some have called a socially based disaster construct that incorporates acceptable attitudes and beliefs about disasters (Weyman and Kelly 2000). This perspective fits in nicely with my own explanation of disaster definition, namely that the mechanism for societal survival comes in the form of institutionalized disaster behaviors. Through the process of risk perceptions, prioritizing such behaviors acts to minimize harm, maximize survival (Krimsky 1995), and maintain ongoing critical social structures (Wildavsky 1990; Earle and Cvetkovich 1997). Indirect evidence in the area of public health seems to support my contention (Gabe 1995; Douglas 1986; Douglas et al. 2000; Douglas and Widavsky 1982), along with findings contrasting risk perceptions on the basis of their national origin (Slovic 1999). If the results of "ethnic" studies on risk perception are included here (Fothergill et al. 1999; Perry and Lindell 1991; Buckland and Rahman 1999), the evidence of the impact of culture or its by-products on risk perceptions would at first glance seem to be overwhelming.

Some controversy does exist, however, as to the degree to which cultural imperatives, in competition with other factors, affect risk perceptions (Sjoberg and Drottz-Sjoberg 1993; Sjoberg 1995). For example, our cognitive ability for rational decision making facilitates adaptive behavioral change; certainly a challenge for the ubiquity of cultural determinism. There is also the "filtering" affect that cognitive processes provide in picking and choosing what is and at what level we seem to be at risk (Dake 1991; Kasperson et al. 1988). Then, of course, there are emotions (Brehmer 1987), which sometimes defy reason but do reflect certain aspects of cultural prerogatives. Given this caveat, culture remains a reliable alternative means to understanding risk perceptions. As a source of societal stability, culture provides a framework in which we can identify and link disasters to their risks, arrive at an assessment of their danger, and act to avoid their negative consequences. As I have previously argued, societies are in the business of survival, and cultural imperatives are a powerful medium through which to do so.

EXPERT VERSUS VICTIMS' RISK

Given these alternative perspectives of perceived risk, the next question that I will pursue is to look at why there appears to be a gap between how experts, in this case disaster managers, and potential disaster victims assess risk. The clues to solve this puzzle have already been laid out in what seems to be an inherent contradiction between how organizations and their clients view the world. The first indication of this was that a serious gap existed between an organization's stated goals and their perception by its stakeholders. An indirect but still important additional clue was a tendency to use traditional rather than official sources of information for disaster role modeling. In their own way, both highlight the constraints imposed on organizational members (the experts). They are, however, largely absent for the potential individual victims of disasters. They show how formalized organizational behavior built on and predisposed toward rational performance-based structures can differ from the way ordinary people see the world. These differences profoundly contribute to the diversity of risk perceptions and their behavioral outcomes. To support this argument I will again utilize the data gathered from the Israel field study but will refocus the emphasis to risk perceptions of emergencies and disasters.

Along with a number of perspectives of what risk is and how it is measured is the sticky problem of defining risk perceptions in order to assure conceptual "validity" of the concept. Before doing so, however, let me set the stage for the analysis by reiterating what the Israeli disaster managers saw as critical in preparing for a disaster. Their estimation and policy priorities reflect their assessment of where the greatest risk lay. Again, their risk estimations must be understood within the recent historical political and military events of Israel, especially the Gulf War, to which the Israel population has been abundantly exposed. Looking back to Chapter 2, the disaster managers were asked what their priorities were for the civilian population so that they would be prepared for future disasters. (See Figure 2.) Each item that was suggested by the disaster managers was separately ranked in terms of its importance. Of the disaster managers who ranked having gas mask kits available, close to three-quarters saw this as critical, reflecting their estimation of the risk of another unconventional war, including biochemical warheads in ballistic missiles. Two-fifths of managers emphasized providing knowledge to civilians and increasing their awareness of the ever-fluid situation, including the biochemical threat. The assumption is that such awareness would increase preparedness. A third of the managers estimated that to reduce the risk of a potential disaster meant having and maintaining a conventional bomb shelter. Apparently, they estimated that the likelihood of an unconventional war was very low, but of a conventional one was high. A fifth

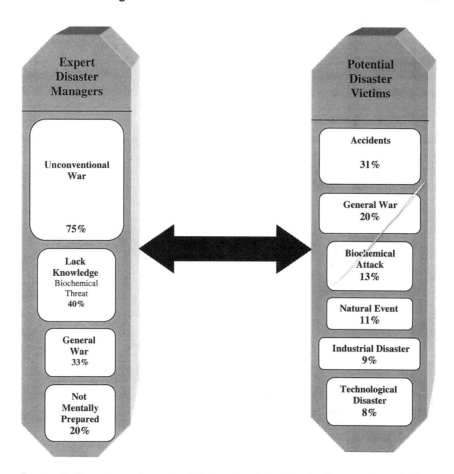

FIGURE 2 Experts versus potential disaster victims' ranked perception of where risks are greatest. Note: Each item was ranked independently on a three-point Like-type scale from very important, to important, to not important. The percentages reflect the rates in each separate category at which experts designated these disaster areas as very important.

recommended preparing the population "mentally," having an emergency kit or plan. What these experts expressed in setting their priorities was their way of telling us how they estimated the risks of another warlike situation. Part of this risk assessment may have been prompted by the fear of critical public repercussions if proper operational measures had not been put in place, but more likely, it was the organizational constraints imposed on evaluations of risk.

ORGANIZATIONAL BLINDERS

Now let us look at how the potential victims of these disasters perceive the risks of disaster events. As the field study relied on open-ended questions for the disaster managers and structured questions for the population, a true disaster-by-disaster comparison was not possible. The disaster scenarios that were used to ask the general population's perception of the chance of war taking place did incorporate basically the same types of possibilities that disaster managers face, however. Not surprisingly, he data revealed that a large gap exists between how experts and the general population evaluate the perceived levels of risks. This was glaringly obvious in the extremely low risk levels attributed by the household sample to the chances of an unconventional war occurring, in sharp contrast to the disaster managers' overwhelming conviction in preparing gas masks for the inevitable chemical and/or biological attack. The representative sample of Israel's population simply put the risk of a biochemical attack occurring at the same low level as a natural or technological disaster, around a one in ten chance. What did appear on the list of disasters that were perceived to be extremely risky were accidents, especially car accidents. Over 30% of the civilian population assigned it a high likelihood of occurrence, even more than the possibility of a general war. This pattern of risk perception fits in nicely with other risk research, which has shown that large-scale disasters are more difficult to assess in contrast to day-to-day events that we come into contact with or experience personally or through our social networks. Who among us has never seen an auto accident? Seeing it or being "entertained" by these sometimes horrendous events in the newspapers and mass media reinforces the perception that it is not "somewhere out there," but could happen to us. How many of us, on the other hand, have seen or been involved in a war, been shaken by an earthquake, or have had our houses washed away by floods? How many of us could even describe what an unconventional war entails? Apparently, it is the everyday or natural-cycle events that we most relate to—those events that have built up our preparedness and response behaviors to assure our survival. For these events we can ascertain a reasonable risk assessment. For events that go above and beyond the scope of these experiences and rely mainly on belief, however, risk perceptions will be extremely problematic (Flynn et al. 1994). This was (and still is to a large extent) the case of technological disasters after the industrial revolution and is now for unconventional warfare and terror (Covello 1983).

GUT FEELINGS

It seems incredibly strange that the Israeli civilians who experienced the Gulf War, saw ballistic missiles rain down on major metropolitan areas, entered sealed rooms, and donned gas masks against potential biochemical warfare, have such low assessments of risk for biochemical and unconventional warfare, yet no one can accuse them of lacking experience. Their skill levels in using unconventional war equipment (gas masks, atropine, sealing rooms) remained at nearly the same level over the ten-year period following the Gulf War (Kirschenbaum 2001a). Something as critical for survival as these skills are not easily forgotten, and the lessons are not easily dismissed. The gut feelings born of experience remain with us for a long time, but in spite of this evidence, how can it be explained that Israelis perceive the risk of an unconventional war as extremely low? They should be more sensitive to it! The most plausible explanation comes from evidence garnered from case studies of disasters that found that there is a tendency to downplay the perceived risks of a life-threatening disaster reoccurring (Hendrika and Sellers 2000). These responses seem to fit a known pattern that despite actual (and sometimes tragic) experiences, the possibility that another horrible event will occur does not seem imaginable. With the potential consequence of an unconventional war involving thousands of dead or injured, plagues let loose, and total disruption of society, perhaps it is best to dismiss the idea that it will happen again, and this is exactly what seems to have happened. It also explains why risk perceptions of more familiar disasters or emergencies, those for which we have a reference point, were given much higher perceived risk ratings. What these results strongly reinforce is that perceptions of risks at the grass roots level, for whatever reason, substantially differ from those of the disaster management expert, who sees the world through his or her organizational prisms. (See Table 1.)

WHAT IS A PERCEIVED RISK?

Now that I have reasonably established that the potential victims of disasters assess risk differently from the expert disaster manager, it is time to go on to look more closely at the concept itself. Until now I have indiscriminately employed the terms risk and perceived risk without clearly defining what they mean. To do so is not easy, but is achievable. In essence, it would require taking advantage of what we already know from the research literature, extrapolating the findings, and proposing an empirical definition for the concept. Like my exploration of the concept of preparedness, the use of risk as it now stands is too broad and therefore too diffuse to use in helping practitioners mitigate disasters. At this point, one man's reason why a disaster incident is perceived as risky may be another's reason not to worry, so what can be done? The first step is to categorize risk in terms of events. This means avoiding the overgeneralized and amorphous situations by asking relevant

TABLE 1 Perceived Risk Levels of Conventional and Unconventional
Disasters Among the Civilian Population

Disaster event	High risk (%)	Medium risk (%)	Low risk (%)	Don't Know[a]	Total (%)
General war	20	46	22	12	100
Chemical	6	33	32	28	100
Biological	7	34	31	27	100
Conventional	7	35	31	27	100
Earthquake	11	35	26	28	100
Industrial	9	19	53	19	100
Technological	8	29	48	15	100
Accident	31	31	12	26	100

[a]The response "don't know," which contributed a fairly large portion of the total responses to the questions on risk, was further analyzed and was not significantly related to any particular demographic group. In addition, this response primarily reflected a lack of concern and knowledge of the situation. Both these conditions were interpreted to mean that the individual perceived of the risks as extremely low.

questions against specific types of disaster or emergency incidents. For example, you might ask what the risk is of a volcano erupting or an earthquake occurring. It is absolutely necessary to link that risk assessment with a specific actual event. More important that event must have some relevance to the individual who is making the risk assessment; so, for instance, asking someone in the Sahara Desert about the risks of flooding is irrelevant! There needs to be a pertinent and clear-cut object that can be related to; otherwise, it will be as if you asked someone about the weather.

A second avenue to pursue is to distinguish between risks to the individual and to the general public. The literature in psychology makes a crucial point that responses can significantly differ if questions are directed toward oneself or "others." How many times have we heard people say when you tell them to be careful while driving that "it [an accident] won't happen to me"; meaning it probably will happen to others who are less capable of driving safely. This type of duality in viewing the world—them and me—is not uncommon, but what it does point out is that we not only perceived and evaluate events differently when benchmarking them against others or ourselves but they affect how we react to and behave in the face of different stimuli and events. For example, when faced with helping or rescuing persons trapped in the rubble of a building destroyed by an earthquake, case study after case study found that family members always choose to look for members of their own family rather than strangers. This happened in Mexico City, Turkey, and in the tornado alley in the United States in which homes were wrecked and roofs blown off. The simple reality is that "blood is really thicker than water." This clear-cut duality between them and me, however, is not as straightforward as it initially seems. This is because most research on disaster behavior has found that it revolves around the family unit (Drabek 1986), strongly suggesting that risk perceptions are also developed in this same fashion. The individual "me" is then a symbolic construct that embraces not only the individual but in many cases extended family members. This makes even more sense when we recognize that the individualistic family nuclear model does not extend much beyond Western industrial societies, as over three-quarters of the worlds population—for example, in China and Southeast Asia—are societies based on extended family relationships. It is for this reason that measuring perceived risk ratings should specifically ask the chances of either the respondent or someone in the respondent's family of being injured while linking these risks to a specific type of disaster.

SOCIAL CONTEXT OF RISK

If we are to examine how the stakeholders in the disaster management game view the risks of disasters, it should be clear what they are talking about. We already know the views of the expert disaster managers, and we have already seen the gap between what they claim as risky and what the potential victims perceive as risky. Are both these groups speaking the same language, however? We already know some of the alternative viewpoints of what risk is, making a definition arguable, but argument is also one way to solve this issue. To find a commonality in language and meaning, I would therefore like to explore a definition of risk that is dependent upon the social framework within which it is developed. Disaster managers make these risk assessments in the context of their organization, while the potential victims do so in a family and or community setting (Hance et al. 1988). This does not mean that bureaucratic disaster managers are not human. On the contrary, their social behavior is very human, but it is severely constrained by the rules and regulations inherent in organizations. This has been well documented in dozens of studies showing the impact of organizational behavior on decision making and risk in particular (Clarke and Short 1993). Interestingly enough, all start out with a basic assumption that the structure of the organization is one of the key factors in how decisions are eventually made (Hall 1996). Bureaucratic structures are not only more formalistic in the decision-making process, but also *less* flexible. Studies in the area of business strategy reinforce this conviction by pointing out that self-contained organizations (e.g., public sector monopolies) with minimum contact with their major clients (stakeholders or consumers) are likely to make decisions disjointed from their clients' needs and impervious to market competition (Bohte and Meier 2001; Boyne 2001; Shoichet 1998). The conclusion I have come to from analyzing these studies is that a clear distinction must be made between the organizational and social contexts, when assessing how risks are developed. (See Figure 3.)

Making risk assessments as individuals also has its constraints. In this case, the social framework of family and community relationships is the key component of how risks are perceived. As I stated, the reference point for disaster behavior is usually the family unit. True, individuals make their own assessments of risk based on their perception of a particular situation, yet many of the components that are integrated into that decision are directly related to the welfare of their families (Kirschenbaum 1992). Very rarely, if at all, would you find, for example, a single driver in a car evacuating an area under severe threat of a flood. What you would see are cars packed with their family members and even neighbors (Ellemers and Veld-Langeveld 1955). In many other cases, risk decisions are influenced by their feelings about their community and relationships with neighbors and friends (Perry and Mush-katel 1984). As we saw in the previous chapter on the strength of traditional role models on disaster behavior, people use informal social networks to help them make decisions about how to act. This also applies to risk assessment. Seeking ways to come to an answer about the risks of a disaster occurring has

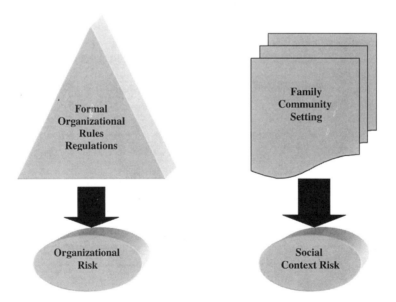

FIGURE 3   Social and organizational context affecting risk assessment.

led individuals to solicit opinions from friends, respected neighbors, or other family members. Here again, the place of trust is crucial, so while the authorities may be providing us with one message, our friends and family may be providing us with another. In each case, the assessment of something terrible happening is based on a perception of risk from two distinct social frameworks. This does not mean that they are inseparable or counterproductive; what may be taking place is that while we may look to our family and friends for information about assessing disaster risk, that information may in whole or part come from an official organization source.

SOCIALLY BASED RATIONALITY

Given this likelihood, there still remains the question of how to approach measuring risk. A first step to do this is to look at the concept of risk as part of our social environment. There is little doubt that from an individual's standpoint that risk is a socially based perceived behavior. We are not mechanical robots that are fed information, chew it up, and spew out a risk quotient, nor do we have perfect information upon which to do so. Whatever information we do obtain is likely to be socially filtered and evaluated through a process that I call *social rationality*. Given these assumptions, the next question becomes. How do we measure perceived risk? Part of the answer lies in formulating questions that measure how individuals assess risk on the basis of both disaster type and the degree it touches them personally. The other half of the measure has to do with the degree to which the risk is perceived to be great or small. The most common types of scales—predominantly found in psychological studies—usually assume that individuals are capable of differentiating the subtle differences in social phenomenon. These scales are, however, fraught with problems. For example, give these kinds of measures of assessing risk to ordinary people and ask them to differentiate between, say, one and two or nine and ten on a scale assessing risk. They would be baffled. More likely the scale would be viewed in clusters; one end of the scale would be "low" risk and the other "high" risk. Practically no attention would be paid to the subtle differences between either 1 and 2 or 9 and 10 on the scale. Above and beyond this is our penchant to generalize. The truth is that risk perceptions are usually generalized and therefore cannot be pigeonholed into scales that assume complete and unambiguous rationality and analytical ability. People are simply not that way! We work with reasonable categories.

MEASURES OF RISK

Taking advantage of the Israeli field study based on a representative sample of urban households, specific questions were introduced to make a judgment of

TABLE 2 Measures of Perceived Risk Based on Disaster Type and Its
Impact on a Personal or Societal Level

Type of disaster	Personal effect	Societal effect
Conventional war	Yes	Yes
Unconventional war	Yes	Yes
Industrial-technological	No	Yes
Natural disaster	No	Yes
Accident	Yes	No

how risks were perceived. It was taken into account that risks are percieved as
being pertinent to "them and me." Also taken into account were disaster-
specific categories. The result was ten separate measures of perceived risk
divided among six basic disaster categories. Table 2 illustrates how these
questions were distributed.

Conventional War

The first disaster-specific category, conventional war, was composed of two
questions. One asked "What are the chances that *you* would be injured by a
conventional attack on Israel by ballistic missiles or aircraft?" This question
focused on the individual and on the two most probable kinds of conventional
war against Israel. The second was more general in nature and asked "What
would be the chances of Israeli citizens being placed in life-threatening danger
from a conventional war during the next five years?" These questions
provided an opportunity to contrast the them and me with the general type
of risk perceptions at the societal level.

Unconventional War

In the case of risk assessment for unconventional war, the personal them–me
question divided into two parts, separately dealing with cases involving
biological or chemical threats. To measure the risks in each, the following
questions were asked: "What do you think the risk would be to you or your
family of being injured by a chemical ballistic missile attack?" and "What do
you think is the risk of your being injured from an attack by biological
weapons?" This distinction is important, as the impact of chemical agents and
those of biological origin differ on populations (CDC 2000; AAP 2000).
Chemical agents usually work on direct contact with the human body—for
example, World War I mustard gas or the spraying of Saran gas in Tokyo's'
subway—and tend to be very localized. In contrast, once delivered, biological
agents have the ability to spread through a wide variety of means, including

human contact. The anthrax episode in the United States showed that this biological substance could be spread through the use of the postal system in innocent-looking envelopes. In addition, chemical agents are immediate in their effect, while biological agents may not be. While both are unconventional, their impact and terror components thus differ. Knowledge about them also differs. For example, the controversy surrounding Gulf War syndrome has led to more generalized knowledge about chemical agents. This same process occurred in Israel because of the preparations for the Gulf War and became very evident afterward with the very real possibility of additional ballistic missile attacks in future conflagrations.

Industrial–Technological

A risk assessment was also obtained for technological–industrial disasters. Here, emphasis was put on specific types of disasters. The first question asked about "the risks from any type of industrial disaster in you general residential area." Another put this same question to those who lived in a neighborhood near an industry that they perceived as potentially risky. A third question was much more general and asked about "the risks that there would be a nationwide shutdown due to a technological disaster such as [then] Bug 2000," the computer glitch requiring software changes to keep major banking, hospital and military systems from crashing.

Natural Disasters and Accidents

In the category of natural disasters, only one question was asked of the respondents; namely, What are the risks of your being injured in an earthquake? This single question in fact reflects the only type of natural disaster of any consequence in Israel. It is for all practical purposes the only type of natural disaster for which disaster agencies have preparation plans. Also, building codes are in place. Other types of natural disasters, such as hurricanes, tornadoes, or monsoons, do not occur. On rare occasions, there is some flooding (such as in the Negev desert), which has little impact on disrupting daily life. Finally, I included the category of accidents. People were asked what they thought was the "risk of being involved in an automobile or similar kind of accident."

COMPONENTS OF RISK PERCEPTION

The theoretical basis for obtaining an empirical definition of risk perceptions can now be said to be in place (in site); not only are there specific types of disasters laid out that respondents can relate to when they make their risk assessment, but there is also a distinction between the degree to which these disaster events affect them personally. To make sense of the responses of the sample, the data were first subjected to a statistical procedure called a factor analysis. The objective is to evaluate not only the sensitivity of the questions, but more important, the degree to which they form common explanatory factors. It could well be that certain questions provoke similar responses, making sense to combine them together to form a new streamlined variable. These new factors could then be used further along in the analysis to gain an even better insight into how risk perceptions are developed.

The factor analysis[1] generated six distinctive types of risk perceptions, all of which are related to specific types of disaster scenarios. More important, they neatly distinguish between the them and me reaction to risks. For example, one factor can best be described as a measure of personal perceived risk. A second factor reflects risk perceptions at the societal level. The re-

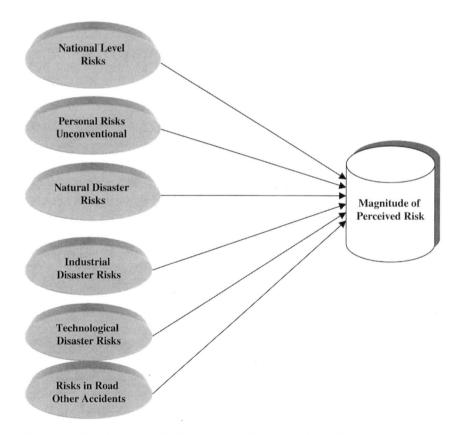

FIGURE 4 Disaster-related factor components of perceived risk.

maining four factors are disaster-specific, covering natural, industrial, technological, and transportation accidents. (See Figure 4.) Each of the factors has a reasonably high reliability coefficient (alpha Cronbach), so that we can trust them to fairly represent the combined variables that contribute to their makeup. They also contribute a large proportion of the total variance among the variables introduced into the factor analysis.

THEM AND ME

A closer look at the factors reveals two extremely important pieces of information that will be critical in understanding why there is a gap between experts and potential victims in the manner in which they perceive risks. The first is that there is an empirical distinction between how people perceive risks at the personal level and how they do so for the general public. If you recall, I argued that experts make their risk assessments within the confines of their organizations, while we as the potential victims do so at the street level. Comparing the factors reveals that we do indeed tend to downplay the risks to ourselves and exaggerate the risk to others. This fact provides an important clue as to why we may not take what disaster agencies tell us seriously. I will also speculate that this difference–them and me–may help explain why the experts, who deal with the public them, perceive of the risks of disasters as being inherently greater than they really are. This means that not only are disaster manager experts constrained by the rules of organizational engagement, but also as individuals, they incorporate into those decisions a bias toward exaggerated risks.

Before I deal with this significant clue, however, the factor analysis also provides one more piece of startling information; namely, that there appears to be no difference at the personal level in how risks are perceived for conventional and unconventional disasters. All the "hype" in the media about the fears, uncertainties, and risks of unconventional attacks may be more a fiction than a reality. The data show that individuals do not distinguish risks involved in a conventional or unconventional disaster and may even use the same set of variables to evaluate each. To them, both are seen in the same light. This finding seems strange at first, but it must be kept in mind that both conventional and unconventional war-related disasters are generated by primarily the same means; namely, ballistic missiles. Such missiles can carry either conventional or unconventional warheads. Knowing this, it now makes sense why the respondents saw little difference is their perceptions of the risks of both; the disaster was simply delivered by the same means. Perhaps if I had distinguished unconventional war from terror (which is predominantly suicide and homicide by conventional means), there may have been a difference. This can only be speculative, as the study was conducted just before the advent of organized terror both in Israel and the rest of the world.

What these data have strongly suggested is that the organizational assessment of risk can dramatically differ from that of the potential victim. This gap is worrying, but understandable in light of how societies have developed the means and methods to adapt to an ever-increasing number and variety of emergencies and disasters. Perhaps this process has gotten off track, however. Have we forsaken our past? Have we reached the point at which formal bureaucratic organizations have broken stride and even divorced themselves from the century-old traditional patterns of disaster behavior that have worked so well? These are extremely difficult questions to answer, but I believe that by looking more deeply at the predictors of risk assessment, answers may begin to emerge.

SOCIETAL SURVIVAL

Given the diversity of opinions of individuals and their cultural backgrounds, a classic question arises: How do we assess the risks that directly affect the survival of our societies? There are, of course, a number of competing explanations. One popular perspective, called the *institutional theory*, posits that societies must maintain a legitimate balance between what the environmental conditions can permit and the social institutions that they support. Any imbalances are followed by changes to maintain a degree of equilibrium and stability (Barley and Tolbert 1997; DiMaggio and Powell 1983). In terms of disasters, this means that if the social institutions that were put in place to deal with threats to societal survival were found to be inadequate, additional or alternative means would be introduced and legitimized. As the gap grows between the ability of social institutions to deal with disasters (at the group, community, or organizational level) and the threat these disasters pose to societal stability, the change will be more rapid. One of the key points in this change is how risk is perceived and assessed. The recent terror attacks on the United States should be considered the most recent classic example of this process. Risk perception at the societal level rose radically when the Twin Towers and the Pentagon were attacked. The institutions that were legitimized during the cold war proved to be inadequate to deal with Islamic terror. This was reflected in the official governmental media message that "terror is a threat to our way of life" and that there is a need to mobilize a "war on terror." The result has been recognition for the need to reorganize government agencies, invest heavily in antiterror efforts, and from the institutional theory perspective, create new and presumably better institutional frameworks to deal with these new forms of disaster, namely the Department of Homeland Security (Rubin 2002).

This example is only the latest in a long line of institutional adaptations that we have been making to ensure our survival. It has occurred over the centuries in different forms. In communities it has been an ongoing process, leading to normative disaster behaviors best adapted to local environmental conditions. With modernization it has taken the form of formal bureacratic organizations. Today, especially in the West, it has advanced one additional step in the creation of a professional cadre called disaster managers. These professionals are housed in the very same public sector bureaucratic organizations that have, for the most part, divorced themselves from traditional community disaster management. How has all this affected how we now assess the risks to our societal survival, however? As we have seen a large part of us continues to rely on traditional sources of disaster behavior, and as I have just shown, we continue to have our own ways of assessing the risks of disasters.

HOW RISKS EVOLVE

There are several alternative perspectives as to how we come to both perceive and assess the level of threatening events. There is of course the biopsychological explanation that puts together chemistry and cognitive processes. The simplistic fright–flight explanation, for example, has an underlying theme involving risk assessment built into automatic behavioral responses through chemical changes in the body. There is also a modified fear and panic behavioral set, which embraces a risk assessment component built on a cognitive explanation of learned accumulated experiences. At the other end of the spectrum are the socially based explanations. Here, social characteristics rather than individual psychological traits contribute toward affecting risk perceptions. Risk perceptions are the outcome of social rather than biochemical interactions. This means that how we view the world of risks depends first and foremost on how we view our own social world. This perpective has been the modus operandi among sociologists, who consider disasters to be social constructs (Quarantelli 1988) reflecting the social milieu within which they arise and how they are defined. The argument goes something like this. Our physical environment is socially interpreted so as to maximize and sustain our long-term survival. Social cues develop to sensitize us to both personal and societal threats, making risk perceptions an integral part of how disasters are socially constructed. Risk perceptions can thus be highly selective, depending on the social source of how specific disasters are constructed. This can be seen in the way in which people who, for example, live in a hurricane-prone area or a flood plain are sensitive to specific cues in their environment that a disaster is eminent. Strangers to these disaster-prone environments who have not yet been socialized into the disaster subculture might not even be aware of these clues.

GROUP ACTIONS

The advocates on both the biological and social sides of the "risk divide" continue to argue their points, but there are no clear-cut or zero-sum winners-take-all explanations What has become accepted on the basis of research for over the last quarter century is that for the most part risks are seen in the eye of the beholder (Grayson and Schwarz 1999). Psychologists put their emphasis on the eye of the single beholder, while social scientists put their emphasis on the collective eyes of groups and communities. The difference is really one of semantics, as individuals do not live in a vacuum, and to one extent or another are influenced by their fellow social creatures. After all, we are from the same species and have built up our survival skills on the basis of group and community experiences. The social mold from which we emerged contains very similar basic ingredients. In the jargon of social scientists, the social mold is primarily based on the commonality everyone experiences during their socialization. With the exception of twins, people brought up in different social environments tend to reflect these environments, in terms of both their individual and social characteristics. Because of this, risk perceptions can also be categorized according to the beholder and assigned to specific groups of individuals with similar characteristics and backgrounds. This basic tenet has wide support in the disaster research literature (Briere and Elliot 2000). For example, individuals collectively categorized by their gender, ethnic, and age group tend to have similar ways of behaving during disasters (Fothergill et al. 1999) In short, groups of individuals who have similar backgrounds or characteristics are likely to perceive risks of disasters in a similar light (Cutter et al. 1992).

Let us take the case of gender as an example of how groups can reflect risk perceptions. Given their socialization patterns, women have been found to perceive and behave differently from men during emergencies and disasters (Flynn et al. 1994; Fothergill, 1996; Morrow and Phillips 1999). Most women were found to be more sensitive to family needs and form social networks that help in restructuring their lives after disasters (Gustafson 1998). This does not mean that all women act this way during disasters; it means that most do. There are always exceptions, and it is precisely these exceptions that have provided us with the statistical concept of a "normal distribution"; that is, groups of persons have a tendency to concentrate around the group average but can still be distributed in such a way as to form pockets of extreme behaviors. This has been popularly called the bell curve, as the distribution tends to look like the shape of a bell. If we translate this into, say, risk assessments, the curve would consist of a small number of extremely high- and low-risk-magnitude assessments at the opposite ends at the base of bell. The overwhelming majority, however, would tend toward the curved apex of the bell, which represents the concentration of average risk assessments. Statistically, deviations from this normal distribution are what tell us if a particular group is significantly different in its assessment of disaster risks from what would be expected under normal conditions.

PREDICTING RISK

Taking this idea that individuals can be collectively grouped or categorized to represent certain social attributes now permits me to examine which variables will predict the magnitude of perceived risks. From a broad sweep of the research literature, it seems that certain classes of variables have been consistently associated with risk. *It is crucial to understand that association does not necessarily mean predictability*, and in the majority of cases, the types of risk studies found in the research literature focus on the medical health field (Ollenburger and Tobin 1999; Minichiello and Browne 2001; Kirschenbaum et al. 2000) rather than disasters. A survey of the literature could thus only provide a surface sweep of potential variables, with at best only a superficial link to disasters. Because of this, it was necessary to select explanatory variables based on their general link to disasters that might theoretically affect the magnitude of a disaster risk perception. Figure 5 outlines these

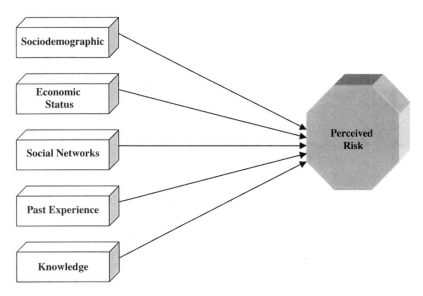

FIGURE 5   The basic explanatory model of risk perceptions, including key predictor variables.

predictor variables. As a start, five categories of variables were incorporated into the analysis: (1) sociodemographic variables, (2) economic status, (3) social networks, (4) past experiences, and (5) knowledge.

Sociodemographic Variables

As we already saw in previous chapters, age, gender, ethnic origin, religion, education, marital status, family size, and health status variables can act as significant predictors of disaster preparedness and traditional disaster role modeling. There is good reason to think that preparedness and risk perceptions are also linked, making common explantory variables potential predictors of risk itself. In fact, this will be examined in depth toward the end of the chapter, but for the moment let me note just two examples. It is reasonable to suspect, for instance, that age or marital status would be good predictors of the level of risk perceptions; older persons would be more conservative in their attitudes toward disaster risk (Leik et al. 1982), while due to their familial responsibilities, married individuals would tend to exaggerate these same risks (Burns and Sullivan 2000).

Economic Status

Along with these are measures of economic status, such as income and home and car ownership. In the case of risk, these measures should be interpreted to mean having "something to lose". Disasters have long been associated with property and business loss, and it is assumed that perceived risk would reflect an assessment that it would entail an economic loss (Dominitz and Manski 1997). Those persons with greater wealth in the form of both fixed and movable property would then be likely to be more sensitive to the risks that disasters pose.

Social Networks

A separate set of potential explanatory variables encompasses those related to social networks. These are primarily related to contact and proximity with family and friends, as well as the community. These networks are the social glue that bonds us and others in the web of social life. Disaster research has long talked about the disruption that disaster causes to these relationships (Nilson 1981; Bland et al. 1997)—how family and community life is torn asunder (Beggs et al. 1996) and postdisaster trauma lingers over long periods of time (Sprang 1999). In light of these studies it makes sense to argue that risk perceptions will be affected by the recognition of what disasters may do to these relationships. The magnitude will certainly be dependent on the intensity and strength of the various social ties. On the one hand, intense relationships provide the potential for more serious disruptions, but on the other, they may form a buffer to these disruptions (Norris et al. 1999).

Past Experiences

A fourth set of variables assumes that past experiences with various levels of disasters can affect the magnitude of perceived risk. The adage "once burned twice wary" seems appropriate here, as logic dictates that those persons who have experienced disasters in the past, either directly or even vicariously, will have a better idea of what to expect (Faupel and Styles 1993). This assumption can, however, go two ways. The knowledge from the past may overly sensitize persons to what might happen (i.e., actually increase the wariness of a future disaster and exaggerate its perceived risk level), or it may desensitize them, reducing the magnitude of the risk. In both cases, these past experiences will affect how risk is perceived.

Knowledge

Finally, there is the hypothetical association of the impact of how much knowledge you have of a potential disaster on your risk perceptions of it. The literature does not provide a clear evaluation of how knowledge can affect disaster behavior (McClure et al. 1999). What does appear is a double-edged sword. On the one hand, greater knowledge about the disaster and its potential destructive ability may filter out imaginary or fictitious scenarios and bring us back to a more realistic assessment of the risks. On the other hand, greater knowledge does provide a more detailed canvas of what might happen, and actually increases the risk factor.

NATIONAL DISASTER RISK

Taking these potential predictor variables of risk perceptions and running them separately against each of the six disaster factors provided a platform to look at what affected the development of such perceptions.[2] The first category of disaster risks was confined to those risk perceptions that were based on what the Israeli respondents defined as a national-level disaster. These risk perceptions were made in terms of the "big picture" and did not relate to the impact on each respondent personally. What was asked was how they saw the risks of an attack on their country (in whole or in part). When the (twenty-nine) independent variables were introduced into the statistical analysis, two categories of variables proved to be significant. These included an economic variable and three social network variables. (See Figure 6.)

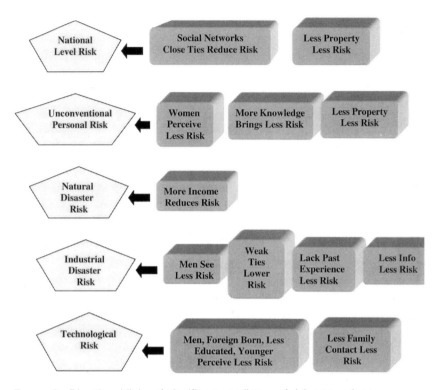

FIGURE 6 Directional links of significant predictors of risk perceptions.

Property Loss

Apparently, risk perceptions at the national level come about through a combination of two key sets of conditions. The first has to do with having some *real property* at your disposal with the possibility of its being lost. This was evident in the significance of the variable "number of cars you own." The sign of the regression coefficient—an indication of the direction of the relationship—clearly indicated that with every additional car there was an additional increase in the magnitude of the perceived risk of a national-level disaster. Perhaps the potential loss of real property sensitizes persons to the risks that such a national level disaster might have upon their own personal possessions.

Social Networks

The second category of variables was associated with *social networks*. One claim was that the fear that such social networks would be disrupted in a disaster would enhance the level of perceived risk. Here, strong networks would increase risk perceptions. Alternatively it can also be argued that tight-knit social ties would act to buffer fears and actually reduce risk perceptions. Both make sense, but which is correct? Now we have a chance to look at the empirical findings.

First of all, it is important to recognize that three network variables proved to be significant predictors of risk perceptions: (1) feeling of neighborliness based on the degree to which the respondents felt their neighbors would help in emergencies, (2) extent of activity in the social and economic affairs of their building complex, and (3) proximity to relatives. These three variables actually represent different levels of social ties: family, neighbors, and residential proximity. That these distinguishing qualifiers appear as a concerted group also attests to the importance of social networking in affecting the magnitude of risk perceptions at the national level. For this reason, I would like to focus on them in more depth.

Strength of Ties

To assess how the strength of social networks affects risk perceptions, I will examine the signs of the statistical coefficients. These positive and negative signs are important clues as to the relationship between the variables and risk perceptions, so when asked if their neighbors would *help them* in case of need, those who responded *negatively* felt the perceived risk of a national-level disaster to be *less*. My guess is that when you feel that your neighbors are really not interested in you, that your relationship with them is minimum, and that you cannot count on them, it leads you to downplay the severity of the risk that a national calamity is at hand. Given the impact of neighbors on disaster decisions (Kirschenbaum 1992), weak social ties among neighbors lead to minimizing the perception of risk.

Unlike the case with neighbors, family ties proved to be different. When asked about the physical *proximity* of relatives—as a measure of the physical density of the family's social ties—the link to risk was positive; that is, the *closer* the respondents' relatives lived to them, the *lower* was their risk estimation of a national-level disaster occurring. Here, strong social ties led to decreased perceived risks. This same pattern also appeared in the third significant social network variable that measured the respondent's *involvement* in the social and economic affairs of his or her residential condominium. Again, the *more* involved he or she was in these building affairs (and with his or her neighbors), the *less* was the perceived risk.

Strong or Weak Ties

What do we make of the link between social networks and risk perceptions at the national level? The answer is really twofold: where the strength of social ties is based on attitudes (e.g., helpful neighbor), weak ties lead to minimizing perceived risks. Perhaps it is because we can't rely on our neighbors that we tend to minimize the risks. When based on actual behavioral ties (involvement, proximity), the outcome is the same in terms of perceived risks, but here it depends on strong social ties. Unlike the attitudinal measure toward neighbors, it is based on a consistent and intense social network—in which social communications about the potential disaster are available and in which social support for decision making occurs. This duality of how social relationships affect risk assessment is complicated, but certainly points out the impact that family and neighborly networks can have on risk perceptions.

PERSONAL RISK FROM UNCONVENTIONAL DISASTER

This second type of disaster category reflects how risks are assessed for both conventional and unconventional disasters that directly affect the personal safety and well-being of the respondent or his family. Here, three distinct categories of variables were found to be significant in predicting the magnitude of the perceived disaster risk. They substantially *differ* from the variables that have predicted the risks of a national-level disaster by the very visible omission of social network variables. The first predictor variable is a *demographic* attribute, gender. A second predictor is a *knowledge* variable that measures the level of knowledge of what a biochemical weapon is and what it can do, and the third is an *economic* variable, car ownership.

Sensitivity of Women

The importance of the *gender* variable is primarily that it opens up a door into how men and women perceive of risk. In this case, the sign of the regression coefficient suggests that women are more sensitive than men to the risks of an unconventional war. From the responses, however, it seems that women perceive these risks to be much *less* than men. Recent case studies of disaster behavior (not risk perceptions) indirectly make this point, but fail to recognize that being a woman in and of itself cannot explain why they assess these threats as being less than men do (Slovic 1999; Smith and Albuquerque 1986). Rather than speculate, I will examine this point in more detail in the next chapter. Suffice it to say that gender is more a descriptive than explanatory variable.

Knowledge Counts

Knowledge is another significant contributor to perceived risk. Having *knowledge* of what biological and chemical weapons are all about and what their potential harm can be affects our judgment. What appears from the signs of its regression coefficient is that as the knowledge of this type of threat becomes more accurate and complete, the perceived risks of personal injury due to an unconventional war *decrease*. This empirical finding is extremely important, as it justifies informing the public about such unconventional weapons. Such information will actually decrease the perceived risk about personal injury, possibly reducing anxiety and fears, and thereby providing a vehicle for preparedness-type disaster behaviors that will be more effective in saving lives and property.

Property

The third predictor, *car ownership*, acts in the same fashion as it did in predicting national-level risks. There is an old Talmudic saying that can be loosely translated as "the more your property, the more your worries!" Here, too, having property affects the perception of risk at a personal level. Having something to lose, in this case reflected in the number of cars owned, heightens the perception of the risk of an unconventional war and personal injury.

RISKS IN NATURAL DISASTERS

An extensive amount of research has been done on natural hazards throughout the world, ranging from floods to hurricanes, droughts, volcanoes, and earthquakes (Natural Hazards Center 2002). These have included studies of risk and disaster behavior. What has been remarkable is that actual disaster behaviors have been consistently similar despite variations in the type of actual disaster, be it a volcano, flood, or hurricane (Drabek 1986). It is for this reason that while the natural disaster-looked at in the Israeli study focused solely on earthquakes as this is just about the only type of natural disaster prevalent in the country, what was learned from it can easily be applied across cultures to other types of disasters.

Buying Safety

When the respondents were asked about the risks of earthquakes, just over 10% thought the risk was very high, and twice as many (25%) as very low. This variability in responses was predicted by only one variable; namely, the level of *income* of the respondent. Income as a part of the general economic status category reflects much more than simple consumer buying power or social status; it also reflects the ability to control situations. Money can buy safety through such means as the purchase of a safety net based on property and medical insurance or emergency and protective

Disaster Related-Risk   **Risk Predictors**

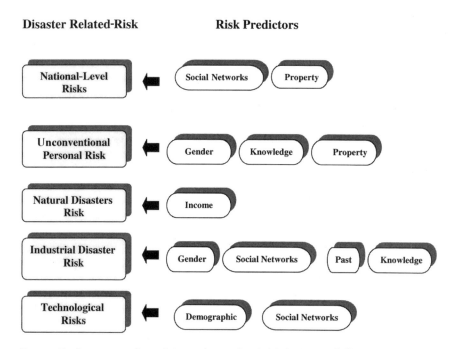

FIGURE 7   Summary of predictors of perceived risk by type of disaster.

equipment, and it can even provide for alternative means of having an alternative shelter and transportation to avoid imminent disasters. In this sense, as the sign of the regression coefficient shows, those respondents with greater income tend to discount the magnitude of the risk of earthquakes. Those who say their incomes are below average are the ones who perceive of the risk of an earthquake (and its consequences for them) to be great. It can be safely speculated that those households in the higher income brackets already have safeguards in place to mitigate this type of natural hazard. (See Figure 7.)

RISK OF INDUSTRIAL DISASTERS

The industrial revolution over the last 200 years has moved us into an era of environmental risks, the potential negative consequences of which are not only global warming but also very local hazards. Seeing smokestacks belch out highly visible pollutants is only the tip of the iceber; highly toxic materials, hazmats, are now of greater concern (Skopek 2001; Edelstein 1988; Kletz 1994). A small, sterile, noiseless, and environmentally pleasant building may contain plague viruses or radioactive material, but as a famous Chicago may or once said, "All politics is local," and so are industrial disasters. Asking the respondents what the risks are to themselves or their families of being harmed by a *nearby* industrial disaster, the best predictors fell into nearly all of the theoretical explanatory categories except economic status. Let us now examine them in greater detail.

Men Count Too

Of the demographic characteristic, *gender* proved to be highly significant. Unlike the results in risk assessment for unconventional war, here it was the men and not the women who were more aware or at least more able to distinguish the perceived risks of an industrial accident. They are, in fact, *less* concerned than women! Perhaps this reflects the macho paradigm of Israeli men, dealing with highly visible external outside threats, whereas women are more concerned with the internal needs of their families. More likely, however, this may be due to the greater involvement of men in that part of the labor market and industrial sector producing hazmats, which increases their awareness and knowledge of this potential threat to their own and their families' welfare. As we saw previously, greater information seems to lead to minimized risks. In general, women are found in public sector white- and pink-collar occupations, reducing their contact and intimate knowledge with hazmat industries and perhaps thereby increasing their fear of them.

Neighborhoods

Three social networking variables also entered the regression model: participating in their *neighborhood* social committee and their relationship with and proximity to other family members. In this case, the coefficient signs indicated that the *less* involved a person was in the social activities of their neighborhood, the *less* seriously he or she took the risk of an industrial disaster occurring. Apparently not being involved socially with other members of your neighborhood deprives you of informal communication in which vital information concerning common interests can be exchanged (Haines et al. 1996; Kaniasty and Norris 2001), especially information about nearby industrial disaster threats. When you don't know about these threats, especially if there are no reliable opinion leaders to verify information, it seems unlikely that your perception of the risk of a disaster will be high. This pattern also follows the "nasty" neighbor syndrome, in which a lack of trust in neighbors also contributed to lowering risk perceptions for national catastrophes.

Fewer Ties, Less Risk

The two significant family variables that best predict the magnitude of risk perceptions are consistent and informative, yet they are contrary to what was found about risk perceptions in the case of national-level disasters. Those respondents who have a "cool" relationship with their relatives and who do *not* live in close proximity to other family members, thus say they perceive of the risk of an industrial disaster to be *less*. Simply put, *fewer ties* among family members cultivate *lower risk* perceptions that an industrial accident will occur.

Why Differences?

Why is this true for industrial disasters but not disasters at the larger societal level? One possible explanation is in the nature of the disasters themselves. National-level disasters are seen to be outside the control of the indiviual, let alone his or her ability to predict. Industrial disasters are of our own making, close by, and more amenable to change and control. The key issue in social networks of information flow is more critical in industrial disasters, during which such knowledge can be used to mitigate the consequences. It is much less so in a national-level disaster. This may be the reason why strong family ties—and with then a greater flow of information—lead to increasing fears of an industrial accident and have litle and even a negative impact on perceived risks at the national level.

TECHNOLOGICAL RISKS

As was noted in Chapter 1, there has been a steady, almost geometric, increase in technological disasters from the four reported in 1950—to 271 in 1999. For the most part, only a small number have attained media exposure because of their notoriety, mainly due to their havoc and devastation. Most likely, there are myriads more that have not been reported (Quarenteilli 2001). To name just a few of the more infamous examples there is the Three Mile Island nuclear leak in the United States and the Bhopal tragedy in India. The most recent of these societywide technological disasters occured with the changing of the millennium, when wide publicity was given to the need to readjust computer systems because of a glitch in the date recording system. This potential disaster became known as Bug 2000. Failure to adjust the dates would, as the experts pointed out, render vital information survival systems such as government, banking, and medical systems inoperative. Taking this cue, the field survey asked the sample of Israeli households how they perceived of the risks of a national technological disaster occurring using Bug 2000 as a reference point.

Demographic Background

Unlike other types of disaster scenarios, risk perceptions of a national technological disaster are predicted almost exclusively by the demographic characteristics of the respondents; namely, their gender, native-or-foreign-born status, educational attainment, and age. The relationship between these characteristics and risk perceptions was obtained from the sign of their regression coefficients. In general, men react to this type of disaster similarly to that of industrial disasters, mainly by downplaying them. Women, on the other hand, perceive the risk of a technological "failure" and consequent disaster as more palpable. Again, it is difficult to put a direct finger on why this gender difference exists and why it remains significant for both industrial and technological disasters. Some might explain it in terms of gender roles, "macho" men versus "feminine" women, or such family cycle attributes as "single" versus "motherhood". Others may attribute these differences to the degree of acquaintance with the sources of these disasters, through their labor market, or by occupational experience. Whatever the possible reasons for these gender differences, they are—as the analysis empirically demonstrates—significant predictors of risk perceptions for technological (and industrial) disasters.

Foreign-Born

A second significant predictor variable was native status. Non-native-born in contrast to those born in Israel perceive of the risk of a national technological disaster as *low*. Again, it can only be speculated as to why foreign-born residents are less concerned about a technological disaster than those born and raised in the country. Several possible explanations come to mind that may be applicable to any immigrant-receiving country. One is that foreign-born persons, especially the more recent arrivals, usually enter into an "up-and-running" developed technological society. In terms of everyday experiences, technology usually works and works well. When you go to work or come home and turn on the lights, they usually go on. The telephone works. Only if something that is linked to technology does not work are we made aware of its presence. As foreign-born individuals were at one time immigrants who probably moved from a country with a depressed economy into a more advanced technological society, the technological marvels of this new society may blind them to the potential consequences of its failure.

Recall the Past

In the case of age, not surprisingly it is the young who tend to *minimize* the risks of technological disasters occurring. It seems that as a person gets older, there is a tendency to become more concerned about technological disasters and to see increasing risks of them occurring. One possible explanation is that the technology that seems so natural to us today only became prevalent in the middle to late 1960s. While the first mechanical computer was designed and working by Babbage in the 1860s, its electronic prehistoric equivalent was in the consumer's hands only at the end of the 1960s. Today's Internet and cell phones were practically unheard of ten years ago. Born before then meant being born in the "dark ages" of technology. Those dark ages were also times of experimentation and failures, something older people recall and apparently use as a reference point in their more conservative assessment of technology. The result is that the risk remains high of something going wrong.

Education

The last significant variable that appears in the demographic category is education. Before empirically testing the impact of educational level on perceived risk, it would have been reasonable to argue that persons with greater education would be more sensitive to the faults and foibles of technology and rate their risks of a technological disaster higher than those less knowledgeable. This makes sense, and the data show that this is exactly the case. Those with less education minimize the perceived risks of a technological disaster, while those more education take it much more seriously.

Connected by Telephone

The only nondemographic variable to be significant in predicting the magnitude of risk of a technological disaster was a social networking factor—the frequency of contacts (via telephone calls) with family relatives. Unlike physical visits, proximity of relatives, or self-reported relationships, contact by telephone allows an objective way to measure strong or weak ties at the family level. Frequency of telephone calls can tell us about the degree to which family relatives reinforce their relationships, even though actual visits may not take place. More important, such indirect contact is an indication of the flow of potential information that passes between them. The signs of the regression coefficient show that when contact decreases—from every day, once a week, once a month, once in a while, to not at all—the perceived risks of a technological disaster are minimized. The more the telephone contacts among family members, the *greater* they perceived the risk of a technological disaster. Less contact led to minimizing the risks. It is possible to speculate that because of its informal nature, this means of communication between family members and their relatives represents a traditional form of role modeling disaster behavior. It is an alternative form of social interaction that bypasses the need for physical face-to-face meetings but still allows everyone to keep in touch. As trust within families is probably greater than with nonfamily members, the information passed along among family members, guided by family opinion leaders and reinforced on a frequent and even daily basis, helps buttress risk perceptions.

RISK AND HARM

The perception of risks of these various types of disasters shows us once again how the expert disaster managers, encased in their bureaucratic organizations, calculate risks on a completely different basis than do their potential victims. As I have shown, the perception of disaster risks is complicated by the fact that it is disaster-specific and can be predicted by the various characteristics and social situations of the victim. There is no single "wonder pill" explanation that can be employed to predict risks. This in itself should make disaster managers extremely wary of how they calculate risks, for even if they discount the potential victims, they must take into account that each type of disaster requires another or different set of risk calculations.

Underlying the analysis of risk perceptions remains an issue that questions if risk perceptions lead to behaviors that will mitigate injury and harm. We always assume that if people think something is risky, they will tend to avoid it (Douglas et al. 2000; Johnson 1992). This seems to be the nature of things. We are always telling our young children not to touch, eat, or smell things that may harm them. We are in fact providing them with risk clues; things that may harm them are to be avoided. Does this type of logic also apply in the case of disasters? To at least open up this bag of worms I will analyze the Israeli data in an effort to evaluate if indeed risk perceptions lead to avoidance behaviors. When individuals do something to prepare themselves for a disaster, they are in fact seeking a way to avoid a confrontation with an event that can harm them (Perry et al. 1981). We prepare our children to avoid harm in a similar way by providing information and sometimes verbal or physical reinforcement. We prepare ourselves for disasters by judging them in terms of their risk of occurrence and potential harm. For conceptual accuracy, such avoidance behaviors will be measured indirectly through levels of preparedness. As Chapter 2 examined the concept and empirical validity of preparedness, what needs be done here is to expand these ideas by arguing that preparedness is an *action* that is aimed at avoiding potential harm. It should be recalled that four basic components emerging from the analysis showed preparedness to be composed of supplies, skills, planning, and protection factors. What will follow is evaluating the degree to which risk perceptions lead to actual preparedness actions. (See Figure 8.)

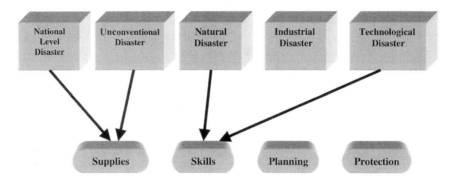

FIGURE 8   How perceived risks of disasters affects actual preparedness.

DOES RISK LEAD TO PREPARING?

The answer is "yes and no." Taking the five basic disaster-specific risk perceptions and statistically regressing them against the four basic preparedness measures clearly shows that only specific types of risks lead individuals to prepare themselves against what they perceive to be high-risk disaster events. Of the five major potential disaster-risk events, four acted as a significant catalyst in explaining variations in the degree of preparation. Only risks associated with industrial disasters did not lead people to prepare. The risk perception that a national-level and unconventional disaster would occur had an important impact on crystallizing individuals' energy to make an effort in *stocking* up on basic emergency provisions. This was not the case for risks associated with industrial, technological, or natural disasters. When there was a feeling that the risks of a technological or natural disaster seemed imminent, however, individuals sought ways of improving their *skill* levels. By doing so they also displayed a very rational set of behaviors that would allow them to avoid—or at least minimize—injury or harm to themselves and their families.

To obtain a better idea of where these disaster-specific disaster risks led in terms of actual preparedness, let me remind you what these preparation encompass. Provisions include such physical items as having a spare battery, radio, water, food, emergency light, copies of documents, emergency numbers, and the ability to seal a safe room. These are basic survival items that would be necessary in case of a national-level as well as unconventional war. Apparently those who perceived the risks of such a conflagration occurring did not distinguish between them. As I mentioned previously, both are simply variations on the same theme—getting attacked by ballistic missiles—except in the type of warhead employed.

The choice of seeking greater skills as a way of preparing for what is perceived as high-risk technological and natural disasters is difficult to understand without a closer look at this category's components. Included are first aid and fire extinguishing skills, which are important in cases of natural disaster, especially earthquakes, which are relevant to Israel, and they certainly are helpful in coping with other types of disasters. The second set of skills are those that have been associated with unconventional war and terror; namely, improving skills in the use of gas masks, sealing rooms, and atropine injections in case of a chemical attack. At this point, it can only be speculated that these are more related to the perceived risks of a technological disaster. Today, asking people about potential technological disasters (even though we tried to specify the BUG 2000 event), may bring to mind such events as nuclear meltdowns and radioactive fallout (Chernobyl style), anthrax or other plague materials accidentally escaping from "safe" laboratories, accidents in highly toxic industries (Bhopal in India, Love Canal in the United States), train derailing, or truck spillage of hazmat material. Being prepared for all these unconventional biochemical incidents makes a lot of sense.

WHAT HAVE WE LEARNED?

The most important lesson that can be gleaned from this chapter and its analysis of risk perceptions of disaster events is that the way risks are calculated by expert disaster managers within the confines of their formal organizational has little to do with how we, the potential victims of disasters, perceive of them. What is particularly worrying is that the gap is so large. It is as if the experts are living on another planet and running the lives of mechanical robots that are devoid of a rich, diverse, and successful repertoire of proven disaster behaviors. Being human means being a social animal enmeshed in an environmental niche that has allowed us to learn from our past mistakes. Our cognitive abilities have even taken us into the future. In this future which we are endowed with the capabilities of perceiving risks and either avoiding them—through preparation—or seeing them as a challenge. In either case, our perceptions of disasters have an impact on our behaviors, for first and foremost societies are in the business of survival, and as individuals our perceived risks of these disasters also affect how we prepare for our survival.

There is also another lesson that can be learned from the analysis. Calculating risk from a technical standpoint by employing elegant "objective" organizational measures is the bureaucratic path of least resistance that completely ignores the complexity of what risk means to its potential disaster victims. As has been amply demonstrated, perceived risk is a complex concept that to a large extent defies a technical definition. As I have empirically shown through the analysis, risk perceptions are disaster-specific and predicted by a mixed bag of variables. Recognizing this has far-reaching consequences for the practical business side of surviving, for if public disaster management agencies continue on their present course, we the potential victims are likely to become its actual victims. Organizations that miss the mark in evaluating the realities of their major stakeholders and reinforce their own internal mechanisms will eventually outlive their usefulness.

NOTES

1. The factor analysis was based on a rotated principal component analysis using a Kaiser normalization procedure. Risk questions were coded on a four Likert-type scale where 1 = high risk to 4 = (don't know) extremely low risk.

2. To determine which of the alternative predictor variables best predicts the magnitude of risk required that risk perceptions be linked to specific types of disasters. The factor analysis above created these disaster categories and they were used as the dependent variables in the analysis. A linear regression model was used independently against each disaster factor in which all the independent variables were introduced. For a more detailed description of the Israeli field survey from which the data were taken, see Chapter 2.

6

The Mother Hen Effect

SURVIVAL BY DEFAULT

A key question to survival during a disaster is who is the best prepared. This requires someone to initiate an action. Government officials want us to belief in disaster management organizations, but disaster management organizations are not what they seem. Although they try to satisfy us and prepare us for disasters, the goals are not those of its client-stakeholders. In practical terms, it means that when emergencies and disasters occur, a large part of our behavioral repertoire falls back on traditional forms of disaster behavior. As I have shown such behavior depends on how we estimate the risks of a disaster occurring. It also rests on the help and care we give to our fellow human beings during a crisis and disaster. Despite what most disaster managers ideally do in their offices, seeking administrative solutions that will guide our behavior, we rarely sit down to systematically calculate a risk of the dangers; we do something much more natural and sensible—we reconnect with our families, friends, and neighbors. It is from them that we draw out both the information and emotional support to help survive. The recent picture drawn from the evacuation of the Twin Towers in New York after radical Islamic terrorists flew suicide planes into them showed the true character of people who are trapped in life-threatening situations: they help each other. True, we also use "official" sources of information, but more likely as a backup and supplemental source to survive. It is the social world we are enmeshed in that provides guidance and succor during times of trouble. A large part of that world revolves around our families. To understand how families are involved and how they affect our disaster behaviors, it is critical that we first understand the role that gatekeepers play in this process.

GATEKEEPERS

From what we have learned until now, it seems that the potential victims of disasters are actually their own best friends; they provide valuable information and help in times of need. On the other hand, disaster agencies only marginally influence individuals and families to be prepared for disasters. Both affect our behaviors. What these patterns of behavior suggest, however, is that the choice of where we obtain information and disaster role models is *not* a random phenomenon. To understand why this occurs, let me revitalize a concept called the *gatekeeper effect*. This term was originally coined by Kurt Lewin, a social psychologist who studied ways of changing household eating habits to accommodate the rationing in World War II. In his study, he discovered that the key to changing food consumption patterns depended on what he called the family's gatekeeper—the wife. She, and not the husband or butcher, was receptive to the government's edict about rationing, decided what to buy, and thereby induced changes in her family's eating habits. This concept was then used in the campaign to get families to abide by the rationing regime. The concept itself, designated the gatekeeper effect, was broadened to encompass various kinds of social situations, especially in groups, in which specific persons determined what and how information was obtained, filtered, and distributed. These individuals were seen to initiate, control, and facilitate the transfer of information (or other material goods) to the rest of the group, thereby affecting others' behaviors. The gatekeeper thereby becomes synonymous with the key decision maker on what information is accepted and what is passed along.

  Whom we chose as gatekeepers, those whom we trust and look up to, can range from official government sources to our next-door neighbor. If, for example, disaster officials tell us that getting vaccinated will prevent us from getting anthrax in a terror incident, we will most likely get in line for the vaccination, but if we hear the information from our long-time next-door neighbor who has a physician friend that happened to tell him that the vaccination could sometimes lead to nasty complications, we might not get on that line. Whom we choose to trust will have a lot to do with whom we listen to. Each gatekeeper—in this case the official disaster organization or local neighbor—collects and disseminates information by different criteria. By selectively providing his or her information, gatekeepers play an important social role in how we make decisions that can affect our disaster behavior and thus our chances for survival (Bell et al. 2001).

BUREAUCRATIC GUARDS

Gatekeepers can be found at the organizational, community, and family levels. In organizations they are found at just about every critical node in the formal communications network in which decisions will be made. As organizations can develop into extremely complex structures, this means that transferring information from one unit or department to another—as part of its operational design—involves many gatekeepers of different abilities and perspectives. This lays open the realistic possibility that even "facts" lend themselves to be interpreted. In bureaucratic organizations, in which paperwork and red tape are infamous, the written word can be as easily distorted as the verbal.

While seemingly innocuous, the most numerous gatekeepers found in organizations are the administrative secretaries who filter information to their bosses or the department managers who report on their work to their superiors. Each decides what is important or not and acts on this basis. The recipients of the filtered information then make decisions. A classic global case of this selective gatekeeper effect occurred during the Vietnam War, when only "good" information was passed along to the U.S. government, information that in hindsight affected political and military decisions. A more recent debate in the United States is now going on about disclosing information that might be used by terrorists. The following news item raises this issue, but more important, it discloses the degree to which members of a public sector organization can filter information vital for civilian use. Notice to whom the information is being passed and where these organizational gatekeeper nodes are located!

> Office of Management and Budget (OMB) officials laid out plans to draft guidance on how federal agencies should handle public access to information that is "sensitive but not classified." OMB staff indicated that the guidance would be focused on how federal agencies should make this new category of sensitive information available to local emergency responders, while shielding this information from the general public, sources say. The sources add that OMB staff said the guidance would seek to limit access to this information without officially making it classified (Tim, American Chemical Association, September 2002).

COMMUNITY GATEKEEPERS

In communities, gatekeepers tend to be associated with opinion leaders because of the centrality of their positions, access to external sources of political power, and the intense social network that surrounds them. As is often said, these people are perceived to be "in the know"; they have the ability to access information and have channels to distribute it. In communities such gatekeepers are usually informal leaders who have gained the trust of community members. Sometimes informal leaders are elected officials, at other times moral or power broker leaders utilizing their position and character. Like their communities, they come in many types and forms and are distributed throughout urban neighborhoods as well as rural communities. In most cases, community opinion leaders play important roles as gatekeepers in activating their communities to potential dangers. In smaller communities, the parish priest, clan head, mayor, and sometimes even the community's patron form channels through which disaster-related information flows to its members. There are also the numerous microcommunity gatekeepers, who are usually your neighbors or relatives.

The importance of community gatekeepers came out in a study I did that showed that the decision to evacuate during an emergency when a gas container depot caught fire depended on getting confirmation from your neighbors to leave (Kirschenbaum 1992). Those at or near the site asked neighbors or went out on the street to talk about what was happening. From these discussions they were able to get information from those whom we discovered were neighborhood gatekeepers. Other got in touch by telephone with friends or relatives in the same area also seeking clarification about what was happening and what to do. The results were that nearly three-quarters of the families left the area hours before an official announcement was made to evacuate!

FAMILIES AS GATEKEEPERS

The gatekeeper effect also involves small groups, such as families. One of the first pieces of research to discover this process was done, as I just pointed out, by social psychologist Kurt Lewin in World War II. What he discovered was that the wife of the household acted as the gatekeeper for what the family ate. This lesson was well learned by marketers in their quest to sell products, but little research or conceptual development of this term was pursued outside product marketing. No one paid attention to this term in the area of disasters, perhaps because of the bureaucratic nature of disaster management agencies, which by their very nature had their official spokespersons. There may, however, have been another underlying reason. To accept the fact that disaster preparedness depended on social processes inherent in the family was diametrically opposed to the rational basis for disaster management agencies. Adding insult to injury, the prime gatekeeper in families were the women, a class of people mainly ignored or excluded from both disaster research and disaster organizations (Bolin et al. 1998). More recently, however, this has begun to change, but in an indirect fashion. There has been recognition on the part of official disaster mangers that the "we know better" attitude has not worked. For this reason community preparedness programs have been set up. A second more revolutionary process has been in an emphasis on gender in disaster research. In the guise of gender studies and disasters (Enarson and Morrow, 1998), the key role that women play in the disaster process has begun to be extensively examined. While stressing that women are the underdogs when it comes to disasters, as discriminated victims, and marginalized as caregivers rather than rescuers, there is also a hidden family theme in these case studies and literature reviews. This theme places women within the cultural context of their families, bringing out their sometimes oppressed state but demonstrating their unique position in family and community disasters. More important, it also shows them to be indispensable in the types of activities that involve preparing for and dealing with the aftermath of disasters. In fact, the combination of household, gender, and kinship has slowly become a linchpin for understanding disaster behavior (Wiest, 1998). The reason for this is the recognition that the family reflects what has been called a "domestic social structure," which provides a framework and link to our behavior before, during, and after a disaster.

Taking this indispensable role of women and placing it within a family context combines two potentially powerful factors that may be able to help explain disaster behavior. First of all, as has been repeatedly claimed, survival of individuals during emergencies and disasters revolves around and depends on the family unit (Drabek 1986). What about the survival of the family unit itself, however? Perhaps this depends on women! If they are indeed the family's gatekeepers, their actions may be critical for the well-being of all the family members. Because families are ubiquitous and run the gamut from small nuclear father–mother–child to extended clan structures, their role in disaster behavior becomes extremely significant. For this reason, I would like to look more closely at the family and discover if the wife or husband is the critical gatekeeper for its survival. Before doing so, let me first focus on gender as a component in family life.

GENDER AND DISASTERS

To get at the family gatekeeper means taking a closer look at how men and women react to disasters. There have been many arguments about why men and women act differently during disasters within the context of a family. Most of us would agree that this seems very natural, but the form that a society's culture has developed and its impact on the structure of families complicate it. Living under the roof of a traditional culture means that the roles of women and men have agreed-upon boundaries that may not be acceptable in a more modern society. Accepting the gender roles imposed by each culture, especially related to the family, has a subtle way of determining what we will do and how it will be done in the face of disasters. The most interesting aspect of the impact of culture on gender roles during disasters is that women and men tend to act out their traditional roles based on a clear division of labor (Drabek and Key 1984; Neal and Phillips 1990; Goltz et al. 1992; Wenger and James 1994). For the most part, women are responsible for childcare and other types of kinship-supportive tasks. Men, on the other hand, take on leadership roles, especially those that require greater physical strength. Many of the case studies have found variations in these roles, but emphasize that women focus much of their energy on their families' well-being (Wenger and James 1994; Millican 1993; Dann and Wilson 1993; Morrow and Enarson 1996). There are, of course, extreme cultural imperatives that have evolved over time in response to a particular religious or cultural environment. The stories of a father saving son's lives at the expense of their daughters, of mothers dying in their attempts to save their children or property, of wives organizing help and care for the sick and injured, and of husbands leaving their families to join disaster search and rescue units demonstrate variations in family gender roles in cases of disaster.

Without getting into the complex question of what a family is, let me take for granted that its most prevalent form includes a member of both sexes and offspring. Various combinations of this nuclear-type family consist of mothers, fathers, uncles, grandparents, and even distant relatives. What is sometimes forgotten is that the vast majority of the world's families are not the typical American or European small nuclear family consisting of a father and mother and perhaps a child. They are in fact large, extended or clan families based on extremely complex relationships that are built into their culture. Most of these families are concentrated in developing nations, and from the scant research of their disaster behavior, there appears to be a great deal of mutual help among family members (Morrow 1997; Bolin 1994). What has been found is that women play an extremely important role in facilitating the survival of their families. Depending on the type of kinship culture in place, women are the primary household managers, preparing and sustaining their households during emergencies. One argument that has been put forward for this is that to survive the higher risks associated with their social disadvantage, women and children have devised all kinds of scenarios making them indispensable during crises.

WOMEN CARE MORE

It is for this reason that women and children are at the forefront in sustaining their family and kin during and after disasters (Able and Nelson 1990; Reskin and Padavic 1994). It is not without reason that the United Nations' International Decade for Disaster Reduction declaration (1995) put an emphasis on women and children as the "key to prevention." In Western nations, in which women are extremely active in both the labor force and community affairs, they have apparently taken these skills into community organizations (Akhter 1992; Eade and Williams 1995; Faupel and Styles 1993). These types of activities run from organizing postdisaster food kitchens and temporary shelters for both victims and rescue workers to initiating women forums to influence political leaders and disaster agencies concerning disaster policy decisions. For the most part, however, they have been excluded from official disaster management organizations, which are staffed primarily by male employees (Noel 1990; Phillips 1990; Fordham and Ketteridge 1998). The reason for this is somewhat vague, but obviously has to do with gender role expectations as both self-selecting segregation and outright gender discrimination. Are these disaster-related behaviors simply playing out expected gender roles of women, or do they hint at something much deeper?

MEN ARE STRONGER

The other partner in most families is a male, usually (but not necessarily) a legal husband. For some strange reason, little can be found on men's roles during disasters. The major source of information we have on men's roles comes from researchers investigating the women's role in disasters while anecdotally using men as a comparison. From the limited data that are available, there is an underlying assumption that male dominance in family life is reflected in aspects of disaster behavior. This starts at the top in terms of formal disaster management organizations, which are (correctly) depicted as dominated by male professionals. Such organizations have a military-authoritarian, command-control organizational structure (Fordham and Ketteridge 1998). In terms of disaster behaviors, this example implicates men in control of the distribution of supplies and resources with the care support system allocated to women. Does this pattern also apply outside the organization to family life? What is painfully absent is actual evidence on how men behave toward their offspring, wives, and kin during disasters. The little information that is available is mixed and mainly anecdotal. For example, let us take the stereotyped picture of men's emotions during disasters. This may tell us in a backhanded way something about men's roles during disasters. The argument goes that men are supposed to be strong and practical but when disasters hit they may lose their traditional family roles as providers and protectors, leading to emotional stress. As they don't have the informal networks to provide succor and companionship that women have developed, their family roles are disrupted (Fordham and Ketteridge 1998). This anecdote is but one example among many that is supposed to describe that disaster behavior among men is one of leadership and determination during disasters but can disintegrate during postdisaster periods. Unfortunately it does not provide very much enlightenment about men's roles toward other family members.

Another problematic example is in the area of risk perceptions. How men and women perceive of risks provides some clues as to how each gender group will behave during disasters. Some case studies have found that men seem to take the threats of a disaster more lightly than women, with men being more concerned with the technical or protective aspects of the upcoming disaster (Szalay et al. 1986; Leik at al. 1982; Palm 1995). The same applies for responding to disaster warnings. Men tend not to hear the warnings, and if they do, especially from their wives, to downplay them (Turner et al. 1981; de Man and Simpson-Housley 1987). What can be made of these case studies is that disaster behavior of men based on their risk assessment is faulty and underplayed, but here again it is not clear what part his role plays in helping his family survive a disaster. From what is said, it appears that it might even be detrimental and that family survival can only be trusted to women!

THE PANACEA OF NETWORKS

Several times when discussing men and women's roles during disasters mention is made of informal social networks. I would like to take a minute to look at some of the basic assumptions associated with the impact of networks on disaster behavior. First, it is assumed that such networks are "natural" to women but difficult for men to cultivate. As such, they help women cope after a disaster by providing support and succor to victims, but as I have pointed out, have little impact on postdisaster trauma reactions among men. Some evidence has even shown that this lack of social networks may be one of the reasons for family violence after disasters (Wilson et al. 1998). It is never clear whether men are genetically antisocial in contrast to women or that their gender roles prescribe such behavior. In labor studies, men are heavily involved in occupations and labor markets that are highly competitive, perhaps imparting on them a less social role than women, who tend to enter protected public sector markets (Kirschenbaum 1999), but it would be an erroneous assumption that only informal networks are important in gendered disaster role behaviors.

Social networks, both formal and informal, allow the flow of information both *before* and after disasters. For men and women who are involved in the workforce or in community activities, there are numerous types of social networks. Some are based on weak ties that radiate out from the workplace or the community, creating a large pool of people whom we know and sometimes call upon for favors or information. Like any other kind of social relationship, however, these social networks have various degrees of trust involved. I may know someone down at city hall or working for the CIA and bump into him or her once in a while. Would I trust him or her with my life or my families' welfare during a disaster? Networks in and of themselves are therefore a relevant fallback explanation for men's and women's disaster behaviors, but there is obviously something more, and that "more" is trust. As I pointed out in Chapter 4, trust is critical in determining disaster behavior. Recognizing this point over thirty years ago was a classic analysis of disaster behavior that showed that the trusting behavior among women of the information passed along by their friends (Drabek 1969) was what convinced them to act sensibly in the face of a disaster. Men, apparently, were not that trusting!

What therefore seems sensible is that the social networks themselves provide a channel of information and social closure that can only be fully utilized when those in the network have a reasonable degree of trust in one another. It is for this reason that informal networks based on neighbors, friends, and family are more influential in affecting disaster behavior than officially based networks, and as women relate to these informal networks more than men, it would be reasonable to argue that women play a more crucial role in helping their families survive in disasters.

MOTHER PROTECTOR VERSUS MACHO MEN

These somewhat stereotypical bits of evidence seem to point toward the view that men are far less concerned with their families' welfare than women. Is their concern, however, simply limited to certain aspects of disasters that only indirectly help in their families' survival? Do women, who carry and give birth to their children, retain their maternal roles as mother hens, doing everything possible to protect their families? Perhaps the answer to this question has evolved in our accepting the macho male or maternal female role as archetypes! Men are the defenders and decision makers of the family and women are the caregivers (Scanlon 1998). Unfortunately what evidence is available on *family gender roles* in disasters is mainly descriptive or anecdotal and in the main not analytical.

Such case studies are helpful, however, in that they provide a window of opportunity to look more closely at how gender roles operate in family survival situations. While these pieces of evidence do not tell us how men or women contribute to their family survival, they do tell us what happens. Here is a good example. When a disaster such as a flood leads to life-threatening situations, it was noted that the husband sought ways to save his only son, even at the expense of his daughters. A similar story focuses on the mother who died trying to rescue the household goods. Now let me put this (actual) story in its cultural context! It concerns an Asian farmer whose village-oriented family culture puts stress on lineage through the male offspring. The mother sought to save all their worldly goods to keep the family intact. It would be extremely difficult to come across such a story in the United States or Europe. The few examples that we have are the recent flooding in Western European cities and the firestorms or mudslides in populated areas of California or hurricanes along the southeast coast of the United States. Here, fathers and mothers put all their efforts into saving their spouses and children, but this disaster behavior on the part of a father (or for that matter, women) may, of course, be a single unusual case or more likely a convenient myth. It nevertheless suggests that family gender roles do have a significant part in helping the family survive disasters. My point here is that there does not seem to be any really solid empirical knowledge of how the family gender roles of men and women affect their behavior before, during, and after disasters. For the most part, all we have are case study descriptions on men and women as individuals devoid of their link to their family obligations.

FEAR OR COMMON SENSE?

As a starting point in this quest to evaluate the roles that men and women play in helping their families survive disasters, I will tackle the oft-held stereotype that women are more emotional (and therefore less rational) than men when it comes to disaster behavior. A number of studies have shown that women take the threats of a disaster much more seriously than men (Palm 1995). They also rely more often on social networks than official sources for their information about disasters (Drabek 1969). Does this mean they are more emotional or irrational and incapable of preparing for disasters? As I have already shown in the previous chapter, as the perception of risk of a disaster increases, so too does preparedness! From this point of view, the fears and anxiety of an impending disaster may in fact be an important catalyst to increase the chances for survival.

In the Israeli national representative field survey, questions were asked about such fears. For example, both men and women were asked about the degree of anxiety they felt during the Gulf War.[1] What was found was a significant gap in reported anxiety levels. For example, three times as many women as men said they were extremely anxious during the war (73% vs. 26%). Of those who reported *not* feeling any anxiety, men outweighed women by more than two to one in reporting no feelings of anxiety (70% vs. 30%). (See Chart 1.)

It should be remembered that these data reflect the emotional state of men and women during the Gulf War, a time in which Iraq was raining

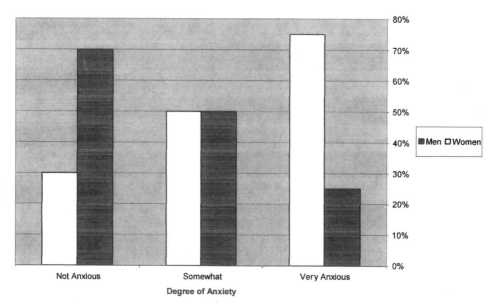

CHART 1 Men's and Women's Degree of Anxiety During the Gulf War.

down ballistic missiles with potentially lethal biochemical warheads on Israel. What the data show is that men and women were not totally blind to the threat on their lives—an equal number of men and women said they were somewhat anxious. It was at the extreme anxiety levels that gender differences really shone through.

Women reported themselves being more anxious than men during a war crisis, but were these anxiety levels due to a personal flaw in women's ability to cope with the situation or men's imperviousness to the attacks? To assess this possibility, I asked what they felt the likelihood would be for themselves or their family being harmed when they heard the warning siren of an imminent missile attack. This question reflected the terrible reality of what was happening, as there was always the possibility of a missile attack (39 actually hitting Israel). The warning gave most people about one to two minutes to get into sealed rooms or shelters that protected them from a biochemical attack. These precautions were less effective from a direct hit by conventional warheads. Both these possibilities existed and depended on the type of missile head that landed, and at the end of the Gulf War, close to 10,000 homes were damaged by these conventional ballistic warheads. Only one person was actually killed by the attack, however.

The responses clearly showed that significantly more women than men made a direct connection between a missile attack warning and the real

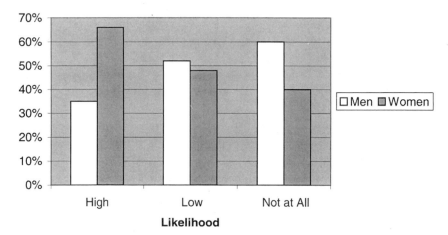

CHART 2   Likelihood of Injury to My Family During an Imminent Missile Attack.

possibility of harm befalling their families (see Chart 2). In fact, twice as many women as men felt there was a likelihood that their family would be injured or killed by missiles. This contrasted sharply to those who felt that no harm would come to their families; men outweighed women by 6 to 4. These results are extraordinary in that they reconfirm how women felt about their families in times of crisis, in terms of both their anxiety and fear that harm would come to their families. At a later point, this concern for the welfare of their families among women will be examined in terms of its gatekeeper effect on family unit survival.

WORDS AND DEEDS

These concerns and fears, and the judgment of the likelihood of death or injury to their families will now be matched against men's and women's assessment of their state of their families' preparedness. As I already pointed out in Chapter 2, gender differences in preparedness were found to be significant only in the case of skill level; there was little difference between men and women in their level of preparedness among the other three components of preparedness—namely, provisions, planning, and protection. In this case, preparedness was based on actual *behavior acts* that experts, disaster management organizations, and researchers defined. Here I will be looking at how these same men and women perceived their level of family preparedness. Don't forget that such perceptions are relative to what they think is important, what their neighbors have, or even what they may have read in a news-

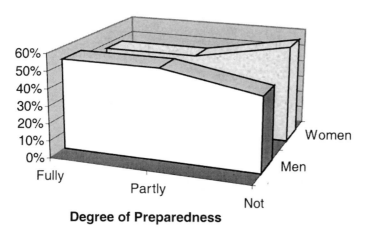

Degree of Preparedness

CHART 3   Degree of Perceived Preparedness by Gender.

paper article. Despite these problematic issues, however, these perceptions reflect their "reality" of how well prepared they feel.

When asked to state how well prepared they felt for a general emergency, there were practically no significant differences between men's and women's responses. Of those who stated they were fully prepared, about half were men and half women. The same applied for those who felt that they were partly prepared. Finally, only slightly more women than men said they were not prepared at all. (See Chart 3.)

What all this says is that the picture that has developed of women being more fearful and anxious than men was not automatically translated into inaction! Women declare, on a nearly equal basis to men, that their households are well prepared for emergencies. They are also almost equally divided on the assessment for their homes being partially or not prepared. Even when preparedness incorporated actual objective measures, the sex of the respondent alone was a poor predictor of preparedness level. (See Chapter 2.) In fact, I would suggest that on the basis of these responses, it would appear that while women were more sensitive to their family's safety and more anxious during the Gulf War, this alone cannot be used as a criterion to distinguish the level of disaster preparedness of their families' households.

MOTHERHOOD AND FATHERHOOD

If gender alone is inadequate to explain levels of perceived preparedness, let me now argue that it might have to do with having children. Underlying most of the studies of disaster behavior by gender is the direct connection between men and women to their family units. While some discussed single-parent families, the widowed, or the divorced, most of the descriptions dealt with family role playing in which *children* are present. In essence, the gender roles of men and women in disasters are not so much as individuals than as family members. When researchers explain their findings by bringing up the protective role of men or caretaker role of women, they are loosely defining family roles, thus to talk about gender roles is, I argue, to really talk about motherhood and fatherhood, and this may be why gender alone does not seem to be adequate in explaining disaster behaviors focused on helping the family survive.

Families that include children are the general format for societal survival. At the most basic level, families are the organizational mechanism by which children are born to replace those who have died. They are the conduit for norms and values as well as transmitters of disaster behaviors. In Western-oriented societies, with adequate food and substantial incomes, smaller families are the rule. In China, with enforced one-child families, this is becoming the case. In Southeast Asia, large families are the rule. The common element in all these families is the essential physical presence of a mother and father. The role obligations of being a mother or father have been passed down and are there to ensure continuity. As we have not yet come to the stage of artificial reproduction as a mass production process, traditional obligations are more or less dictated by cultural imperatives. Some of these are reflected in strict laws that punish abusive parents or that provide the grounds for removing children from problematic families. Children may have rights, but parents have obligations. The extent of these role obligations can sometimes be simply heroic, with mothers and fathers going to extraordinary lengths to protect and succor their children. I would submit that having children—by being a father or mother—is a decisive criterion as to why some families are more prepared than others, and being more prepared may be due to who is the family's survival gatekeeper.

GENDER OR CHILDREN?

The first step to evaluate my proposal is to investigate whether gender and having children make a difference on family-related disaster preparations. To evaluate this, I resorted to comparing if being a women or man made a difference in family-related activities directed at potential disasters (in this case various types of disasters, including unconventional war). In addition, I also went on to investigate if having children or not having in the family also made a difference in these same activities. (See Figure 1.)

What I chose to be the criteria were three basic activities involving the participation of both partners in a decision concerning a potential emergency

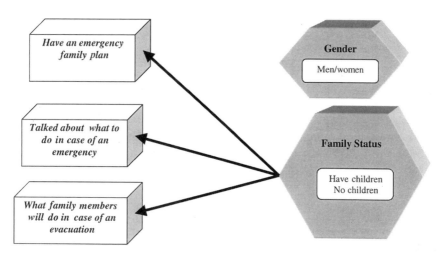

FIGURE 1 Does gender of parents or is having children at home more important to family-related disaster prevention measures? *Note*: Gender based on respondent's sex. Male = 1, female = 2. Children based on dichotomy if children were absent (1) or lived (2) in the household.

or disaster. The first had to do with having an *emergency plan* that included all of the family (in some cases even close relatives). The analysis showed that no difference in the extent of having these plans could be discerned by gender; neither men nor women had a monopoly on such plans. When I sought to find out if households with or without children made a difference in this activity, however, the analysis clearly and strongly pointed out that having children in the family makes a significant difference. Families with children are much more likely to have an emergency family plan than those without children. This empirical finding provided the first important clue that perhaps the link of parents to their children—rather than individuals—affects disaster behaviors aimed at family unit survival.

The second family-related activity dealt with *discussions within the family* about what they would do if and when a disaster or emergency occurred. This question was aimed at tapping an important aspect of how families relate to the possibility of a disaster having an impact on them personally. The analysis once again demonstrated that gender differences alone could not reasonably explain the frequency of such family-related discussions. Having children present was very significant, however. Here, too, when children are present in the family, discussions about what the family would do in case of a disaster were much more prevalent than in families without children.

The third disaster-related activity dealt with the question of what family members would do in case they had to *evacuate their home*. Here again there is a basic underlying assumption that spouses are involved in making this kind of decision, and again it is directly related to the well-being of the family as a unit. This approach to evacuations, however, is rare, even though critical problems in getting families to evacuate and why they don't are almost constantly brought up in the research literature (Kirschenbaum 1992; Perry and Lindell 1991). Interestingly, except for problems involved in evacuating special groups, there seems to be an almost universal assumption that evacuations take place by family units and not individuals. Returning to the data shows that once again gender makes no significant impact on these discussions. Neither men nor women as individuals prevail in these discussion; both are equally likely or unlikely to engage in this type of disaster behavior. What does matter is if the family has children present in the household or not. Those families with children are significantly more likely to have these discussions than childless households, and because of them to be better prepared for a disaster.

Now we know something important that was only hinted at before, that children make a significant difference in whether or not their parents will engage in family-based disaster preparedness. Families without children apparently are significantly less likely to initiate any of the three family-related disaster behaviors. It is possible to speculate that childless family units do not have the incentive to prepare for disasters on the basis of noncommitment to family-related roles as mothers and fathers. Families with children, on the other hand, activate parental role obligations for the safety and well-being of their children, thereby prompting them to engage in disaster-related behavior for the survival of the entire family unit. More important, gender in and of itself does *not* create the conditions for the initiation of family-related actions to reduce the chances that the family will be harmed during a disaster. Overall, children seem to be the essential element that will help identify the gatekeeper of family unit survival.

CHILDREN AND NETWORKING

These results prompt another line of thought that seeks to understand what it is about having children that leads to more active disaster behaviors as a way of ensuring family unity and stability in case of a disaster. I had mentioned that one of the possible ways to understand gender roles in relation to disaster behavior was through the way men and women form their social networks. This could also apply to the presence of children! Anyone who has (or had) children knows the degree to which they have been pulled into a separate, wonderful social world associated with everything "children," from meeting other parents at the physician's office, to going shopping for toys, gossiping at the playground, going to kindergarten meetings, joining parents associations, and so on. This children's world directs us to other parents (and even grandparents) with whom we, for better or worse, can form social networks. We all have something is common—the welfare of our children! It forms a common ground upon which we can start up conversations and make contacts. As I have already noted, such networks are focused not only on children, but also on their welfare, and as such these networks can become prime sources for information about disaster behaviors. (See Chapter 4.) Given the kinds of common interests involved may also engender trust, a precondition for accepting advice. The question that I raise here is perhaps more complex. Does having children in and of itself act as a catalyst in prompting us to actively do something to prepare our families in case of a disaster? Alternatively, does being a mother or father set the stage for a special kind of social networking that triggers these family-linked disaster behaviors? To test this alternative argument, I first looked at the influence of having children on the intensity of specific types of networking components. (See Table 1.)

To do this, I compared the degree and type of social networks that families were involved with on the basis of having children. These networks

TABLE 1 How Having Children Affects Creating Social Networks

Network component	Children[a]
Acquainted with neighbors	0.00
Neighbors helpful	0.71
Neighborly relations good	0.17
Neighborhood watch	0.31
Community center	0.78
Building committee	0.67
Neighborhood committee	0.44
Relatives within proximity	0.53
Visit relatives often	0.35
Telephone relatives often	0.18

Note: The analysis is based on the chi square (χ^2) statistic of the Pearson correlation between the two sets of variables. Network variables based on a Likert-type scale from "very high" to "very low" or equivalent scale and children coded as absent = 1, children present = 2.
[a] The scores represent actual p values of the chi square test.

included those that were associated with neighbors, friends, relatives, and formal social organizations within their community framework. The objective was to try to tap into a variety of social networks that might be formed on the basis of either strong or weak ties, based on the families' common interest; namely, having children. A look at Table 1 reveals that whether or not children are present in the family has very *little* impact on the vast majority of networking components. For one thing, it does *not* significantly affect neighborly relations. It was supposed that when such relations are friendly, there would be more social contact among neighbors, thereby generating a wider social network and greater access to disaster-related information. This did not turn out to be the case. A similar pattern occurred in terms of social networks formed on the basis of being active in neighborhood community affairs. Again there was no significant difference in these networks when children were or were not present in the family. The third set of network indicators focused on the impact that children have on their parents' relationships with relatives. In terms of visiting or being in contact by telephone, children made little difference. Let me now make sense of these results. What all this means is that the various sets of social networks parents participate in through direct or indirect contacts with neighbors, friends, or relatives is accomplished just as well with or without children.

The only exception to this general rule are social networks generated in our daily social intercourse with our neighbors. If we take a step back at my depiction of how the world of children encourages us to meet other families in various situations, my guess is that neighbors more easily engage families with children than single or childless couples. There are large number of common points of conversation and interest. This type of contact may be more likely to happen, but as the data show, these contacts are not strong; rather, they are dispersed and widely spread out. It's the case of bumping into a neighbor at the playground or at a kindergarten meeting. They are people who have a common set of interests and who are available when advice may be needed, but they play only a very minor part in daily living. The upshot of this "exception" is that it really is not an exception but re-emphasizes that children do not in themselves create the basis for generating social networks!

THE PUZZLE

The causal chain linking children to social networks that act as the prime catalysts for family unit disaster behavior does not hold much promise. I am still left with the puzzle about how families survive as a unit. What are the mechanisms that provide disaster behaviors that increase chances for survival? We now know that the children-network argument is spurious. Again, sex-related gender roles have been shown to be inadequate. Having or not having children within the family framework independent of other matters has also been inadequate. Leaning on social networks has shown little promise. Now I would like to get at the heart of the matter by exploring if, indeed, motherhood or fatherhood and the roles that have evolved around them can explain why some families are more prepared than others.

Let me backtrack briefly by reiterating that the concepts of fatherhood and motherhood are culturally bound and therefore not only have a wide breadth of meanings between cultures but even within the same culture. The example I gave about the farmer who saved his son at the expense of his daughters prescribes a certain role that fathers play in family life. The same also applies for mothers. Fathers and mothers in a different culture may adhere to a different set of role obligations whereby they might save a daughter rather than the son, but rather than look at these extreme cases, I would like to focus on what I believe is the general role obligation of all fathers and mothers in various cultural settings; namely, the institutional normative obligation of societal survival through procreation and the actions that mothers and fathers take to ensure that their family survives. In the case of the farmer, he did this by making sure his son survived to maintain the family lineage. Others may do the same thing in a roundabout manner by focusing resources on smaller families to ensure not only the physical survival of off-spring but also their social success. In both cases, fathers and mothers take on a role that is based on providing sustenance and protection for their children.

GENERATIONAL CONTINUITY

One of the critical elements in this role playing is to effectively utilize traditional knowledge handed down through the generations. One universal example can be seen in how mothers tend to help their daughters (or relatives) when they give birth so they can be near them through the first critical days or months after birth. They provide useful knowledge and experience to the new mother, who in turn will do the same for her children. This continuity, from mother to daughter, has its basis in a socialization process that ensures that family role obligations are passed down. It is also present for fathers, who have traditionally passed down other types of family-related survival skills to their sons. At one time these were primarily occupational skills, such as hunting, fishing, or farming, and to a large extent in the nonurbanized world have remained vocational skills. Today, in more urban, industrial-based nations, these skills have become nearly superfluous, but fathers continue to pass down other kinds of skill values that continue to affect their sons' niche in the occupational structure. It should not come as a surprise that the sons of physicians tend to become physicians or work in related fields, while those of factory workers tend to become blue-collar workers.

There can be little doubt that both fathers and mothers contribute to their families' survival. They do so not only by fulfilling the role obligations as protectors of their children, but also by passing along vital survival information that their children will utilize when they themselves form families. Part of the knowledge that is passed down has to do with disaster behaviors. This is clearly spelled out by a Jamaican Red Cross worker in the Caribbean, an area hit by hurricanes and volcanic eruptions. Here there is a saying that the best way to survive is "to listen to what Grandma said" (Clark 1995).

SELECTIVE GATEKEEPERS

To say that our mothers and fathers are the single most important source of disaster behavior role models that facilitate the survival of our families is at this point only a supposition. True, the evidence strongly points toward this conclusion, but the need remains for a more empirical confirmation. This can come about by taking the analysis a step further in its sophistication. Right now all we know is that families with children tend to discuss topics in their households that are directly related to disaster-type behaviors aimed at helping the family survive a disaster. What is still unknown—at least empirically— is whether or not these sources of information are generated through the mother or father—or both! While most of us would bet on the mother, which seems most natural, given her general familial role as caretaker, there still is the possibility that the father may also provide such information (or they may share in what is passed down). This led to an reanalysis of the three critical areas of family discussions that were touched upon previously: family discussions about emergency plans, what to do in case of a disaster, and what to do in the event of the need to evacuate. What I did was to look closely at whether men or women who have children present in their households are significantly more likely to engage in such discussions. (See Table 2.)

What the analysis of the data provided was a picture that the parents of children, both fathers and mothers, are more involved in their families' predisaster preparations than men and women who do not have children. In terms of the degree of significance, mothers appeared to be significantly more involved in family discussions over family emergency plans than fathers, but in terms of the remaining two areas of predisaster family discussions, both mothers and fathers apparently take these types of family discussions very seriously and are jointly involved in them. Simply put, men and women without children in their households are much less likely to deal with these predisaster discussions than mothers and fathers. What makes these results of special importance is that for the most part it seems that these issues are not confined to the realm of (or initiated by) one parent or another; both fathers and mothers take an active part in these disaster behaviors.

TABLE 2   Family-Related Disaster Prevention Measures
for Fathers and Mothers

Type of family measure	Fathers	Mothers
Emergency family plan	0.195	0.000
Talked about what to do	0.006	0.000
What to do for evacuation	0.007	0.000

Note: The analysis is based on the chi square (χ^2) statistic of the Pearson correlation between the two sets of variables. Family preparedness activities variables coded as "yes" to "no" and fathers and mothers coded as dichotomous variables. The scores represents actual p values of the Pearson correlation chi square test.

If this is the case, I have narrowed down the potential gatekeeper(s) who are key to family unit survival during disasters. Don't forget, however, that these results only focus on predisaster behaviors and are based on internal family discussions. As we all know from our own life experiences, talking about things does not necessarily mean that we will do something about them. A large body of research in fact has repeatedly shown that discussions of this type do not directly lead to appropriate behaviors. What is important, however, is that such discussions take place. They show that these disaster-related topics are important to families and that parents of children are concerned and take these topics as a serious threat to their families. By discussing these events, parents provide a basis for a more informed decision about what to do in case of an actual disaster. As I showed in Chapter 4, there is a serious search for appropriate disaster behaviors through both formal official and informal social networks that, as is now suggested, is primarily done by fathers and mothers. Such a search may have predated the family discussions or come about as a result of them, but in either case what mothers and fathers do is provide a guideline or benchmark for what they may do in order to help their families survive intact.

ACTUAL PREPAREDNESS

Until now I have looked at that part of the family "experience" that has been involved in the preliminary stages of disaster behavior; namely, the family discussions of the "what if" questions. The next step in trying to discover the degree to which fathers and mothers are gatekeepers of disaster behavior was to examine not just what they discussed but what they did. I emphasize the "did" here, as only if the outcomes of these family discussions lead to actual preparations for a disaster can we say they have been successful. Only if they lead to actual disaster behavior associated with preparedness can we begin to uncover if one or both of the principle family members are truly the family gatekeepers. Certainly more critical for family unit survival are what kinds of verbal disaster behaviors are translated into actual disaster-related activities. It's all well and good to talk about plans or evacuation schemes, but it will go only so far when faced with an actual disaster. This especially applies to family unit preparations when actions and not only words are needed.

The argument that preparedness is a crucial component to discovering the family gatekeeper comes not only from the need to look at actual disaster behaviors (rather than attitudes or discussions), but also from underlying historical lessons. I have continually argued throughout this book that behaviors that were learned and adapted to survive disasters have become part of our community and family heritage. They are called upon in time of need, and for the most part, are action-oriented. Things are done. People purchase emergency equipment, stock foods, build shelters, and under dire circumstances evacuate their homes. This has been the case in the past and it remains the case today. To make concrete steps in preparing for a disaster, such socially based communications as warnings are necessary, as they are in all social actions. In contrast to disaster preparations, however, they represent only a very minor part of the survival behaviors that families utilize. How and what to prepare is already imbedded in our social heritage. This can be added to or modified through our trust of information provided by others. Who are these other people? Primarily family, friends, and neighbors who provide us with the support for specific disaster behaviors. They don't force us to be prepared, however; only we ourselves can do that. This was clearly seen in Chapter 2, in which the analysis of social networks—a classic measure of social communications—show such networks not to be all that omnipotent in their ability to predict preparedness. The bottom line is that network communicating and even family discussions are only a preliminary stage in actual disaster behaviors aimed at helping the family unit survive. How these various pieces of information and advice become a reality in terms of actual family preparedness depends on the family gatekeeper.

KEY PLAYERS

It is for this reason that I now turn to examining who the key players are in preparing the family for disasters. In laying the groundwork to discover who contributes the most toward family unit survival in a disaster, I have slowly examined sets of potential gender characteristics to narrow the focus on the family gatekeeper. Those who have argued that successful family disaster behaviors are due to sex–gender roles have been shown to be inadequate. Being a man or women, and by implication exhibiting the gender roles associated with being manly or feminine, is not nearly enough to explain differences in family-oriented disaster behavior. Moving away from specific male or female gender roles to a household status determined by having or not having children in the family did show some promise. Taking this cue, the next logical step would be to ask is if being married (being a husband or wife) would make a difference.

Let me start by assuming that marital status represents the existence or absence of a basic family unit. Single persons are not the basis for a family, while married individuals form such a basis. For most of the world's population, stable family life is usually accompanied by a change in personal status, which we label as being married. Most societies link this change to a religious ceremony or civil contract, while others take various types of stable relationships as enough to be considered a family (e.g., consenting partners). Once such a family unit exists, I would expect that men and women would start to take on broader family rather than narrower sex–gender-oriented roles (Smit 2002; Feldman et al. 2001). Single individuals would simply continue to play roles they were socialized into upon gaining independence from their parents. Married couples, however, find themselves with additional sets of obligations, not only for themselves but also for their partners. This initial stage of family formation through marriage is likely to provide relevant clues as to the gatekeeper of family unit survival in the face of disasters.

GENDERED GATEKEEPER ROLES

One possibility for the role of family gatekeeper is the married woman. This first choice is hard to ignore as it is blatantly implied in the research literature on gender and disasters. Married women's role in disaster as described in case after case makes it almost impossible to ignore their possible role as gate-keepers, as those who decide what disaster-related information is relevant and its actualization into being prepared. The reasoning behind this stems from the supposition that when women get married, they extend their "natural" nurturing, caretaker roles as females into the realm of their family. In most societies, based on a division of labor by sex and status, married women also may have a vital economic stake in making sure their partner stays healthy and safe (Fothergill 1998).

There is of course the counterargument that married men should be considered for the role of family gatekeeper. The logic here is also convincing, as it combines a similar transfer of the typical male role of defender and leader into the realm of family life. Here the stakes for the man are twofold: to protect his wife as a stable sexual and work partner and as the potential progenitor of his future kin. To do this, he will probably be extremely sensitive to information about situations that might harm him or his female partner. If so, there is every reason to suspect that he will then take appropriate preparedness actions in case a disaster occurs. Both actions are typical of a family gatekeeper.

These two alternative possibilities rest on the assumption that being a family gatekeeper depends solely on fulfilling the status of a married man or women. In light of the arguments for each, both seem reasonable, but there is another alternative explanation—not only being married, but being a mother and father to children. This status position is much more complex, as it involves not only thinking about the welfare of your partner, but also of your children. As I have already noted, mothers and fathers—in contrast to childless partners—are active participants in their families' safety. Both hold discussions that are directly related to their families' disaster survival. They are not only concerned as married couples, but extend their role obligations to assure their children's welfare. The end result is that mothers and fathers play two complementary roles, that of married partners and that of parents. It is this double role that makes them potential family gatekeepers.

Let me be more explicit about how I link this family status to the role of gatekeeper. The obvious assumption I make is that the verbal disaster behaviors associated with motherhood and fatherhood will somehow be translated into actual disaster behaviors; that is, parent will put into action what they discussed about being prepared for disasters. Who will do what is difficult to predict. Taking what we know of the basic gender roles, however, some sort of division of labor should evolve between women and men as mothers and fathers. This division of labor would then be apparent in the "whom" and "what" of family preparations. What I suggest is a distinct division of labor in these preparations, with the father focusing on the physical, protective components of preparedness and the mother on honing planning and skills. In such a case, the role of family gatekeeper may not be filled by single individual, but by a subtle combination whereby both parents take on specific facets of their family's survival.

ACTION AND NOT WORDS

All of the above hypothetical arguments—of who the family gatekeeper is—still face the inevitable empirical test based on the data I have collected. To do so, I will focus on examining the levels of preparedness of each status–being a husband or wife and being a father and mother to children. As actions speak louder than words, it seems more than reasonable to make use of disaster preparedness measures. This concept reflects actions, simply those things that individuals do to prepare themselves for emergencies and disasters. The measures are based on actual behavior and material items that can be objectively counted. As I pointed out in Chapter 2, preparedness is a vague concept that has different meanings to different people. To get at its underlying empirical meaning, I analyzed how disaster experts, researchers, and organizations defined it and established that it is composed of four basic components: having basic survival provisions in the home, having emergency skills and training, having family unit plans for possible disaster scenarios, and having the basic physical protective structures in cases of extreme types of disasters. As the facts emerged, these four distinct characteristics of preparedness could be explained by different sets of factors. This being the case, I retained these four meanings of preparedness and sought to find out if being a husband or wife or father or mother would make a significant difference in preparedness levels. If differences did appear, I could then go on to state that one or more of these status levels definitely affects how well a family is prepared for a disaster.

By logical implication, these results would also allow me to take a further step by saying who the family gatekeeper probably is. It should be remembered that the concept of gatekeeper that I proposed represents a family member who not only selectively accesses information but also puts it to the best use for his or her family. By focusing on the status of who enables the family to be better prepared, the source of the family gatekeeper can be revealed. It is to this that I now turn.

WHO PREPARES THE MOST?

There are several alternative possibilities as to who may be the family gatekeeper. The first stage in discovering who the family gatekeeper is requires that I compare the different levels of family status. This meant creating four different status categories: husband, wife, mother, and father.

Each of these family role status categories is actually built on contrasting the internal status that it represents. For example, the husband category represents men who are either married or not married. This also holds true for wives. In the case of father and mother, the status levels that are compared are between men and women who have or who do not have children. By tackling these status levels in this way, I can expand the analysis to focus on not only family status roles but also sex–gender roles. (See Figure 2.)

The next step was to run a series of statistical tests based on linear regressions for each status level of the four family roles. What this meant was that for each specific family role status an evaluation was done to see if it was a significant predictor of any of the preparedness components. For example, the husband family status—which is composed of married and unmarried men— was matched against the preparedness component "provisions." What this test did was explore if this family status was any good at predicting various levels of provisioning for disasters, and if so, if it made any difference if the

Potential Gatekeepers

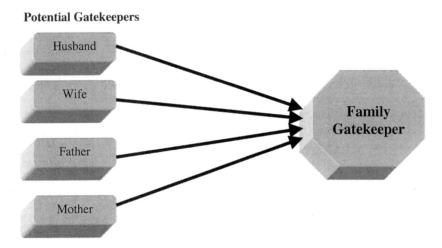

FIGURE 2   Potential family gatekeepers based on family role status.

man was married or not. This same type of analysis was also done in the case of having children, with men and women separated by the fact that they had children in their households. This statistical test was done independently for each of the four family status roles that then allowed me to compare each of the family status roles as predictors of preparedness. What are the results? (See Table 3.)

THE MOTHER HEN EFFECT

The only question that has guided the analysis and arguments here has been who in the family initiates and activates the family to ensure its survival as a

TABLE 3   Parental Status as Predictors of Preparedness Components

Preparedness factors	Husband	Wife	Fathers	Mothers
Provisions	0.844	0.095	0.740	0.010
Skill level	0.860	0.888	0.762	0.375
Planning	0.467	0.520	0.342	0.014
Protection	0.119	0.713	0.439	0.062

Note: The levels of significance are based on a regression model in which each parental status was regressed separately. Men and women were coded as a dichotomous married/not married variable with fathers/mothers coded as having a household with children/without children.

unit.[2] The results of the analysis in Table 3 go a long way toward unraveling this complex question. Incredibly, the answer seems to be that family unit survival during disasters depends on what can be labeled the "mother hen effect." In short, mothers with children are the source of family survival. I believe that my coining of the phrase mother hen effect reflects this ability of mothers in several ways. First and foremost are the role obligations that have become an integral part of motherhood. In nature, protection of offspring is a basic evolutionary mechanism for species survival, and can range from genetic hormonal behaviors in nonprimates to what appears to be more social group behavior in higher primates. Sometimes this protection can even lead to extremely high risks on the part of the mother. In its modified form among humans, mothers invest a tremendous amount of their energy and resources into their children. During such disasters as wars, mothers have gone to extreme lengths to save their children.

It is easy to argue that what the results of the analysis showed can in retrospect be said to be "obvious." Of course mothers protect their children! All the clues were even in place in previous research. Why was it missed? What seems to have happened was that an ideological filter (i.e., Western ideologies toward individual rights and egalitarianism) tended to overemphasize individual "women" in disasters and not their role in the family as a basic survival unit. The arguments and counterarguments about the role of women in disasters somehow missed the crucial point of women enacting the role of mothers, who are the master designers of their families' survival. In contrast to other family members, mothers best prepare their families and who apparently initiate seeking and sifting the information that provides them with a risk assessment matched to their actual preparedness actions. In short, family unit survival depends on mothers who fulfill the social role as mother hen and family gatekeeper.

CULTURAL FRAMEWORK

The mother hen effect, however, may be a bit more complicated than just isolating mothers and tagging them as gatekeepers. For one thing, being a mother may be a necessary but insufficient condition for preparing families to survive a disaster. One reason for this depends on the degree and strength to which the role is played. Not all mothers are totally dedicated to the welfare of their families. Variations exist, and it is my contention that it may have to do not so much with the personality of a particular mother, but with the social constraints imposed on mothers within their familial cultural setting. Cross-cultural studies have showed how both cultural and ethnic differences have an impact on family disaster behavior. The underlying impression from these studies is that these cultural and ethnic differences impose different roles on family members, especially mothers, and these obligatory roles foster or dampen the degree to which mothers also attend to their families' disaster preparedness. This, of course, is only an informed opinion at this point. To test its robustness, I will combine two approaches. The first will be to look at what I call *familism*, or how close families are socially. The assumption is that traditional families maintain stronger ties among themselves than modern families. The second approach will look at "ethnicity" as a proxy of "traditional" and "modern" family structures. As both complement each other in attempting to describe the ideal forms of traditional and modern families, it will be possible to assess if external factors affecting family processes indeed have a part in the mother hen gatekeeper effect on family preparedness. Before doing so, it is crucial to understand the rationale behind this thinking. (See Figure 3.)

To some extent, we already know that cultural and ethnic characteristics affect disaster behavior. We already saw this to be true in Chapter 4 when I looked at how Jews and Arabs, immigrants and natives, choose their source of disaster role model behaviors. If this is the case, it can be expected that

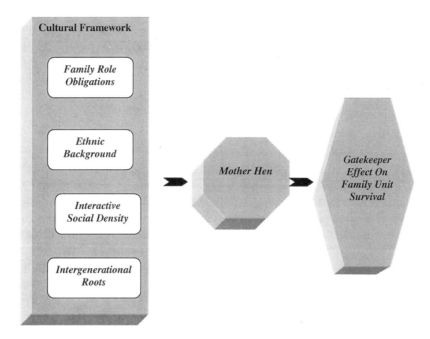

FIGURE 3 Cultural and ethnic factors that might affect a mother hen's gatekeeper ability in preparing her family for disasters.

mothers whose ethnic background are more closely aligned with traditional or modern family structures should prepare their family for disasters somewhat differently from each other. Many of the case studies I have cited actually make a point of how women are expected to take care of specific matters in case of disasters, be it to gather up agricultural tools or construction materials in the case of rural farming families or to initiate volunteer helping organizations in Western urban societies. In general, the ideal traditional family, based on extended family networks and close relational ties, is usually depicted as patriarchal in structure with a very clear sex role division of labor. Modern family units, based on the nuclear unit, have less clear lines of sex role demarcation and tend to be seen as more egalitarian. These depictions are difficult to find nowadays because of the encroachment of modernization into even the most isolated areas, resulting in researchers falling back on a number of alternative measures of traditional or modern family types. One used most frequently is employing ethnic group affiliation as a proxy.

ETHNICITY AND FAMILISM

Ethnicity in its broadest sense is a culturally based demographic characteristic (Berthoud 1998), and for this reason has been used as a proxy for traditional and modern family types. Certain ethnic groups display family characteristics that go a long way to matching the ideal traditional family, while others more closely resemble the modern family type. It is for this reason that ethnicity may provide a springboard to understanding the mother hen gatekeeper effect in disaster preparedness. To do so, however, requires that we provide a more common definition of this variable, one that can be accepted by laymen and researchers alike (Aspinall 2001). The majority opinion of what ethnicity is all about rests predominantly on a cultural perspective (Halualani 2000; Wink 1997). In these terms, ethnicity is the outcome of the general cultural atmosphere that pervades a society. Some societies are homogeneous and others heterogeneous, thereby promoting singular or multidistinct types of groupings. Imposing particularistic cultural behaviors to one or more of these groups leads to their distinctive character and what we tend to call ethnicity.[3]

Most researchers agree, however, that ethnicity and familism are to a great extent interchangeable. They both represent some form of group identity and way of life. Because of this ethnicity has been technically measured in terms of a person's country of origin, which under certain circumstances can extend along generations. The underlying assumption is that people from different countries express their social and cultural behaviors in different ways. In some cases, even indigenous population groups, such as Native Americans or African Americans, have been designated as ethnic groups due to their particularistic past cultural artifacts and norms (Reese et al. 1998). In Israel, it is even more complex, because of the large number of immigrants and mixed ethnic marriages (Israel Central Bureau of Statistics 2002). Because ethnicity is such a broad-based concept and can act as a proxy for family relationships, it provides a number of diverse and alternative channels to explore its relationship with how mothers influence their families' ability to be prepared.

Despite the theoretical and practical potential of employing ethnicity to understand disaster behavior, the actual number of studies that have sought to empirically link ethnicity to preparedness is extremely small and inconclusive.[4] In one way or another, all of these case studies have attempted to tap into the concept of ethnicity as an indirect way to explain family-related disaster behaviors. For the most part they are primarily descriptive in nature and provide an unclear link between ethnic characteristics and disaster behavior. They certainly neglect how mothers as gatekeepers are influenced by their familial and ethnic backgrounds. I will now try to rectify this gap in our knowledge.

TRADITIONAL MOTHER HENS

One of the core characteristics of traditional family structures is the intimate and strong physical contact that family members have with one another. This would be particularly true among the women of the households. This is not to say that this is totally absent in modern family life, but is less the case in modern, structured, nuclear families where members often live great distances from one another. Using this cue of physical contact, *mothers* were asked about family *visits*. The scale on visits ran from visiting family members every day to never. When asked about how much they visited their relatives, the picture that emerged was that close to three-quarters of the sample respondents keep in very close touch with other family members. About one-fifth (20.1%) responded that they visited their relatives every day, over half (54.4%) at least once every week, a sixth (17.5%) once a month, and about a tenth (10%) rarely or never. This overall pattern seems to side with the notion that Israeli families tend toward traditional extended family relationships, even though the country is highly urbanized and modern.

Taking these results and now imprinting them on ethnicity should provide some notion if such family visiting patterns and ethnicity coincide. This was done by asking the respondents from the sample where they were born (country of origin), and if born in Israel, whether or not their parents were natives or immigrants. In this way, three levels of intergenerational ethnicity could be arrived at: immigrants, first-generation natives and second-generation natives. The assumption was that those mothers closer to their immigrant roots would be more likely to have traditional family structures. A tenth (10.4%) of the *mothers* were native born to parents who also were born in Israel, close to half (47.6%) were first-generation natives whose parents immigrated to Israel, and about two-fifths (42.1%) were immigrants. When matching visits with the ethnicity of the mother, *no significant* differences could be found (chi square 0.40); that is, it did not statistically matter what ethnic group you belonged to when it came to how strong your family ties were (as measured by visitation). Both native-and foreign-born individuals had very similar patterns of visitation to their relatives. To reconfirm this, a simple Spearman bivariate correlation was run to assess if an ethnic group could be matched with a particular type of visitation pattern. The results likewise yielded anonsignificant positive coefficient of 0.37. Putting these results together was a clear indication that the intergenerational measure of ethnicity was *independent* of the measure of family closeness through visitation. Apparently, visiting relatives is a part of the overall culture and not related to one ethnic group or another.

ETHNIC ROOTS

Another possible approach to exploring the impact of the ethnicity of mothers on being prepared was to rely on the "intergeneration social distance" measure from one's immigrant roots as a proxy for the intensity of ethnicity. Again, the assumption was that mothers who were second- or third-generation natives of immigrant parents would exhibit fever ethnic characteristics than those of their immigrant parents or grandparents. A series of statistical analyses were then performed to determine if different generational ethnic groups had an impact on whether or not mothers who were affiliated with specific native or immigrant generation groups acted differently when it came to preparing their families for potential disasters. Again, it should be recalled that what was sought was if ethnicity–mother behavior went beyond just random behaviors. The results showed quite clearly that intergenerational-based ethnicity does *not* significantly explain any of the preparedness factors. (See Table 4.) This was quite surprising, given what seemed to be a clear set of indications—both theoretically and empirically—that ethnicity and its implications of tradional–modern family structures would have an impact on the intensity to which mothers would act to prepare their families from disasters. The facts proved differently, however. Here, too, I set out to reconfirm this nonassociation. In this case I employed another form of ethnicity which decomposed the intergeneration measure into its single ethnic origin groups (e.g., Asia; Europe/America; Russia; Israel-born: Asian parents; Israeli-born: European parents). This was done out of concern that the combination of ethnic origin groups might have whitewashed out differences between each of

TABLE 4   Mother's Level of Disaster Preparedness by Intergeneration Ethnicity

Ethnicity	Supply	Skills	Plans	Protection
Intergenerational[a]	0.46	0.51	0.98	0.48
Country of origin[b]	0.22	0.64	0.88	0.61

Note: The figures represent the significant levels based on the chi square statistics.
[a] Includes separate categories for native born with native born parents, native born but parents foreign born, and foreign born.
[b] Includes separate categories for native born whose parents emmigrated from Asia, Europe/America, or parents born in Israel and those born in Asia, Europe/America, and Russia.

the separate components. Here, too, *no significant* ethnic group differences were found in explaining levels of preparedness.

RETURN TO MOTHER HEN

These results show a clear and consistent *rejection* of the notion that ethnicity based on intergenerational detachment from immigrant roots affects a mother's ability as family gatekeeper to prepare her family for disasters. All the arguments, implications, and clues that have been tossed about in the research literature that have hinted at this can now be seen as having been extremely problematic. The plain fact is that ethnicity as a proxy of the characteristics of traditional and modern families does not exert any meaningful influence on family disaster preparedness. What has and continues to do so is the mother of the family. Despite the ethnic character of the mother, despite how close the families are as a unit, the greatest influence on disaster preparedness remains the mother hen. The weight of the evidence makes us once more return to the ability of mothers to act as gatekeepers in selecting, processing, and acting to ensure the safety and preparedness of her family.

What all this means is that the key to successful preparation for disasters is primarily in the hands of mothers. This is not to say that fathers or men or women without children do not do an adequate job at preparing themselves for disasters. It means that if we compare them, most bets would be placed on the mother as the key person to successful survival. Perhaps this is one of the reasons why women are more prone to postdisaster trauma, as they may feel responsible or guilty for not fulfilling their family role obligations as family protector (Fordham and Ketteridge 1998). The implications of these findings are manifold. First, they strongly reinforce the idea that family unit survival is the basic building block upon which group, community, and societal survival depend in the face of disasters. The family unit should be looked at as the "first line of defense" against disasters—as the core organizational form in which disaster role model behaviors are relevant. Second, families are more likely to survive disasters than nonfamily units. Given the fact that families with children and a mother present are more prepared than other family types means they will have a better chance at minimizing the negative effects of disasters. Third, as gatekeepers, mothers are the vital link in transferring crucial disaster-related information to other family members. This form of communication is not dictated by bureaucratic rules but by informal social norms, making the transfer, acceptance, and compliance more effective.

Taken together, the discovery of the mother hen effect calls into question the organizational means used by disaster management agencies to prepare us for disasters. The assumption that providing all the relevant "facts" to the public will release disaster agencies from their obligations does not match what has been found in the analysis. Simply providing the facts has been shown over and over again to be ineffective. What we now know is that disaster-related information is filtered and selected by mothers through traditional informal social networking sources. It is the mother who acts as the gatekeeper and repository of disaster role behaviors. In short, the key to family survival depends on the mother hen.

SUMMARY OF VICTIMS' PERSPECTIVES

The past three chapters of the analysis have focused on a side of disaster management that to a very large extent has been ignored by disaster management organizations. Each has explored a critical part in the complex relationship between individuals and disasters. All have touched upon the social foundations of disaster behavior and in doing so have, I hope, shown the powerful effect that the social world outside these organizations has on such behaviors. The arguments that were presented in these chapters not only looked at disasters from the perspective of the potential victim; they also highlighted the gap that exists *between* official disaster management organizations and their clients. For the potential victim, disasters are not artificial administrative directives. Disaster management is not related to preparedness of the organization. For us, disasters are real threats to our safety as individuals, family, or community. Our perceptions and reactions are deeply embedded in the social world around us. Our behaviors are socially based and not administratively directed. For disaster management organizations, these factors play only a minor role in their decision basis. It is this gap that the analysis has focused upon.

The first chapter of this section raised a basic question concerning the viability of the traditional ways we have utilized for millenniums in case of disasters. These traditional ways have historically been associated with seeking, obtaining, and utilizing sources of *social* information generated by family members, friends, and neighbors. Such social information, based on a trust generated through social interactions, provided us with a framework to devise disaster role models of what to do and how to act in case of disasters. These sources of information were, however, at odds with information generated by public sector disaster management organizations.

This clash between organizational and traditional sources of disaster-related information formed the crux of the analysis. The end result was that traditional sources of information concerning disaster role behavior were alive and well. The implication was that despite the omnipotent scope of formal public sector organizations over the area of disaster management, people continued to rely on traditional social forms of disaster role modeling. (See Figure 4.)

In contrast to the views of disaster management organization experts, the second test of the vitality of our disaster behaviors was evident in the way in which the risks of a disaster were assessed or evaluated. Again we saw that there was a wide gap in what disaster management agencies saw as a risk and how we perceived of these same events. It became apparent that the organizational constraints and priorities of disaster management agencies were not those of the potential victim. As the analyses showed, we evaluated the risk of a disaster not on the basis of sterile probabilistic calculations but in

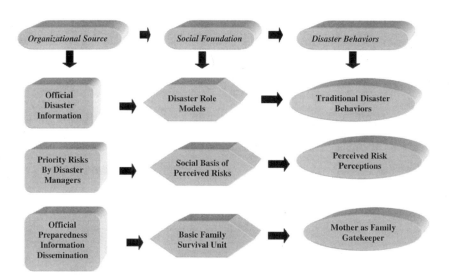

FIGURE 4 Summary of potential victims' disaster behavior in contrast to official disaster management organizations.

terms of our social environment. Disasters were assessed on the basis of *risk perceptions*. These risk perceptions were not uniform, but varied by the social backgrounds of the individuals. Also, we did not evaluate different types of disasters equally. In short, our perceptions of risk were profoundly immersed in the social worlds within which we lived. These risks also had an effect on our actual preparedness for disasters. The higher we felt the risks, the more we were prepared. These empirical findings once more confirmed that there is another separate world of disaster management outside the formal public sector organizational boundaries. It is a world built on everyday perceptions fostered by social discourse with our fellow man.

A final evaluation focused on the family unit. Here, too, the effort was to empirically demonstrate how the victims' social world affects disaster behaviors independently of disaster management organizations. The emphasis on the family was due to its ability to act as a successful survival unit. In understanding why this was so, I developed the concept of the mother hen gatekeeper. Such gatekeepers selectively filter, process, and implement information to increase the survivability of their families. The official dissemination of disaster information might be irrelevant if it did not pass through the family portal guarded by mothers. The analysis not only confirmed the ability of mother hens to prepare their families for disasters, but also clearly showed them as a serious rival to disaster management organizations. As a primary directive of such organizations is to inform the public, there is a very good chance that not only will the information disseminated be inappropriate, as it reflects the assessment of disaster managers, but it will never reach its intended destination, so here, too, the power of everyday social processes that are embedded in the family can act to ignore, divert, or reinterpret what the experts have to say to us.

Overall, the results of the analysis have provided us with two important lessons. First, the world of disaster behavior continues to be based on social processes that have been with us since time immemorial. They are generated in the daily social discourse we have with others and are institutionalized in our social fabric. Second, the fact that socially based disaster behaviors have operated and continue to operate in parallel with the formal organizational framework also helps explain why these organizations have not been as successful as their mentors were hoping. In the next series of chapters, I will examine and suggest an alternative organizational format for disaster management.

NOTES

1. It is extremely important to remember that the "war" was in fact an attack solely on the civilian population of Israel. It is for this reason

that like natural, technological, or industrial disasters, the Gulf War
was another form of disaster that led to the disruption of Israeli
civilian society.

2. Before getting into the details of the results of the statistical analysis,
    it is crucial to recall that the object of this chapter is to look more
    closely at who is best prepared for a disaster and how such a state of
    preparedness came about. On the second issue of the mechanisms
    for preparedness, disaster management organizations have been
    extremely lax on several levels. Their goals are not in tandem with
    their client stakeholders. Their assessment of risk does not match
    the general population's. What apparently is the result is that people
    fall back on traditional modes of disaster behavior, and as I have
    forcefully argued, do so within their family framework.

3. Variations on this theme exist, but on the whole are marginal ad-
    ditions of specific descriptive characteristics that make each group
    distinctive in its social behaviors. For example, some researchers
    focus on perceptions (Laaksonen 1996). Here the emphasis is on
    how each group perceives of itself as distinctive. It results in how
    ethnicity clouds perception's of other types of social behavior. For
    example, we use the concepts of "barbarian" or "civilized" as a
    measure of our own ethnic groups' self-perceptions of how one
    should behave. Others scholars have put an emphasis on how per-
    sonal relationships are structured (Gaines et al. 1997). This more or
    less relates to the social pecking order within groups, which dictates
    who interacts with whom. Certain ethnic groups have laid down
    what can be euphemistically called "lines of respect," which even
    determine power relationships within the group. For example, a
    family clan's head or council of elders is the final arbitrator of
    disputes. There is even a measure of in-group closeness (Uleman
    2000). The idea behind this is a mix of social group behaviors, but
    basically relies on the solidarity, tightness, and reinforcing
    interactions of social networks. In a sense, it's a sort of group
    incest by which members only interact with other members of the
    same group. An additional characteristic that reflects ethnicity is
    dependent on language differences (Piette 1997). This seems an
    obvious trait, but as language is also a significant device to transmit
    cultural attributes, especially emotional and nostalgic reminders of
    the origins of the group, it can also be considered a singular
    differentiating mark of a group. The degree of its power will depend
    on the intensity by which it will be used; for everyday usage or only
    on special occasions or ceremonies such as in church (Latin) or
    synagogue (Hebrew).

4. One such study was done about a year and a half after a major devastating earthquake in 1992 in a medium-size town in Turkey (Ruestemli and Karanci 1999) This study looked at sets of cognitions that affected preparedness behaviors. Another study, but this time in the United States, also indirectly linked ethnicity and preparedness, but through the medium of social networks (Haines, et al. 1996). Case studies have also focused on ethnic differences in evacuation compliance (Perry and Lindell 1991). Other studies put the stress on ethnic differences in postdisaster behavior (Bolin and Bolton 1986; Khoury et al. 1997) and postdisaster trauma (Perilla, et al. 2002), and in a few cases by children's reactions to disaster (Jones et al. 2001). Not surprisingly, researchers seemed to use the ethnicity construct as a catchall concept for race (Bolin and Klenow 1988). This also appears to be the case with religion (Schmuck 2000; Gillard and Paton 1999) and immigrant status based on national origin (Rubin 1981).

7

Disaster Communities as Survival Mechanisms

A FALSE MESSIAH?

Relying on our ability to organize has been the secret to our successful survival over thousands of years. The recent and abrupt transformation from small family group and community survival modes to formalized organizational ones, however, has torn out the very heart of the social process by which we have succeeded in adapting and learning how to survive. The social language and behaviors that have evolved in response to disasters are still latent in the community but are no longer part of the repertoire of official disaster or emergency behaviors. They lie in artificially constructed organizations that have a completely different set of rules and regulations about how disasters can be prepared for, mitigated, or coped with. There are those who will argue that the complexity of modern society requires the establishment of public bureaucratic agencies to act as brokers for us in the ever-continuing struggle against disasters. They further argue that we now reside in highly urban and industrial societies and not small agrarian communities, making disasters a national matter rather than a local one. We also hear that only such large bureaucratic organizations have the resources and ability to cope with the intricate complexity of disasters. Perhaps they are right! How, then, can you explain why the number, intensity, and damage done by disasters has been rising?

There is, of course, an alternative option, and that is to go back to basics, to refocus on the community, which has for so many thousands of years provided us with the ways and means to face disasters. Undoubtedly there are many disaster behaviors found in communities. When understood and taken advantage of, these disaster behaviors will act as catalysts for helping us prepare for mitigate, and cope with disasters. Some of these disaster behaviors have been recorded in numerous case studies and certainly warrant review-ing—I will mention some later in this chapter—but the most promising are studies that in one way or another focus on community-based disaster behaviors. The most prominent are "emergent" group actions during di-sasters (Wolensky 1983) and those associated with disaster "subcultures" (Granot 1996). Underlying these concepts is a clear recognition that disaster behaviors are an essential part of community life.

Let me first look at the idea of emergent groups. In such cases research-ers have found that during disasters, groups seem to organize spontaneously to save themselves and their neighbors. As such actions are contrary to sce-narios envisioned by the organized disaster management establishment, it is assumed that people who engage in these types of disaster behaviors are a hindrance rather than a help to successful disaster management. In fact, con-siderable resources are put into making sure such emergent group behavior at disaster sites are minimized, and when this cannot be accomplished, forcibly restrained. A good example of this scenario occurred in a major earthquake that shook Mexico City to its foundations (United Nations Economic Com-mission 1985). Thousands of citizens in the affected area "emerged" imme-diately after the quake to take part in trying to rescue people trapped in the rubble. When the authorities finally arrived, they stopped such lifesaving ac-tivity, claiming it hindered their professional efforts! These emergent groups are not doing anything particularly unusual, however. They are in fact the true first responders. They are putting into action dormant, normative behav-ior based on tried and true methods of organizing that have evolved in their communities. They are falling back on what seems the most natural way to behave in the face of a disaster—to use historical precedents in organizing along lines that have been set down in blood and experience and that have been proven to work. The bottom line is that emergent groups are a stellar representation of the richness of normative disaster behaviors found in com-munities.

In tandem with emergent groups is the idea that disaster subcultures form an integral part of community life. This concept takes for granted that different "communities" have different views and normative expectations when faced with disasters. Individuals and groups in some communities will relate and react to the same types of disasters differently (Turner et al. 1981). In Chapter 6 I presented several examples of how culture can affect disaster behavior among families, especially among women. The same principle applies here; namely, that particularistic community subcultures embedding institutional norms affecting disaster behavior differ from one community to another. In short, disaster subcultures are an artifact of the characteristics of the community's population and their experiences with disasters. Taken together, the concept of disaster subcultures is a reaffirmation of the significance of communities on disaster behavior. The many case studies of such subculture-related disasters as hurricanes (Gillard and Paton 1999), floods (Mamun 1996), and earthquakes (Ishizuka and Hirose 1983) are witness to how the intricate mixing of social networks and disasters within communities generates the seeds of what we will do and how we will act in the face of disasters. More important, it again shows the relevance of communities in understanding disaster behavior.

MISSION IMPOSSIBLE?

Where does this all lead? Are communities a better bet at managing disasters than disaster management organizations? Is there no hope that formalistic public sector disaster management agencies, whose mission is (as they themselves state) to prepare us for disasters, will be able to rise above their inherent and intractable problems as bureaucratic organizations? Are all their efforts doomed to failure? If so, this will almost certainly hit a nerve among the many thousands of people involved in disaster management, but rather than enter into political or social polemics, I would suggest that we remind ourselves to look at the facts and not what we would like to see. Just knowing that these disaster management organizations are not as effective as they should be does not mean that they cannot be improved or that the organizations' goals cannot be amended.

Improve and amend are easy to say but extremely difficult to implement, as organizational change is a tricky business, especially in public administration, in which most disaster management agencies are positioned. One of the critical problems stems from the need to coordinate multiple agencies and resolve interorganizational conflicts (Perry 1995). To give an idea of what is involved is the following case of a "simple" local disaster that required an emergency management employee to

> identify all the "generic" federal, state, and local player organizations and determine what each agency can bring expertise and equipment to a unified command response; a "go to" list of personnel and equipment for various aspects of the fire (excavation, environmental hazards, extinguishing, personnel safety, disposal, natural resources, etc.). There is no way this will ever be complete, but I am trying to hit

the big targets within the agencies. Expected equipment resources by agency type is the biggest gap so far in this effort. For example: United States Environmental Protection Agency (USEPA)—Provides On Scene coordinators for incident management, air monitoring and sampling personnel and equipment. USCG—National Strike Force teams provide specially trained personnel for site assessments, safety planning, action plan development, and documentation for both inland and coastal zone incidents. They can bring pumps, boom, air monitoring equipment, communications equipment, etc. The other responding agencies (and their specialized personnel) I have identified have included (there are others that I haven't even thought of I am sure): 1. State and local Police, 2. Public Works agencies, 3. State Department of Emergency Management Offices, 4. Regional offices of the Federal Emergency Management Agency (FEMA), 5. Environmental Protection Agency (EPA) Environmental Response Team (ERT), 6. State Division/Department of Natural Resources or State Forestry Agency, 7. State Fire Marshal's offices, 8. Department of Interior—US Fish and Wildlife Service, 9. OSHA—worker safety, 10. ATSDR, 11. NOAA Scientific Support Coordinators, 12. PIAT 13. Regional Incident Coordination Team (RICT). What did I miss? (Debbie, IAEM, November 2002).

GOING BACK IN TIME?

Imagine trying to coordinate these agencies, all of which want a piece of the disaster pie to justify their organizational objectives and keep in the competitive running against their rivals for budget allocations! It is for this reason that I will move cautiously by first looking at the basic social units that are the major players in the disaster survival game. Here I am referring to the community and its complex balance among family, friends, and neighbors. Let me start by first reiterating that disaster behaviors reflect our ability to find satisfactory organizational solutions to threats to our families, groups, and communities. This process was refined over the centuries and is an ongoing process. Critics will argue that these processes were all well and good for an agricultural, pastoral society but have no place in a highly urban, industrial world.

There is, however, a basic flaw in saying communities are no longer alive and well. First there is a large portion of the world population that is not urbanized (United Nations 2001). In China, for example, close to 80% of its 1 billion 300 million citizens are not urban dwellers. More important, researchers keep on rediscovering that a diversity of communities of all sizes and shapes exists even within the most populous of cities. The image of the small town or village as the last bastion for community life in highly urban nations is, it seems, mainly a nostalgic media creation. Most of these urban communities are composed of populations that have something in common, be it similarity of religion, race, class, occupation, or family life-cycle stage. People adopt names to the geographic areas they reside in, mental maps are created among neighbors, and neighborhood boundaries are delineated. Ask someone where he lives and he or she will inevitably give you the name of his or her neighborhood. Along with the physical proximity that fosters a gambit of social activities are social networks, leadership, and community services. Most important as far as disaster behaviors are concerned, the community forms a social reference point that can be utilized to make decisions. As we have already seen, for example, disaster risks rarely evolve in a vacuum; they are predicated on the strength of social ties among family, friends, neighbors, and the community. We also saw that individuals ask their neighbors, friends, and family members about appropriate disaster behaviors. These facts are overwhelming in their support of how the community is a vital ingredient in affecting disaster behaviors and perhaps the key organizational format in stimulating greater sensitivity to the dangers of disasters as well as preparing for them.

DISASTER STUDIES IN COMMUNITIES

Both scholars and disaster managers have generated a large number of case studies of communities that have gone through one kind of disaster or another. This may be due to the fact that communities are convenient research units to assess and provide an acceptable notion without having to precisely define their boundaries. While there are different approaches to doing these types of studies, the underlying assumption is that something can be learned and eventually applied to the organization and application of disaster management. It can also be said that the range and quality of studies vary, and in many cases they have explicit political or organizational agendas (Quarantelli 1986; Perry 1995; Taylor-Adams and Kirwan 1995; Scobie 1997). Like many practitioner-driven fields, there are "ideologies" about what is best, and these come through the various "schools" of thought and in their reporting. A recent book on "what is a disaster" exemplifies these various points of view and provides a glimpse into the deep-seated disagreements fostered by ideological and personal perspectives of one of the most basic concepts in the field of disaster research (Quarantelli 1998).

While concern has been raised about the reliability of the data used in statistical analysis in disaster research (Quarantelli 2001), rarely have researchers asked the simpler question of what a community is, always assuming that we know! Some studies have focused on communities from a geographic–ecological boundary perspective, and others on political boundaries. The majority simply uses the name of the place in which the disaster occurred as coterminous with community. Just to name a few, there is the Loma Prieta, California, earthquake (Bolin 1993), the Centralia, Pennsylvania, strip mine fire (Kroll-Smith and Couch 1990), the St. Louis, Missouri, flood (Solomon et al. 1989), the Yungay, Peru, mud slide (Oliver-Smith 1982), the Aberfan, Wales, coal waste debris flow (Couto 1989), the Ephrata, Pennsylvania, fire (Fisher et al. 1995), the tornadoes in White County, Arkansas (Marks et al. 1954) and Woodstock, Canada (Stewart 1982), the Three Mile Island nuclear meltdown (Goldhaber and Houts 1983), the Love Canal toxic pollution event (Levine 1982), the Times Beach toxic contamination (Goodman and Vaughan 1988), the Mount Saint Helens volcanic eruption (Warrick 1981), the Mt. Usa, Japan, volcano (Hirose 1982), the Sidney, Australia, industrial explosion (Britton 1991), the Crest Street community relocation (Rohe and Mouw 1991), and so on. In some cases, the studies of these community disasters are accomplished by ethnological, anthropological, or sociological methods. In too many cases the reports are more anecdotal than systematic and laced with generalized conclusions for consumption by disaster managers.

These reports are nevertheless a treasure-house of examples of how people and organizations function under the exigencies of emergencies and disasters. The major repository of such studies is the Disaster Research Center now at the University of Delaware (DRC 2002), which has been accumulating them for close to fifty years and in a large sense reflects the development of disaster management as a scholarly endeavor. Members of this center have studied over 450 community disasters of one kind or another. Of the 13,500 references to disasters that are found in the Natural Hazards Center at the University of Colorado in Boulder, which acts as a clearinghouse for disaster research, close to 850 can be referenced under the key word community. Several compilations of these studies have appeared as either annotated bibliographies or in books that extensively utilize these community case studies of disasters. Unfortunately, as they do not share a similar methodological approach or standards of analysis, generalized implications from these studies are highly suspect, as findings from one study may not be applicable to others. While this is not the place to critically review specific studies, it is important to recognize these methodological constraints, for they place on hold the conclusions and implications of their findings.

A COMMON THREAD

What has emerged from these community studies, however, is an important framework composed of common sets of disaster behaviors that seem to reflect what victims do even under various circumstances, places, and disaster scenarios. This means that disaster behaviors during earthquakes, volcanoes, floods, and industrial accidents have something very much in common; they elicit similar types of behaviors that have been honed to increase survival. While these behaviors are practiced on the individual level, they are in fact incorporated into a community framework. Even if each of the specific studies uses a community baseline that varies, there is the clear recognition that something about communities provides the raw social data for understanding disaster behavior. This is an extremely important point, as it suggests that there may be a common benchmark of disaster behaviors at the community level that can be utilized to predict how we will act during disaster events in the future. This argument has several important consequences for both disaster research and its implementation, as it serves as a practical guideline for policy makers.

From the standpoint of using community characteristics or social processes that are common to all community activities as predictors of disaster behaviors, a strategic research door opens up into the world of disaster behavior. Rather than looking at the specific type of disaster, specific individual behaviors, or communities that happened to experience a disaster, it is now possible to examine how communities in general are linked to disaster survival. It takes the analysis a large step forward by looking at the components of community processes and how they are associated with disaster behavior. As I pointed out in the first chapter, communities have a basic set of social behaviors that distinguish them as collective social units. It may be that these community-linked behaviors are what lead to better preparation and coping when faced with disasters. The logical consequence of this is the ability to test the argument that community-level analysis may be one of the best ways to understand disasters and formulate ways to face them.[1]

COMMUNITY-LEVEL ANALYSIS

To provide some framework of how disaster behavior can be examined from a community-based perspective requires a great deal of stamina due to a large reservoir of material that has been written about communities. These materials have dealt with an extremely wide range of topics, in deference to the focal point that communities have in our lives. From my perspective, communities are also the bedrock of successful disaster behavior. To get a "feel" of this, I have devised a flowchart of how communities have organized around the need to adapt to the physical and social environment to increase the individual's chances for survival. (See Figure 1.)

The model is fairly straightforward. Adaptation to the environment is partly biological, but predominantly social in nature. Through the advan-

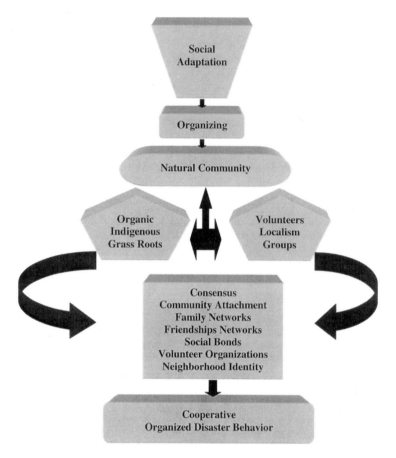

FIGURE 1   Organic community model for disaster survival.

tages of learning from the past and the cognitive ability to imagine the future, people have accumulated a storehouse of survival skills. Like the individual strands of a rope, these individual skills can be immensely strengthened when put together, and this is exactly what happens when individuals organize. The result is what I describe as a natural community, a place in which social norms devised to increase survival are incorporated into the institutions that make up the community. The classic types of these institutions are all familiar to us, as they invoke images of "grass roots," "indigenous groups," "organic development," "volunteerism," and local orientations. These institutions are supported and in many cases reinforced by community-based social processes. Among the social processes that emerge are those that give "character" to the community. There is a feeling of attachment and identity to the physical place or neighborhood based on social imaging (Orellana 1999). These can take the form of rating, labeling, or stigmatizing the community as a "good" or "bad" place to live. Living on the other side of the tracks, in rich neighborhoods, or in slums are ways in which "identity" and "attachment" are fostered. A community's character also comes about when family networks are established through marriage, births, and deaths. Who marries who has always been one of the most important components in establishing family networks that reinforce community ties by establishing the rules of social discourse and power relationships in communities. Friendship and neighborly ties are established through both proximity and cultural events, leading to various types and intensity of social bonds among the community members. These, along with family networks, create an intricate yet orderly social fabric that can be identified as a community. From these multilevel interactions and social patterns emerges the basis for cooperative efforts to increase the survival quotient in case of disasters. The basis for cooperation has already been provided in the very way in which communities are structured as viable and adaptive social units. There is no need to artificially create or manipulate disaster behaviors within the confines of disaster management organizations, as they are already embedded in the social history and consciences of the community members. In this sense, the community can act as an ideal medium to discover disaster behaviors.

WHAT IS A DISASTER COMMUNITY?

Given the wealth of disaster research that has focused on communities, we should easily be able to identify patterns of community disaster behaviors that can be relevant to disaster managers, but this assumes a consensus in the definition of a *disaster community!* Some community disaster studies cover specific segments of larger communities so that they concentrate only on the specific area affected by a disaster. In many cases this means that only a small physical part of a community is examined. These studies basically define a disaster community in terms of the physical and geographic boundaries within which a disaster occurs. For example, studies have looked at the populations in flooded areas, in the fire-devastated neighborhoods, at the residential site of a toxic spill, or in the path of tornado.

In other cases, the entire community affected by the disaster–both directly and indirectly–is considered (Karanci and Rustemli 1995). This extends the concept of disaster community to embrace contiguous physical areas under the assumption that disasters are not only a physical but also an important social event. The importance of this distinction cannot be overestimated, as what it says is that a disaster community is first and foremost a social community, one that may or has already experienced the devastation of a disaster. It also implies that the consequences of a disaster affect an entire community—both those who are directly affected as well as those who, through the web of community social networks, are also indirectly affected. In practical terms this would mean that anyone linked to a specific family, friend, or neighborly network affected by a disaster would also be affected, even though not directly hurt by the disaster.

The implication of this definition of a disaster community is that the boundaries of the physical threat may be only a small part of the actual damage to the social fabric of a community. This perspective downplays the physical damage caused by disasters or to only those directly physically harmed by the devastation. Seeing wrecked or destroyed homes or torn-up infrastructure in the media only reflects a small part of those enmeshed in the disaster community. This is not to say that the physical destruction is unimportant or should be excluded in its entirely. Physical damage, by creating economic, environmental, and human losses, also has an impact on the social structure of communities (Harvey et al. 1995; Jones et al. 2001). When a disaster wipes out a downtown business area or destroys a school or health facility, the very social foundation of a community is put in jeopardy.

RIPPLING EFFECT

The definition also implies that a disaster community has a reserve of potential disaster behaviors that allow its members to survive, cope, and eventually revitalize the community. We have already seen this in the case of Chinese widows remarrying after a particularly devastating disaster that killed large numbers of men. Other studies have consistently found that disaster communities that are characterized by strong community-based social networks bounce back quickly (McFarlane et al. 1987), are better at coping with losses (Bravo et al. 1990), and learn the bitter lessons for potential future disasters. These results can be interpreted to mean that when a large number of socially interactive components of communities are in place the consequences of disasters are modified. Communities that undergo a disaster without the strength of social ties contributing to greater community solidarity and identification fare much less well in cases of disasters. As for understanding the behaviors that we associate with disasters in a community, I can thus make the argument that there is something about the totality of a community's social fabric that can affect how individuals react to disasters. In a sense, disaster communities are constructs that reflect real-world actions. Disaster behavior—before or after a disaster actually occurs—seems to be built on the same principle that occurs when we throw a rock into a pool of still water. The result is an ever-widening ripple effect. This seems to be the case in disaster communities; the ripple effect is enhanced through the medium by community social networks. The result is that the effects of the disaster touch people who are not even directly or physically involved in the actual disaster (Perilla et al. 2002).

WHOSE COMMUNITY?

The argument that a disaster community is one that touches its members one way or another still requires us to come up with a reasonable definition of community. Complicating this problem is the broad range of disaster behaviors and community types that are looked at by researchers. This makes it extremely difficult to claim that there is a pattern of disaster behavior common to all communities. It may very well be that certain disaster behaviors appear only in certain types of communities and not in others— even when the type of disaster is similar in both! In many cases, these problematic methodological issues overlap, but the bottom line is that disaster researchers rarely provide a definition of community. They are really not to blame, as community researchers in general face the same conceptual problems in defining community (Beck 2001).

The most common definitions are those first suggested by the giants in sociology, such as Weber and Durkheim. Both took into account the social processes that were leading the world in an abrupt transition from small rural village life into the dense urban industrial jungle. They suggested that in both rural and urban areas communities thrived, but on a different basis. Rural village communities were defined in terms of intimate social relationships conducted on a consensual, face-to-face basis, reinforced by family networks and common economic interests. These same social relationships operated in urban areas, but through a different medium, primarily on secondary tiered relationships and a division of labor glued together by interdependence and specialization.

In both cases, communities stemmed from a member's self-identification with a physical area or socially identifiable group. This self-identification develops from intricate social networks. A recent compilation of journal articles in a special issue on the problems of defining communities and a need to re-evaluate the concept agreed that communities are place-based and develop through locally oriented interactions of the residents (Beck 2001). Over the years other researchers have added more sophisticated components to the definition of community to deal with the heterogeneous and segregated character of urban and rural areas. Among these have been differentiating communities based on mutually shared language (Karam 2000), the use of particular semantics and having a common history and culture (Piette 1997), and most important, the distinct cohesive ties developed with family, friends, and neighbors (Bastida 2001). If we take all these components together, we thus may be able to declare that a community is an ecologically bounded area that is a community based on its social character, be it a rural village or an identifiable urban neighborhood in a large metropolitan area.

MULTIPLE DISASTER COMMUNITIES

Now the question arises if it is possible to make use of these measurable definitions to evaluate the degree to which disaster behaviors can be tied to community life. In Chapter 6 compelling evidence was found to point to the relevance of the mother as gatekeeper of her family's ability to be prepared for and survive a disaster. This finding is in itself important, yet it also is relevant in providing a surprisingly important potential clue at something much broader; namely, the cumulative role of mothers in establishing and sustaining a community's social basis. This is based on the assumption that being a mother goes beyond just the ability to act as a gatekeeper; it means having a broad social network of family, friends, and neighbors, all of whom are the building blocks for a community. There is no doubt that this networking may entail having both strong and weak ties, but such ties nonetheless are the basis for a viable community and can be expressed through a myriad of interlocking social networks.

While the mother as gatekeeper contains the kernel of potential disaster communities, the actual community emergence comes from the gatekeeper *process* itself; namely, the manner in which information is processed, filtered, and passed along. More specifically, gatekeepers attain a broad spectrum of information from a variety of social sources. They also provide a broad range of disaster-related information to targeted family, friend, and neighboring networks. By taking a small leap of faith, it can be postulated that these members who are linked with each other socially in such networks form a potential disaster community. Those enmeshed in a particular network's web—which may be physically located alongside different social networks—form a distinct disaster community.

What should be distinguished here is that there is the possibility that the larger disaster community may contain numerous disaster subcommunities. This is not far-fetched, as communities have numerous networking systems. Some of these networks are fairly self-contained, while others overlap. It is more than possible that some but not all of these disaster microcommunities will be affected by a disaster event, thus the construct that I have called a disaster community may actually be composed of multiple subcommunities based on the varying social networks. If this is the case, research on disaster communities will need to take into consideration both the existence of and distinction and overlap of these microdisaster communities. This idea is illustrated in Figure 2.

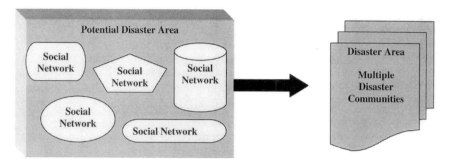

FIGURE 2 Multiple-disaster communities based on distinct internal social networks found in a potential disaster area.

COMMUNITY SOCIAL STRENGTH

In addition to the likelihood of multiple disaster communities based on various social networks, it is important to recognize that these social networks may be loosely or strongly connected. For example, some networks may be strongly bonded together because of family ties. Other networks may be more porous and less stable, such as network interactions composed of neighborhood acquaintances. In the terminology of network researchers, the density of the social networks and their reciprocal interactions are a telltale sign of a group's social strength. The existence of multiple social networks in communities from the stand point of disasters lays the foundation for the idea of disaster communities having varying levels of social strength. One of the arguments made by disaster researchers is that such social strength helps explain a community's resilience and provides its members with the ability to withstand and cope with disasters (Karanci et al. 1999; Kaniasty and Norris 2000). These arguments support the supposition that successful community-based disaster behavior is not only a matter of historical trail and error but also is built on social strength generated through the medium of organized social networks.[2]

These examples—with all their shortcomings as community case studies—provide a platform from which to justify thinking about disaster communities as predictors of disaster behavior. By viewing communities as social entities having a particular set of characteristics, disaster behaviors leading to community survival are thus open to investigation and prediction. This argument goes well beyond what is being done at present, as it emphasizes the significant nature of place-based patterns of social relationships in determining disaster behaviors.

URBAN COMMUNITIES

Until now I have made a series of assertions. The most general was that communities are alive and well even within the most heterogeneous and dense metropolitan areas. I further claimed that this would mean that the normative and institutional patterns of disaster survival behaviors still lie dormant, *even* in urban communities, waiting to be called upon when needed. To support these assertions, I will again make use of the field survey based on a representative national sample of urban households in Israel. The emphasis that I would like to put here is on *urban* households, as this tells us that we are dealing with individuals who do not live in rural towns or villages. They are not associated with any particular community disaster case study; they are people who live in and among diverse and heterogeneous urban populations in ninety-seven separate municipalities composed of at least 10,000 persons.

A first step to buttress these arguments is to examine varied sources of social networking and decide if they can contribute to help us distinguish disaster communities. This will be helped considerably by the survey data, which included a series of questions that measure various forms and intensities of social networking. The sample was asked, for example, with whom they socially interacted as well as the intensity of these interactions. Questions were asked about their relationship with family, friends, and neighbors, and their participation in general community activities. All this information was aimed at determining if in fact I could discern the existence of urban disaster communities.

From responses to these questions it became apparent that the individual household repondents perceived their own communities as a relatively compact physical place inundated by various social, cultural, and political activities, something akin to a microneighborhood. Even from the limited number of social network measures I looked at, there seemed to emerge a large number of discrete potential disaster communities. With over 800 individuals in the sample, each representing a separate household in close to 100 distinct urban centers of varying size, the number of such potential discrete disaster communities based on each household's networks could theoretically match the number of respondents. Close to 80% of the sample not only were socially involved with their neighbors, which in itself helps form microneighborhoods, but most felt these relationships were positive in nature, thereby reinforcing the social network in which they were involved.

This image of multiple disaster communities, each infused with a rich social life, seems to be the norm rather than the exception. As I will empirically demonstrate below, people are acquainted with their neighbors. They interact with them, and in this process probably have clearly defined mental maps as to their neighborhood's boundaries. Each household is in fact a mirror of a distinct community based on social networks that are apparently reciprocated by those in the same area. What these findings from the field survey in Israel clearly demonstrate is that the image of the large urban and anonymous aggregate is actually made up of multiple sets of microsocial networks. This picture is easily verified by a simple taxi ride through large populous cities in Southeast Asia, China, Europe, or the Americas, all of which have highly dense urban centers. Every few blocks we enter another neighborhood in which physical and social clues accentuate segregated communities and neighborhoods.

These initial results raise some disturbing questions. First, why is it that researchers have tended to define a disaster community in terms of a specific physical area rather than sets of patterned social relationships? In every sense, disaster communities are a combination of both. More troubling, why is there a reluctance to include urban areas in disaster community studies? Are they seen as problematic, as they do not fit the classic rural community ideal? Finally, comes the validity of the assumption that disaster communities are monolithic physical entities enveloping only those directly falling into harm's way. Those in harm's way, however, are also socially linked to others outside the path of destruction. Are they not deeply affected as well?

DISASTER NEIGHBORHOODS

These questions led me to think about an alternative approach to viewing disaster communities. It starts with what we already know. As I showed in Chapter 4, the residue of *traditional* community survival processes that are initiated through family, friends, and neighbors are still fully operative today. This one overridding assumption that community life directly affects our disaster behaviors and chances for survival can be derived from the pattern of relationships developed by its own residents. This means that the people of a particular community have or are capable of devising socially based ways to take care of themselves. As we have just seen, such neighborhoods exist in urban settings. By logical extension, so too should their ability to take care of themselves.

On this basis, each separate family household was employed as a basic building block of a disaster community. The rationale for this argued that such communities developed through the intricate social networks that families build up through social contacts and interactions. In this framework, a disaster community is formed when networks intersect, there is an overlap of these networks, or when one family's extended network meshes with another's through mutual friends or neighbors. From this perspective, lines of communications are in place that provide the vital disaster behaviors to other members of the network, allow gatekeepers to filter and pass along this kind of survival knowledge, allow for rapid organization to prepare, mitigate, or cope with the actual disaster, and finally provide the comfort and caring after a disaster to members of the network.

To a great extent this approach views the concept of disaster community as primarily dependent on what I call a "disaster neighborhood." This is because a large number of our social contacts outside work are usually with persons or families within close proximity of our residence. These contacts are not limited to only those living next door, as social networks can extend well beyond these borders. When a disaster does occur, it thus affects members primarily in the disaster neighborhood, but may continue to affect the larger disaster community. This approach incorporates into its framework a rippling effect on the interlocking social components of social networks that comprise disaster communities. A good example of this kind of thinking would be the World Trade Center terrorist attacks. Post-September 11 studies showed that not only were the residents of the immediate neighborhood traumatized, but thousands of relatives, friends, and acquaintances of those who experienced the collapse of the Twin Towers were traumatized as well (DRC 2003). These "collateral" damage victims are in fact part of the disaster community, thus one consequence is that disaster behaviors are no longer restricted to the disaster area itself. In addition, disaster behaviors are not necessarily a direct result of the potential or actual disaster, as they are not restricted solely to the actual disaster victims. A good example of this would be the Holocaust, which has affected even second generation children of the actual victims of Hitler's attempted destruction of the Jews.

NEIGHBORING TIES

As a first step in evaluating this approach (and some of the arguments I have made), let us go back to the Israeli national field survey data. The survey included a long list of questions aimed at discovering the existence of social networks and their influence on disaster behaviors. The questions ranged across the various types of potential networks—from family to friends and neighbors—and included the intensity of these ties. One set of questions dealt specifically with ties to neighbors and their neighborhoods. As you can see from Table 1, not only do most of the respondents know who their neighbors are, but they also find them helpful and have good relationships with them. Apparently, at least at the disaster neighborhood level, we see that these individuals have already built the springboard for a microneighborhood-based community way of life. This picture is strengthened by the fact that over one-fifth have other family members living nearby, thereby increas-

TABLE 1   Measures of Community Involvement

Measure	Positive
Know most of your neighbors	81.8
When request, neighbors help	80.8
Neighborly relations good	86.9
Active in building coop	21.5
Active in community center	6.6
Active in neighborhood watch	5.2
Active in community committees	6.1
Family members live close by	24.6

ing their ties to the neighborhood and also expanding their community social networks. Being active in the social and economic affairs of their coop buildings likewise adds to their community involvement, as does (albeit at a much lower level) being active in their community centers and neighborhood watch.[3]

The portrait that is presented here is a social community built on social ties that form the basis of a potential disaster community. For example, the networks that have been developed provide a reliable path for the rapid dissemination of disaster-related information. Not only can neighbors just call each other by telephone or meet in the hallway, but as platforms for information exchange, networks also have a strong semblance of mutual trust built into them, further facilitating transfer and belief of the information. In addition, such networks form a repository of accumulated disaster experiences. Such historical knowledge of disaster survival behaviors and techniques is the lifeblood for role modeling behaviors for survival. Taken as a whole, this knowledge, which can quickly traverse through the disaster community's social network, forms the basis upon which family gatekeepers protect their families.

There is an additional remarkable advantage that social networks provide us with; namely, the ability to rapidly organize when facing a disaster and to cope with the consequences of its aftermath. As I pointed out above, disaster managers seemed to be surprised at the prevalence of emergent groups that arose to help and cope with disasters, yet this rapid display of organizing probably came about from previously intact and viable disaster neighborhood social networks. This is not to say that group formation during disasters can only come about if networks were already in existence (i.e., that groups had been previously trained in disaster or emergency help activities), but it would make it less problematic, as these networks would facilitate rapid organization. For example, the seemingly artificial social networks that are created during training courses for volunteer first responders enhance their effectiveness precisely because they put in place the catalysts for organizing. This is done because both the formal and informal networks provide lines of command, communication pathways, specific job performance requirements, and a large dose of group trust. While not as rigid as formal organizations' training programs, community-based social networks have these same characteristics. People know others in the network, are familiar with them, have had contact with them, have developed different levels of trust, and have formed a social hierarchy of status. When the potential disaster is over the horizon or at their feet, these networks already have the basis to rapidly organize. When this happens, they do so with the accumulated disaster information and behaviors that have been part of their social and educational history, thereby increasing their chances for survival.

COMMUNITY PREPAREDNESS

Emergent groups whose disaster behaviors reduce chances of harm and death are certainly not new. They have been overshadowed by organized disaster management agencies, however, making it difficult to identify them during disaster events. The visibility, noise, and media photo opportunities of dozens of disaster and emergency units and agencies simply shroud their presence. They don't have high-tech equipment or spokespersons. This also does not mean that such emergent disaster groups are equally capable of promising a disaster-free environment or that each has the potential ability to reduce the negative effects of disasters, and yet they are certainly there. In fact, they are available as latent groups ready to be organized even before the actual disaster. This is a point that I would like to emphasize, as it has a direct relevance on disaster communities' preparedness for disasters. This is because even in a state of hibernation, such latent groups—through network interactions—provide predisaster knowledge and role model behaviors about what to do for upcoming disasters. In times of relative "quiet," such knowledge is probably low on the list of priorities, but as risk perceptions become more acute, this knowledge and potential group actions will likely move to the forefront of social discourse in disaster communities' conversations. In short, disaster preparedness originates from within the disaster community.

One reason for this assertion is that each disaster community is endowed with certain social features based upon and reinforced by its internal social networks. If these relationships are intense and the social networks are dense, bringing about strong social ties among it members, it can be assumed that organizing in the face of disasters will be more rapid and effective—certainly more so than if these ties are weak. When such social networks are based on recognized normative behaviors, such as those displayed by family, friends, neighbors, or acquaintances, the strength of the ties will also differ. Here, too, as I have shown in previous chapters, the degree of sensitivity to disaster preparedness will differ. Taken together, chances of survival are not likely to be evenly distributed among disaster communities, for each disaster community has a different social network base upon which it relies. Given these underlying arguments, I expect that some disaster communities would have a better basis to prepare for, mitigate, and cope with emergencies and disasters than others. This may explain why certain communities fare much better than others in disasters; namely, due to their degree of social strength based on the intensity of social ties that shape the disaster community.

LEVELS OF COMMUNITY STRENGTH

In order to evaluate if the social strength of disaster communities has an impact on disaster behaviors, especially preparedness, it is first necessary to come up with a reasonable measure of community strength. To do so, I will focus on social networks. The reason for this is that different types of social networks are one of many indications of the level and web of social interactions that are taking place among individuals and groups of persons. For example, interaction with our closest neighbors forms what can best be described as a microneighborhood disaster community network. This network may be very circumscribed, because most of our neighbors are just as they are described—they are friendly and live within close physical proximity to us. (See Figure 3.) They are the ones from whom we borrow sugar and with whom we exchange information about health and children, and by sheer probability–they are the ones we are most likely to bump into nearly every day

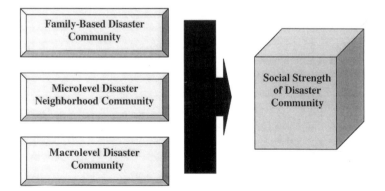

Figure 3 Types, boundaries, and levels of disaster-community strength on the basis of interactive social networks.

in the local grocery store, the elevator, or the parking lot. Our neighbors are also the ones from whom we get neighborhood gossip about other neighbors, reinforcing the links to this network. They are the people on whom we tend to rely in terms of mutual help, and our neighbors will probably be the first responders if a disaster occurs (Smith et al. 2000). Most important, our neighbors provide and confirm disaster information that affects our own disaster behaviors. The simple fact is that our neighbors are in the same proverbial boat with us; they are just as likely to experience and suffer from a disaster as we are! Proximity dictates this. We therefore have a lot in common when it comes to disasters. Case studies have indirectly shown this pattern of behavior among neighbors in cases of evacuations (Kirschenbaum 1992), but it is also likely to affect other types of disaster behaviors, such as preparedness and coping (Rubin 1985).

In the case of networks based primarily on the give and take between families and relatives, the boundaries of the community can extend way beyond the actual physical area in which a disaster occurs. Among most of the world's population, family members tend to live in proximity to one another, either as extended family units or in larger clans. These patterns are typical even in densely urban areas in Asia and Africa. This is much less the case in Western industrial-urban societies in which both residential and labor mobility scatter family members. Even here, however, despite the distance, the links within these networks remain intimately connected. The old saying that blood is thicker than water seems very true, so that attachments among family members remain a powerful glue that maintains kinship social networks. The strength of this glue, however, determines the level of intensity of family-based interactions. Even if disputes occur, family relationships, however weak, still remain. This stems from the fact that family membership is an ascribed status, one that we are born into. We can pick our friends but not our family. In cases in which family proximity is the rule and not the exception, in which family members are within reasonable communications distance from one another, family social networks can be extremely robust. In this state, they radiate an intensity and viability that certainly can affect disaster behaviors.

There is a third type of social network that seems to be relevant to this discussion; namely, macroneighborhood networks. In one sense these networks are much more diffuse than family and microneighborhood disaster communities, but they nevertheless provide a connection between an individual or family unit and its community (Carter et al. 1979). Here the network link is through community-based services, which more or less define the outer boundaries of the disaster community by acting as a center radiating out toward those within its radius. The network provides a loose link to the overall community, one that is certainly less intimate than family networks or microneighbor-based neighborhoods. What does remain, however, is putting people who use community services in touch with each other. At the very least this allows them to communicate disaster-related information, but primarily through weakly linked social ties. It also broadens the physical area of their disaster community.

DISASTER COMMUNITY NETWORKS

Identifying these three basic types of disaster communities opens up a window of opportunity that has evaded researchers; namely, to evaluate the impact of community-level characteristics on various disaster behaviors. By differentiating communities in terms of their social networks, a key to unraveling the link between disaster behaviors and a community's characteristics may be at hand. This concept of a disaster community based on social networks incorporates two important elements in understanding disaster behavior; namely, the boundaries and social strength of a disaster community, Both not only define disaster communities but provide a benchmark to compare how different types of these communities affect such behaviors as disaster preparedness. The research literature suggests that a community's social strength should affect its preparedness, resilience, and coping ability in the face of a disaster. It can therefore be expected that strong disaster communities will be more prepared than communities with weaker levels of social cohesion. To actually test these assertions, however, requires a definition of what is a socially strong or weak disaster community. The answer to this question lies in my previous arguments that the boundaries of such communities are based on the type and intensity of their social networks. These characteristics make them at once coherent and flexible.

This is not to say that the distinct social networks that make up the family, microneighborhood, and macrolevel disaster communities cannot be absolutely separated. As I have pointed out, there is likely to be a meshing of these networks so that family members may well participate in neighborhood- or communitywide networks. Each of these separate social networks, however, continues to represent a distinct disaster community, as they interconnect people in discrete, recognizable social relationships. In addition, the social source that generates these networks—be it the family, neighbors, or community services—exposes the cohesion and social strength of the disaster communities. The underlying assumption to my arguments is that there is an ordinal decrease in a disaster community's social strength as one moves from communities built on family-, neighborhood-, or service-based social networks. Family networks thus mirror disaster communities having strong, viable social ties. This is followed by a lessening of the strength of ties that are found among persons whose networks are founded primarily on neighbors in microneighborhoods. These networks are less strong than those among family members, as they are bounded primarily by physical proximity and not the normative obligations that bind families. Finally, and the least in strength, are those social networks found at the macrocommunity level. Given these distinctions, it is possible to compare and evaluate which of these disaster communities have the greatest impact on being prepared.

NETWORK IMPACT

In Chapter 2, I discovered that the overall measure of social networks did have a significant predictive value on preparedness. It affected only one component, however, namely, planning for disasters. While certainly hinting that social networks should be looked at more carefully, the measure was a composite that included ten separate types of network criteria, making any definitive assertion of the link between networks and preparedness problematic. To avoid this problem here, I have decomposed the original measures into three separate components representing the three levels of social networks discussed above; namely, family, neighbors, and community services. These measures, transcribed into specific questions, required the national field survey sample households to indicate the degree to which they had contacts with each of the three types of social networks. In this way, I was able to build up a composite picture of these disaster community networks. Once this was accomplished, I then sought to find out if there was a relationship between the level of social strength (or as others would call it, social cohesion) of disaster communities and their ability to be prepared for disasters. The first step in answering this question is by utilizing a correlation analysis that seeks to discover if changes in one component are associated with changes in a

TABLE 2 Community-Level Correlation Analysis Based on Type of Social Network by Specific Preparedness Components

Community networks	Supply	Skill	Planning	Protection
Family-based community	0.21[b]	0.10	-0.01[a]	0.05
Microneighborhood	0.15[b]	0.04	0.09	0.11
Macroneighborhood	0.12[b]	0.04	0.13[b]	0.02

Note: The preparedness components are based on their factor loadings that ranged above and below zero. These ranges, which differed for each component, were divided into four levels, ranging from very positive to very negative. These were then correlated with type of disaster neighborhood.
[a] Correlation significant at the 0.05 level (two-tailed).
[b] Correlation significant at the 0.01 level (two-tailed).

second component. For example, will a family-based disaster community be more prepared if its social network ties are stronger? The results are found in Table 2.

FAMILY-BASED NETWORKS

The summary results in Table 2 begin to unravel this mystery. By once again looking at preparedness from the standpoint of its four basic explanatory factors, we see that disaster communities with intense family social networks tend to be much more prepared than those communities with much weaker family networks. As the data show, however, they are more prepared only in terms of being supplied with essential survival goods and materials and in having plans that will help them either evacuate or avoid an actual disaster. There appears to be no significant difference in the impact of socially strong or weak family network-based disaster communities in the area of having disaster-related skills or providing protective means in case of a disaster.

What seems interesting here is that the sign of the planning component is negative, suggesting that stronger family ties may actually hinder the actualization of a disaster or emergency plan. I can only speculate, but it seems that strong family-oriented networks induce an unconditional reliance on other family members to help out in case of a disaster. This is probably what dissuades people from coming up with a disaster plan; they can simply trust and rely on their families. On the other hand, when family ties are weaker and reliance is in doubt, families will prepare such plans. What seems important here is that we have a first indication that the strength of the social network does have an impact on that disaster community's level of preparedness.

MICRONEIGHBORHOOD IMPACT

Assessing the strength of the degree of relationship between microneighborhood disaster communities and their level of preparedness once again confirmed that this particular characteristic of communities has an impact on its preparedness. In this case, a community's social strength is measured in terms of neighborhood-level social networks. The attributes of this measure were devised so as to ask specific questions about neighborly contacts and relationships, with the results explicitly showing that the link to being prepared was significant only for one of the four preparedness components; namely, having adequate supplies. The stronger the social ties among members of a microneighborhood, therefore, the more likely they are to be better prepared for a disaster—but only in terms of supplies. While the direction of the relationship among the other preparedness components did hint that greater levels of social strength in this disaster community lead to having higher levels of skills, more preplanning, and more protective equipment and shelters, the analysis did not confirm that it was significant. It might be that these types of disaster preparedness behaviors may be considered as only of marginal concern among members of microneighborhood disaster communities.

COMMUNITY SERVICE NETWORKS

Like the two previous types generated by either family or neighborly relationships, the third level of disaster community social strength also proved to be important. In this case, the disaster community is seen at its broadest level, as a network encompassing links to the basic community services that are usually available in most urban neighborhoods. Networks based on common interests dominate this link. It is not unusual that people involved in this network may have started out by simply joining clubs or other types of groups at community centers. These points of contact then led to the social networks that put diverse and very loosely linked persons together. It is for this reason that it seems sensible to view this type of social network as the weakest and most diffuse among the three that have been analyzed, yet despite this loose and perhaps even fragmentary picture of its social network, this type of disaster community also has an impact on its members' preparedness. Again, there appeared a distinctive general trend in which stronger network ties led to greater levels of preparedness. The data analysis convincingly demonstrates this to the case, both when it comes to being supplied for disasters and in the area of planning (see Table 3).

What the results of the analysis have shown so far is that the social character of disaster communities can affect their level of preparedness for disasters. *Disaster communities with strong, interlocking social networks at all levels create conditions in which their members are prompted into being better prepared than those communities in which networks are less robust.* What I have shown in addition is that this is the case for the most stalwart of social networks built on family relationships as well as on the more diffuse networks found at the macroservice-based community level. This generality applies to the three levels of disaster community networks that I have examined, but it must be remembered that the overall trend does not apply equally to the preparedness components for each of the disaster communities.

PREDICTING COMMUNITY PREPAREDNESS

The original proposal that disaster communities generated from different types and intensities of social networks can affect disaster behaviors can now be said to be a very realistic proposition, but it also opens up a possibility that the type of disaster community a person resides in can predict his or her being prepared for disasters; that is to say that there is something about social networking configurations that sets in motion behaviors to make us better prepared for disasters. To investigate this possibility requires the use of a statistical analysis, a linear regression model, which is aimed at comparing the three basic disaster community types with each other and seeing which best predicts each of the components of preparedness. (See Figure 4.)

Figure 4 illustrates which of the three types of disaster communities can best potentially predict the preparedness behavior of its members. In addition, it allows us to compare the clout of each of the disaster communities in affecting its members' willingness to be prepared according to one or more of the preparedness components. This analysis allows me to go far beyond establishing that a relationship exists between the strength of a disaster community and its ability to be prepared for a disaster. Here we can actually begin to look more deeply into how disaster communities as macrosocial units affect and predict their members' behavior.

The most visible expression of the impact of disaster communities on preparedness behavior can readily be seen when examining each type of community separately. The underlying assumption is that being in a partic-

TABLE 3 Significant Components of Family Ties, Neighborliness, and Community Social Networks Significantly Correlated to Specific Levels of Preparedness

Networking component	Supply	Skill	Planning	Protect
Family-based networks				
Family members live close by	.16[b]	.04	−.01	−.05
Contact family by telephone	.11[b]	.01	−.08[a]	.07
Frequently visit family	.17[b]	.07	−.05	.01
Good family relationships	−.01	−.02	−.12[b]	.08[a]
Microneighborhood networks				
Familiar with neighbors	.07	−.02	.04	−.01
Neighbors are helpful	.07	−.04	−.03	.06
Relations good between neighbors	.11[b]	−.04	−.00	.01
Active in building coop	.05	.04	.11[b]	.06
Macrocommunity networks				
Active in community center	.07	.03	.12[b]	−.01
Active in neighborhood watch	.06	.06	.07	−.04
Active Neighborhood Committees	.09[a]	.01	.11[b]	.02

[a] Significant at 0.05 level (two-tailed test).
[b] Significant at 0.01 level (two-tailed test).

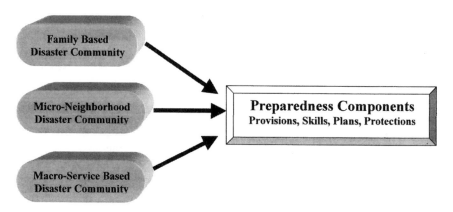

FIGURE 4 Disaster preparedness behaviors predicted by different disaster communities.

ular type of disaster community fosters certain types of disaster behaviors. The way in which this can be determined is to take each preparedness component (e.g., being prepared by having a sufficient supply of basic survival goods, such as water, food, and batteries) and evaluate the ability of each of the disaster communities to predict it. The regression analysis will allow us to ask and answer the question "Which of the disaster communities can best explain and predict whether or not a person will be prepared in a specific way?" The results should provide a clear indication of which of the social networks generating the disaster communities can then be examined in greater detail to learn more about the social mechanisms affecting disaster behaviors. By employing such an approach it becomes possible to compare the predictive ability of each of the disaster communities on the preparedness of its members.

PRIORITY EMPHASIS

The results of the analysis seen in Figure 5 are revealing. For one thing, each of the disaster communities predicts a different set of preparedness components. This can be interpreted to mean that there is something about each of the disaster communities that leads its members to put more priority on certain types of preparedness components and less on others. At a first glance it would seem that there is a good possibility that one of the consequences of the interrelationships fostered by social networks is in persuading people to adhere to certain kinds of normative disaster behavior. This seems very reasonable for the simple fact that we are indeed influenced by those around us. Once in a network with the desire to remain "inside" for all kinds of social and status reasons, emulating what is thought to be "proper" and "reasonable" makes sense. I would therefore argue that the various disaster communities, through their basic social networking systems, actually set different disaster behavioral priorities. Each pressures its members into conforming to what the majority feels is important or relevant to their survival.

In order to confirm these arguments, let me return to the results of the analysis. For households caught up in family network disaster communities, preparedness behaviors focus on having supplies available to them in case of a disaster and the variety of skills to prepare for an emergency. Planning or providing protective shelters is not significantly predicted, thus being a member of a family-oriented social network (and the disaster community it generates) acts to promote only these specific kinds of disaster behaviors; namely, supply and skills. Microneighborhood disaster communities, on the other hand, only predict being prepared in terms of their members preparing protective shelters. Built around social networks derived from neighborliness, these disaster communities provide a completely different picture of their members' preparedness behaviors. In this case, it is only a concern for supplies; learning emergency skills or even planning is of marginal interest

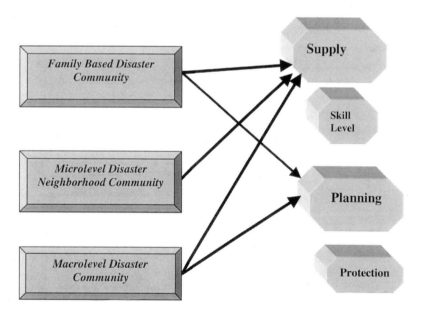

FIGURE 5 Significant relationship between disaster-community social network levels and its members being prepared for disasters.

for its members. When it comes to the macroservice-based disaster community in which social links are primarily based on common interests, having both adequate supplies and some plans for action in case of a disaster are the predominant disaster behaviors among its members. Taken together, I can only conclude that different disaster communities do indeed foster different types of disaster preparedness behaviors for their members. For a summary of these results see Figure 5.

A CLOSER LOOK

Highlighting the relevance of disaster communities on disaster behavior (albeit associated with being prepared) leads to exploring the underlying social mechanisms that may contribute to these differences. To do so, I will now suggest taking another direction in the analysis—focusing on the specific components of each disaster community. I have already pointed out that each disaster community is based on a composite of social network measures. Figure 6 provides the specific measures that were employed to obtain an index average 4 for each of the disaster communities. Each disaster community composite index was based on a minimum of three independent measures of social networking. These were disaggregated into their original single measures and used in the analysis. Here again I employed a correlation analysis as the best means to decipher if the strength and/or intensity of the specific social network can be related to being prepared.

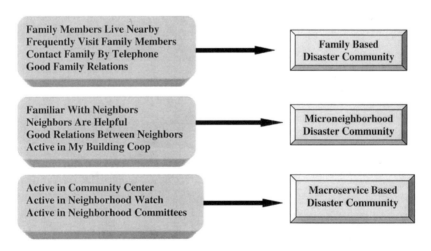

FIGURE 6   Specific social network measures of each disaster community.

TABLE 4 Linear Regression Analysis of Disaster Community Type by Components of Preparedness

Community Type	Supply	Skill	Planning	Protection
Family-based community	0.174[b]	0.084[b]	−0.015	0.038
Microneighborhood	0.093	0.019	0.055	0.089[b]
Macrocommunity	0.086[b]	0.033	0.111[b]	0.004
Model F	[b]	[a]	[b]	[a]

Note: The regression analysis provided both standardized regression coefficients and their level of significance for a two-tailed test. Each preparedness component was regressed separately, with each model found to be significant.
[a] Significant at 0.05 level.
[b] Significant at 0.01 level.

Looking at Table 3 gives us a better idea of what types of social networks are associated with the specific components of being prepared.[5] It is important to understand that Table 4 highlights those variables that are statistically significant; that is, the relationships are *not* due to pure chance. It does not negate the fact that there continue to be substantial relationships between preparedness components with the remaining explanatory variables, however. The importance of being statistically "significant" is that we are shown that something is very unusual about the relationship. This makes the relationship more important and gives us a great deal more information upon which to come to substantive conclusions. Given this brief explanation, I will now focus on the significant relationships as a means to further understand the link between disaster communities and disaster behaviors.

PROMOTING OR REDUCING PREPAREDNESS?

As a start, I will examine those social networks based on family links. The data in Table 3 clearly show that one or more of the family network measures affect three of the four components of preparedness, primarily concentrating in the area of supply and planning. More specifically, all but one of the family network measures is significantly correlated to the supply component of preparedness. The signs of the relationship are also very important here. A positive sign indicates a parallel association, while a negative signs indicates a reverse relationship. As all the significant links in the case of supply are positive, it can be concluded with confidence that with every increase in the strength and intensity of a family-based relationship there is likely a corresponding increase in preparedness. What this means is that nearly all forms of family networking, be they through visitation or phone contact, positively affect their level of preparedness in terms of the adequacy of stocked supplies that members of this network have at hand.

Looking further at the impact of family networks on preparedness shows an interesting contrary pattern, in which having a good relationship with family members and being in touch by telephone actually brings about a *reduction* in the preparedness of disaster plans. On the one hand, tight-knit family networks induce one component of preparedness (supplies) while at the same time reducing it in another (plans). The networks members make this pattern of disaster behavior a bit more complicated by the fact that having good relationships with family members increases the level of protective behavior exhibited. The end result is very instructive, as we can see for the first time that disaster communities based on family social networks do not automatically bring about greater preparedness. In fact, they can even reduce some types of preparedness, as was the case in making disaster plans!

WHAT'S EXCLUDED?

In contrast to family networks, the pattern for microneighborhood or macrocommunity network disaster communities is fairly straightforward. For example, of all the components that are used to measure microneighborhood networks, only two were found to have a significant impact on preparedness. The first is a measure of how well the neighbors get along. This was measured by questions asking the respondent if "good relations exist among your neighbors." Apparently, the better the relations the better prepared the households were in terms of stocking survival supplies. These neighborly relationships also had a significant positive impact on the number of protective items that were available to them. What is the reason for this association between neighborliness and preparedness? The answer probably lies in the fact that such positive neighborly relations can only lead to increasing the number and intensity of interactions among neighbors, and these interactions allow for the easy flow of information about what to do in case of disasters as well as stimulate peer group pressure to conform with majority opinion.

The second preparedness component has to do with being active in the financial and physical operation of their residential cooperative buildings. It should be recalled that a majority of the sample live in such cooperative residential units in which the buildings' public areas are part of the common property of all the private apartment owners. This means that those who are active in the upkeep of the building are very likely to meet neighbors, participate in committees, and be involved in the physical maintenance of the building, including the bomb shelters. Those individuals who were more active also tended to be better prepared in terms of planning "just in case." What these results seem to imply is that patterns of reinforced face-to-face contact with members of your social network make a serious contribution to your being better prepared. There seems little doubt that actual social interactions among those in this disaster community have an impact on their disaster behaviors.

These results are also interesting because of what is excluded. Half the measures—specifically, familiarity with and helpfulness of neighbors—did not come into the equation! True, all the relationships are positive, suggesting that increases in the strength of neighborliness do lead to being better prepared, but only two are relevant in terms of their statistical potency. This absence strengthens my argument that the more amorphous types of social networking have less of an impact on disaster preparedness. Apparently, simply knowing of, hearing about, or listening to third-hand gossip cannot replace face-to-face interactions in terms of their impact on disaster preparedness behaviors.

SERVICE-BASED NETWORKS

The association between social networks based on links developed through common interests in the larger disaster community and preparedness focus on being active in one way or another in the larger community's affairs. This is reflected in the positive significant relationship of those who are active in their local community center and in neighborhood committees. Both these areas of social activity are places for establishing connections to others who have similar interests. On the other hand, they are also "neutral" areas that intersect with various other types of social networks. In a sense, they act as focal points outside the usual attraction of family and microneighborhood, yet as with family and microneighborhood disaster communities, this type of disaster community covers social interactions that are more diverse and physically dispersed. This is because such communitywide activities encompass large physical areas and are aimed at including the heterogeneous groups living within their boundaries. Despite their amorphous character, service-based disaster communities do have an impact on their members' disaster behaviors.

The results reaffirm that greater levels of social activity do indeed lead to being more prepared. More specifically, the results tell us that being active in neighborhood committees has a greater impact on preparedness than being active in a community center. This may be due to the fact that the respondents interpreted "being active" to mean different things—in the community center by availing themselves of the facilities and clubs and in neighborhood committees by being concerned for the welfare of the entire community. This may also explain why being active in neighborhood committees leads to substantially greater degrees of preparedness in terms of both stockpiling supplies and having predetermined plans in case of an emergency, while community activity is only in the area of planning.

NETWORKS AND ETHNICITY

What do these results show us? For one thing, they confirm that no matter what type of disaster community is looked at, the stronger the social ties within these communities the greater their members' preparedness for disasters. The specific types of preparedness components that are significant may vary for each of the three types of disaster communities, but the overall pattern remains the same. Also of interest are signs that the correlations between the specific disaggregated social network measures that make up each of the disaster communities are overwhelming positive. This means that even those measures of the disaster community's social strength that did not turn out to be substantial continue to reflect the positive relationship between a disaster community's social strength and its levels of preparedness. Due to the specificity of the measures, the specific significant associations between a disaster community's social strength and its preparedness could be further explored.

One example of this—which I will only look at briefly—would be to examine in greater detail the sociodemographic composition of these disaster communities. As an example, I will explore two key characteristics that might hypothetically affect disaster preparedness outcomes. The first is ethnic origin. As I already pointed out in the previous chapter, ethnicity can be viewed as an important characteristic that reflects a host of social values and norms likely to affect preparedness behavior. In fact, one of my arguments here is that social networks and disaster communities can find a common intersect in terms of ethnicity. As I have shown elsewhere, "like units tend to cluster" (Kirschenbaum 1984), and it might be that the link between disaster communities (built on social networks) and preparedness may be influenced by the ethnic character of the communities themselves.

To test this possibility, I first looked at the link between ethnic groups and social networks. The ethnic group categories among the sample included foreign-and native-born. The foreign-born were categorized into three groups by country of origin, and native-born by the status of three generations. A first step toward investigating if there was a link between ethnic origin and disaster community was based on simple statistical tests of significance (e.g., chi square statistic). The results led to the conclusion that significant ethnic differences were only found in disaster communities that were formed on the basis of family social networks ($p = 0.041$). This meant that the impact of ethnicity on preparedness was very limited and did not extend beyond family network disaster communities. Ethnic origin had no influence on either microneighborhoods' or macrocommunity-disaster communities' levels of preparedness. (See Figure 7.)

A second possible characteristic of the members of social network disaster communities that might have an impact on preparedness is education. Several studies of the impact of educational levels on various types of disaster behaviors have come up with mixed results (Ecevit and Kasapoglu 2002; Schmidlin and King 1995). The arguments for and against education as a key influence on disaster behavior stems primarily from the notion that our educational level constricts or broadens the types of information that we have access to but also affects how we understand the information. Education is thus in many ways a proxy for our perception of disaster knowledge. Again, the assumption is that this knowledge will affect how we react to and what we do in cases of emergencies and disasters. In Chapter 2, I found that educational levels did affect preparedness, but only in terms of having sufficient skill levels to increase the chances for survival during a disaster. This meant that educational level might—through the composition of the different social networks making up the disaster communities—affect preparedness behaviors. On this basis and employing the same technique as I used for ethnicity, it was possible to understand if different educational levels are typical of the social networks that make up the disaster communities. If so, what would be education's impact of these networks on preparedness?

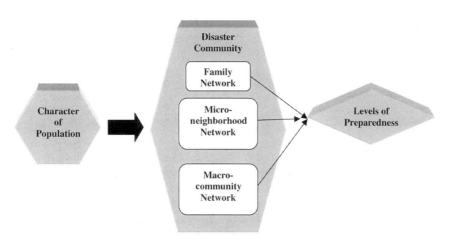

FIGURE 7   The hypothetical link between characteristics of the disaster community, its social networks, and components of preparedness.

The results of the analysis showed that there was *no* significant statistical difference or association between educational level and the three different types of disaster communities. What this meant was that the education of disaster community members did not have an impact on their levels of preparedness. This same procedure can also be employed for other sets of socioeconomic variables that theoretically could—through the social networks that generate disaster communities—affect preparedness, but the most important lesson that can be learned from this approach is that the concept of a disaster community is a viable empirical construct that can be extremely useful in understanding disaster behavior.

COMMUNITY SURVIVAL

In this chapter I have tried to present a convincing case as to why disaster communities should be seen as viable empirical constructs to understand, predict, and ultimately change disaster behaviors. This effort was based on an underlying premise that the use of the disaster community construct in disaster management will provide an alternative perspective to that foisted upon us by public sector disaster management organizations. The step-by-step arguments and formal analysis of both the literature and the data have afforded us with a great deal of substantial evidence in favor of thinking about disaster communities as basic social units that have an extraordinary influence on how we perceive and act in the case of disasters. Just as we learned that traditional ways of obtaining disaster role models are still very much with us and that a family's preparedness depends on the mother as gatekeeper, so too is the disaster community an ever-present factor in influencing our disaster behavior. The difference is that by focusing on disaster communities I have moved the analysis in a step-by-step fashion from disaster behaviors based on individual decision making to that of family units and now to a community macrolevel approach based on social networks.

Defining disaster communities as social networks is based on a compelling logic that our lives and survival are woven into the fabric of community life. This is how individuals survived in the past, and there is no reason to doubt that this kind of organizing continues to be a powerful ingredient today. *Disaster communities, defined in terms of their social networks, have an extraordinary influence on how we perceive and act in the case of a disaster.* We need to concede that the simple social interactions made by ordinary people through circumstance of physical proximity or common interests are the genetic material generating disaster communities. It also means that there is a multiplicity of disaster communities even within the same physical geographic area, with social networks that may intersect and even overlap. As I have argued, such social networks have distinct characteristics which are dependent on their social source and the intensity of the relationships. Such a distinction makes sense, as it taps into three inclusive networks that reflect different levels of social activity and discourse among its members For the purpose of the analysis, I focused on family, microneighborhood, and community service-based networks as the basis for distinguishing disaster communities.

THE PAYOFF

This approach seemed to pay off handsomely. In the analysis it became quite clear that disaster communities do have an impact on disaster behaviors. In general, what I discovered was that the greater the intensity or social strength of a disaster community, the more prepared its members were for a variety of disasters. This finding puts into place a cardinal principle that through their complex sets of social relationships communities affect our individual disaster decisions. In addition, variations in the types of disaster communities affect these decisions differently. We have before us the ability to look at disaster behaviors as the output of disaster communities whose ever-changing boundaries are determined by different social networks.

Finally, I can make the claim that disaster communities are relevant to the study of disaster behavior. These are not the same communities that are bantered about in the hundreds of case studies of specific disaster events. They are not towns or villages. They are social units that have a common denominator. Throughout, I have been arguing and attempting to empirically demonstrate that the concept of a disaster community not only exists but can provide an extremely useful tool to understanding disaster behaviors. One of its major advantages is that this concept reflects the historical adaptation process and ongoing concerns for community survival in the face of disasters. What we have apparently managed to learn and implement over thousands of years has been passed along to us through community-based social institutions and reinforced through the intricate interrelationships that generate social networks. These social networks are the fundamental building blocks of disaster communities, and disaster communities are the fundamental social entities that have a direct influence on individuals' disaster behaviors.

WHAT'S NEXT?

With the discovery and empirical verification of disaster communities and their relationship to disaster behavior comes the million-dollar question: How can disaster managers utilize this information? Managerial implications must be intimately linked to the empirical propositions that are generated as we look more closely at the relationship between disaster communities and actual disaster behavior. In short, every practical managerial decision must be backed up by an empirically relevant proposition. Without this empirical basis, anybody's guess is relevant.

NOTES

1. Doing so through sophisticated meta-analysis techniques, for example, might provide some universal types of community behaviors that could then act as a stepping-stone to provide a sounder theoretical and practical framework for dealing with a whole range of disaster-related behaviors. This point—looking for common or universal types of community-based disaster behaviors—is crucial.

2. Many studies of social networks outside the community, especially in work organizations, have also consistently found that networks not only exist but also have a profound impact on work behaviors. Apparently, such networks are universal and may have similar impacts on the organization of behavior, be it the workplace or community.

3. There will be those who will argue that such neighboring ties are unique to Israel due to the system of home ownership that favors residential condominiums. Such housing arrangements, along with the necessity to form a building committee, could possibly promote neighborliness. Such housing also includes rentals as well as absentee ownership, however. An analysis of those in rental units or their own apartments showed that no significant differences were found between them in their levels of neighborliness. This signaled that such housing arrangements might not by themselves be crucial for neighborliness. What was not available in the data was the physical status of the residence as a single home or in an apartment complex, which might have further complicated this issue.

4. The composite index of the ten networking measures was first combined and attained an alpha Cronbach measure of .47, allowing their use as independent measures. The alpha measures for the "neighborhood disaster community" was .50, for the "family disaster community" .61, and for the macrocommunity .40. These alpha measures are borderline reliability scores allowing for a judgment call on whether to use them as separate indexes or as independent variables. In the decision to build them into an coherent index to represent various disaster communities, the principal guideline was to combine variables on the basis of their similarity of social networks.

5. The four major components of preparedness were originally generated through a factor analysis. (See Chapter 2 for the details.)
   For the present analysis, the factor loadings were used as the basis
   for a four-point scale from highly negative to highly positive. As
   the range of the factor loading for each preparedness factor
   differed, each separate factor range was independently divided into
   four equal parts, with 0 acting as the midpoint.

8

Privatizing Disaster Management

WHAT IF?

This final chapter will take what we have learned about how the potential victims of disasters organize chaos and attempt to look at alternative forms of disaster management. This will not be an easy task, as nearly all disaster management today falls under the rubric of public sector administration. If you ask the thousands of public servants who in one way or another are involved in disaster management, I doubt that any could conceive of another way to deal with disasters. What you will hear said by both senior managers and those at the front lines of disaster management is that what we have today may not be the best and certainly can be improved, but it is all we have. Some others fall back to the simplistic arguments that try to justify these public agencies on the basis of tradition or political expedience or by asserting that the organizational forms now in place work, but as we now know, they do not work as well as can be expected. The reason appears to be based on the fact that there is a large gap between how members of these organizations, however well meaning, perceive of and deal with disasters, and how we, the potential victims, deal with disasters.

But what if? What if there were alternative organizational forms from which to choose? What if we take a chance at trying something else? Of course, there is always the alternative of letting people take care of themselves and do what they have always done, organizing and coping with disasters in what can best be described in a "natural" and generally successful way!

Let us imagine just for a moment that we have all the resources in the world, no political restrictions, the best advisors, and the support of the populace to devise a scheme that will assure us as individuals and as a community of the ability to survive disasters. What do we do? As a start, it is likely that someone would advise us to look at what has already been done, and if we just looked around, we would see that disaster management is for all intents and purposes in the hands of public sector employees. We would see dozens of government departments and local government agencies having the word disaster or emergency in their titles. Here and there we would come across private companies that fill the lower end of the disaster management chain, such as private ambulances, volunteer firefighters, and private medical services. Before long, our survey would lead to the conclusion that disaster management is organized, controlled, and financed as a public sector enterprise. There are no other serious forms of alternative organizing that seem apparent.

Then we begin to look at the research literature and discover that this form of disaster management is a relatively recent professional activity embedded in public organizations, and from a number of specific case studies, does not seem to be very successful. Researchers seem to point out all kinds of organizational problems. The usual turf wars, interagency discord, problems in coordination, overlapping, and redundant services, and of course political power struggles. What seems to be the rule is that as the number of agencies involved in a disaster or emergency increases, the effectiveness of these agencies decreases. In some cases, the consequences of the disaster multiply in terms of damage and death.

Then we begin to look carefully at the research about the victims of disasters. As most of the research has been done primarily within the confines of Western urban industrial societies and mainly on natural disasters, we tend to get a biased view of disaster behaviors. Little heed is paid to the billions of people who live in developing countries and have a non-Western cultural perspective and philosophy of life. In addition, no attention is paid to the rising numbers of unnatural disasters that are technical, industrial, or war-related. Ironically, most of the case studies emerging from research centers in the United States, in which over 80% of the population lives in urban areas, focus on natural disasters in towns and villages. Add to this the numerous studies dealing with postdisaster behaviors, sometimes on an anecdotal basis, which further compound the uncertainty of what disaster behaviors are. Then there is the dearth of broad, empirical studies of the antecedents of such behavior or how it socially manifests itself. In short, understanding disaster behavior still remains in its infancy, clouded by descriptive rather than robust analytical investigations.

A CRITICAL INTROSPECTION

Now comes the irony! Against all that we know from the literally thousands of studies and opinion articles that have been written about disasters and their management—however rigorous or anecdotal—there has been practically no critical analysis of the disaster management system as it now exists. There are the usual complaints about bureaucratic bungling, the need for more and better equipment, and what I consider the most revealing, the quest for more power in the halls of government. The most recent and visible example of this phenomenon is now occurring with the creation of the Department of Homeland Security in the United States. In and of itself, these types of social behaviors can be expected, yet this desire reveals the flip-flop of priorities for organizational aggrandizement, budgets, and recognition. It also reflects how the disaster management profession tries to gain legitimacy to impose its ideology on disaster management in the name of being able to provide better disaster management practices. If successful, the result will be bigger and more complex disaster management organizations, but will it mean better services leading to fewer deaths, fewer injuries, and less damage?

As I said, it is taken for granted that the best way to deal with disasters is through the complex bureaucratic systems of organizations that have become part of our civil lives, but let us now step aside for a moment and take a closer look at disaster management agencies. By re-examining their basic core concepts, questioning their effectiveness, and then looking at them from the outside—at how we the potential victims perceive of our "big brother"—we may learn a few important lessons. The first and most critical, as I have tried to show, is that at least in their present form these organizations have been pointedly unsuccessful. They have failed on several accounts (see Figure 1).

First, these types of organizations have built-in structural inconsistencies and contradictions that do not allow them to fulfill their mission of preventing, mitigating, or preparing the population for disasters. Those professional disaster managers who fill the job slots in these organizations are also put into an impossible situation by the administrative constrictions placed on them. When everyone is contending for funding to aggrandize their empires, little thought is given to what these organizations were originally set up to do. Take this remark by someone in the midst of the ongoing battle between professionals and bureaucrats.

> The post 9/11 scramble to obtain government financing and to "get rich quick" from Homeland Security projects and opportunities sickens me. As a long-time professional in the field of ICS [International Crisis Studies] emergency response, and (especially) threat and vulnerability assessment, I'm astonished at the politicization of funds and the agency-level scramble to grab for dollars in this near-paranoid frenzy (David, IEMA, August 2002).

FIGURE 1   Inherent flaws in public sector disaster management.

Also consider the statement made by firefighters who faced the bureaucratic maze of rules and regulations imposed by administrative restrictions:

> Orders, Protocols and Procedures exist for many reasons. Knowing when to ignore them is always the toughest decision. Mostly you pay with a kick-in-the-ass, sometimes you pay with peoples lives and once in awhile they give you a Medal and rewrite Procedure (Michael, July 2002).

Second, the conceptual basis employed by disaster managers that guides their actions is dependent on muddled understandings of core concepts in disaster management. Just imagine what considerable resources and manpower are being put into preparing for worst-case scenarios on the basis of a misunderstanding of who they should be directed toward and what they should be prepared for. Scarce resources are primarily being used to prepare their own organizations and not the potential victims of disasters. What could be more appropriate than the war against terror?

> Terror threat overblown, says expert "...argues that policymakers should be taking a closer look at just how great a risk is posed by terrorist activities, as well as how much effort and money should be committed to address that threat, versus the other risks faced by society" (United Press International, IEMA, August 14, 2002).

Third, disaster managers' understandings of their organizational goals are out of kilter with their major stakeholders' perceptions of what those goals should be. The practitioners are always complaining that researchers and academics do not understand what goes on in the field. These same disaster managers are partners in determining the organizational goals, which, as I have shown, are a far cry from what the potential victims in the field think are important! Disaster managers plan for one type of disaster and throw many of their resources into it, only to find out that its clients do not respond. Instead, clients perceive of and prepare for what they think is of relevance. The classic case, of course, occurs in official evacuation scenarios. This big brother attitude can be seen from the following announcement:

> The Veteran's Administration has produced an Emergency Management Program Guidebook. The introduction states, 'This Guidebook provides a process to develop a fully functional [Emergency Management Plan] and contains extensive examples of plans, policies, contingencies and solutions for problems that every VAMC (Veteran's Administration Medical Center) may face' (Gregory, IEMA, May 23, 2002).

Fourth, despite the omnipotence of public disaster agencies, large numbers of people continue to rely on traditional, socially based means of deciding about their disaster behaviors. Family, friends, and neighbors form social networks that are the conduit for time-honored knowledge about how to act in disasters. These are still chosen over information sources delivered by disaster agencies. People pass on this type of information by face-to-face contact or by simple telephone calls. This raises the embarrassing question as to why so much money is being thrown at bringing the most up-to-date technology in communications into organizations. The obvious answer is that they use it to communicate with themselves and not with those who are to be disaster's victims. Just look at how it's done:

> The Federal Emergency Management Agency will coordinate all federal wireless communications projects in a bid to ensure interoperability and standards while avoiding stovepiped systems (*Government Computer News*, June 5, 2002).

Fifth, the potential victims of disasters turn the way which formal organizations assess risk on its head. As I have shown, there is a large gap in what disaster managers see as areas of high risk and what the victims perceive. This gap not only pertains to the types of disasters but also to the way the risks are assessed. More important, risk assessment was found to affect how people prepared—what they did to increase their chances of avoiding injury and death. The bureaucratic system of prioritizing risks on the part of the disaster management agencies would siphon valuable resources away from where people feel it is needed and where it would provide them with maximum benefit, but this is the way public agencies operate:

> Conducting such analysis [vulnerability assessments, cost-effectiveness test of risk versus security-value added] is a daunting task; one the administration acknowledges has only just begun...In the meantime, however, what Washington has got is a partisan wrangle over whether employees in the proposed department [Homeland Security] can join unions. Sydney J. Freedberg Jr. and Siobhan Gorman, (*"National Security*: Are We Safer?" *National Journal*, August 9, 2002).

Sixth, by concentrating on the needs of disaster organizations and assuming people will automatically listen and respond to their directives, disaster managers are leaving out the most critical part of the survival puzzle— the gatekeepers. In my analysis of the mother hen effect, it became increasingly clear that disaster survival is not a random phenomenon; it depends to a great extent on the efforts of family gatekeepers who act in the best interest of their families. Families have always been important in the pre- and post-disaster events and again show their strength as key elements in effectively utilizing disaster behaviors that are available. Mothers, it seems, are the strategic gatekeepers through whom both disaster information and disaster behavioral choices must pass. It is perhaps for this reason that disaster management organizations have failed in their mission to prepare us for the inevitability of disasters, as they have appointed themselves the gatekeepers of this process.

Seventh, there is a cynical use of the concept of community by disaster management agencies in their race to rectify their lack of effectiveness in dealing with both the physical and social consequences of disasters. Community disaster management, or in its newer version the "citizen corps," has simply become an acceptable bureaucratic creation, much the same as the big brother approach. In the world of bureaucratic parlance, priority resources are reassigned to another department (within the existing disaster management agency) to solve an urgent problem. In reality, such a move breathes life into a redundant agency and justifies greater budget allocations. An example of this can be seen from the following announcement:

> National Citizen Corps Council Launched At White House... FEMA announces $21 million in grants to states to support citizen homeland security efforts...announcing the formation of the National Council, which brings together leaders from first responders

groups, emergency management agencies, volunteer service organizations, state and local governments and the private sector to engage citizens in homeland security and promote community and family preparedness across the country (December 2002).

Eight, there is another critical problem of the use of community in the jargon of public disaster management agencies. This arises from the fact that like the definitions of disaster that are devised to increase budgets, manpower, size, and departmental power bases, *community* serves the same purpose. Communities tend to be artificial physical areas that by some special coincidence overlap political constituencies. It is difficult to claim that these bureaucratically created communities have a lot in common with what scholars have defined as communities. It is certainly a far-fetched definition compared to that of the construct of communities based on social networks, which I analyzed in the last chapter. This confusion is compounded by the inconsistent and sometimes contradictory use of the term community even by disaster researchers. The result is that disaster management agencies missed a golden opportunity to utilize communities in managing disaster behaviors.

THE QUICK FIX

Given this long list of inherent problems that are built into public sector disaster management, there arises the inevitable search for a solution. Three alternatives come to mind. They can be best described as approaches advocating "tradition," "seeking an organizational fix," or "manipulating disaster behaviors through social engineering." For each, a long list of the pros and cons can be brought forward showing its unique benefits, yet they all have the same goal—of helping people survive disasters. *It is from this generic goal that I hope to be able to forge an alternative perspective about disaster management.* (See Figure 2.)

Tradition

This particular kind of approach of doing nothing and letting nature take its course is typical of the neoclassical conservative laissez-faire economists who leave everything to general market forces. If there is too much demand in one place, the push and pull of the market will bring it back into equilibrium. Malthus used this type of rationale to explain the links between food and population growth. If population grew too quickly, natural constraints (such as food supply and disasters) would get growth back into line with a society's ability to feed itself. In this framework, disasters are part of the natural order, and like the ecosystem, have rules that regulate the relationship between people and nature. Like wages, jobs, and population growth, disasters are

FIGURE 2   Alternative means to improve disaster management.

thus simply another cog in a large social and ecological system that affects our survival. Like everything in nature, there is neither good nor bad, but the relationship between disasters and people is something different. It deals with survival, and as such is based on learning from our experiences and passing them on to future generations. We simply face disasters as humanity has throughout history; when mistakes are made we pay with our lives or property. When we learn from the mistakes, we survive. These accumulated experiences are the basis for disaster traditions.

Adapting this perspective, we make an assumption that over time individuals, families, and/or communities have figured out what is best for them. The results of the analysis in Chapter 4 clearly demonstrated that people do seek out traditional disaster role models as their prime source of information in the hope of increasing their chances for survival. There is thus some optimism that leaving us to own abilities and our own wits will not mean an automatic death sentence. In fact, the emergence of community-based voluntary organizations that deal with all kinds of emergencies and disasters is a testimony to our collective ability to take situations into our own hands. This point, I believe, has been amply demonstrated in the previous chapter about communities.

This remarkable ability for communities to deal with disasters has, however, been ignored and to a great extent marginalized by official disaster management agencies. Such an approach, according to its advocates, can upset the delicate balance between people and disasters by artificially interfering in this "natural course of events." For example, subsidizing housing or providing a safety net of automatic insurance in disaster-prone areas may actually boomerang by artificially attracting people to live in them. Take an even more innocuous way. Local authorities under pressure to obtain more tax money will redefine residential building codes to allow housing to be built in areas near toxic or hazardous chemical plants, in floodplains, or in hurricane regions. Assuming the authorities are keeping an eye on the best interests of their constituents, especially their health and well-being, most people don't think twice about taking up a good deal. The inevitable immediate or long-term results will be deaths, injuries, and damage. This situation would probably never have happened if knowledge about a potential disaster in the making were known and local authorities took heed of it.

Organizational Fix

A second option is based on the laws of inertia. If we already have a disaster management organization in place, why destroy it? Why not just make it better? The basis for this approach stems from the belief in the power of public sector organizations as the modern engine of progress in providing public services. Its existence evolved in the attempt to cope with a more urban and industrial world after the industrial revolution. This belief assumed that complex formal organizations are the epitome of rational social organization. Public sector service organizations, run on administrative autopilot, are assumed to be clones of this model. If by some chance there are flaws discovered in them, it is possible under the assumption of rationality to rectify the problem. These same principles can therefore apply to disaster management organizations. What the original authors of these ideas found to their chagrin was that the perfect world made up of perfect organizations simply did not exist. All the efforts at improving upon the original design failed for the simple reason that organizations are also composed of people, and people cannot be relied upon to be wholly rational. In organization terms, there are both formal and informal structures in all organizations that to one degree or another are at odds with each other. The result, as I pointed out in Chapter 1, is a built-in conflict mode that can sometimes have devastating effects on the workings of the organization.

For those who argue for an organizational fix to improve on disaster management organizations to make them more efficient and effective, the task is daunting. Not only do you have to contend with the way public organizations operate internally and with each other, but there is also the sticky problem of organizational behavior among its members. Remember that such public sector organizations are very political. Let us take one of the more prominent "flaws," namely, organizational coordination. Case study after case study has pointed out that this problem is a serious block to any effective disaster management program. Disaster agencies virtually run into each other; they contend for control and fight over turf. It's all part of a day's typical disaster response! Can this flaw be fixed by providing better communications equipment, more preplanning meetings, cooperative tabletop training? Perhaps it can, but perhaps it cannot. Even if it does, will that mean that the disaster agency will be more effective in terms of saving lives and property, or will it simply provide the organization with more resources to aggrandize itself?

What is clear is that there is no fast fix! Organizations are simply not a set of blocks that can be rearranged by color and size. *Organizations are made up of people, and to change how an organization behaves means first and foremost changing how the people behave in the organization.* In a sense, to fix up such pubic sector organizations is akin to making what already exists better—like trying to make a better mousetrap. Such attempts have been marginal, and they usually end up doing the same thing at diminishing rates of success. This does not mean, however, that it is hopeless. Some of these attempts have been pointed out in Chapter 1, primarily my emphasis on the New Public Management approach. In addition to considerable literature in the area of organizational behavior, human resource management and the sociology of organizations can be utilized to try to bring about organizational change. Overall, success in making such public sector organizations more effective has not been too successful, leading to demands to actually privatize these services. This point will be discussed in detail below.

Social Engineering

As the name implies, the idea behind this perspective is basically to use scientific and engineering methods to manipulate social behavior. As bad as it sounds, this method is grounded in the very basics of scientific inquiry and is used in all forms of social discourse. The most recent widespread use of such a perspective was in the 1990s, when the term re-engineering was used in an attempt to restructure for-profit organizations along engineering principles as a way to cut costs and increase productivity. There is no reason, however, to look far afield to realize that social engineering is being used every day. For example, forms of social engineering are used daily by marketers and politicians to sell products or to persuade us to vote for someone or some issue. Teachers use it in classrooms and in seminars. Disaster managers use it to gain more leverage in their workplace. In fact, we all use such manipulative practices in our lives every day, so why does it sound so loathsome? One potential explanation is that the concept of social engineering implies a cold-hearted ability to determine behavioral outcomes by manipulating situations or social conditions. It is sort of like adding *a* to *b* and predictably getting *c*. While sounding coldblooded, this ability is what science is all about—the power of predicting. The difference between our everyday use and a researcher's use of social engineering is that the former is based on a one-to-one basis (and is very difficult to replicate), while the latter is based on predicting collective group and organizational behaviors.

This ability to affect individual or collective behaviors provides a key device in disaster management. As an alternative to public sector organizations, social engineering can offer to disaster managers a powerful tool to manipulate behaviors in order to increase rates of survival and lessen harm and damage. Here again, there is an underlying assumption that surviving disasters lies primarily with the potential victims, in their ability to be prepared and cope, but even if this is not completely true; being able to persuade or manipulate people to act so that their lives will be saved or at least minimally disrupted would make any disaster manager's day a success! To accomplish such a feat requires a great deal of socially based research and a consensus among scientists as to the reliability and validity of the results. To a large extent such research is being done—take this book, for example—but there are problems with standards of research and consensus about the results. Simply put, if social engineering methods are to provide a means to improve on the disaster management already available in public administrative agencies to reduce the number of disaster victims, research will have to be put on a firmer scientific basis.

A DIFFERENT PATH: PRIVATIZATION

Unlike the above alternative means to improve on what we now call disaster management in public sector organizations, let us now explore a different path of thinking; namely, privatization. The ideological basis for this perspective is a running assumption that the private market, at less cost and at greater efficiency and effectiveness, can replace public monopoly services (Rondinelli 1989; Pack 1987). This approach has been tried all over the world with various degrees of success (Farazmand 2001; Cowan 1990). For a combination of ideological, political, and economic reasons, governments have used all types of mechanisms in an attempt to divest public service agencies (Armstrong et al. 1997; Samson 1994; Massey 1993). Not only have they tried to divest budget draining and highly subsidized government monopolies in such industries as gas, oil, coal, communications, and transportation, but other services as well, in the areas of education (Bennett 2000), mental health (Upshur et al. 1997), art, and culture (Campbell 1999).

Figure 3 provides a general picture of the basic argument in favor of or against the privatization of such public goods as disaster services. The arguments center primarily on the effectiveness of market competition in making the supply and quality of disaster services better for the end user than

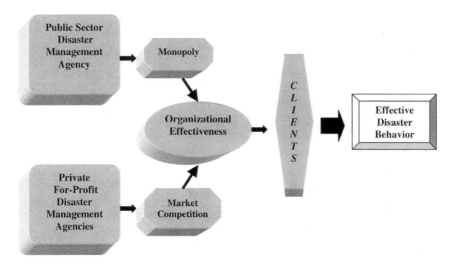

FIGURE 3   Privatization as an alternative path for effective disaster behavior.

a monopoly market. To a great extent, the measure of the success or failure of the privatization process depends on the ideological perspective of the beholder (Drakeford 1997; Froud et al. 1996; Feigenbaum and Henig 1990). For senior members of a government's treasury department, success means that such moves to privatize public services may substantially cut public expenses, putting less strain on budget requirements, reducing inflation, and even increasing employment! On the other hand, privatizing may inadvertently create private market monopolies, which like their public big brothers, are not very well attuned to the needs of the public (Sclar 2002).

As the saying goes, there are two sides to every coin, and in the ideological battle over privatization, this is certainly the case. Much criticism has been laid on the ways in which privatization has been implemented, but rarely on the process itself (Whitfield 1992; Vernon-Wortzel and Wortzel 1989). Despite these reservations, the trend for privatization has been a hallmark in the last two decades (Poole and Fixler 1987). It has been put into place all over the world, from developing economies to more advanced service- and knowledge-based societies. Public services that have in one form or another been privatized include a wide range of locally based public agencies encompassing local educational systems, transit systems, correctional facilities, and health care. There have even been successful attempts to privatize prisons and police forces, the paradigm of public service institutions (Benson 1998). Interestingly enough, disaster management agencies have remained faithful to

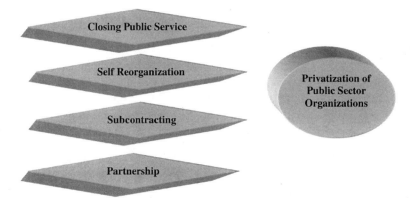

FIGURE 4 Options and strategies for the potential privatizing of public service agencies.

their organizational mentors and budget providers, the public purse of governments.

The extensive literature on privatization is more or less split along "ideological" lines buttressed by anecdotal arguments or the rare empirical evaluation, usually dealing primarily with saved or lost costs to the public (Sclar 2002). Social scientists tend to espouse the ideas of public good from the perspective of privatization's social impact, while economists stress economic savings and efficiency. Few actually take up the banner of the quality of the service to the public, mainly due to the fact that the basic underpinnings for privatization are economic in character, but despite the sometimes acrimonious debates, the arguments in both the popular press and scientific journals have made the idea of privatization more open to debate and criticism. This has resulted in some very good ideas and proposals about how to combine private and public services to the benefit of the general public. I will now review some of these options. (See Figure 4.)

PRIVATIZATION OPTIONS

In the debate over privatization have come several possible options, ranging from complete privatization at one end of the spectrum to some form of partnership between public and private enterprises at the other. I have tried to categorize these options in Figure 4. At one extreme is total privatization, which can be accomplished by cutting loose, by completely disbanding a particular public service. This is usually done under two types of circumstances.

The first is when the government initiates a new service that without public largess and oversight would not be initiated in the private market. The second can occur when such services already exit in the private market and it seems reasonable and less costly to close the service department down. One example is private sector production in the areas of crime prevention and protection (Benson 1998), an area normally under public control and scrutiny. Another has been the wholesale transfer of public assets and services to private sector companies in such areas as highways, transit, water supply, and even education (Poole and Fixler 1987).

Another possibility is to create conditions in which public employees act as a semi-independent public cooperative that has to compete in the private market. This may entail allowing the employees of a particular public agency to recast their organization as they see fit and then apply all the tools at their disposal to compete in the marketplace. A good example of this occurred for the fleet services of Indianapolis. Its unionized public employees were threatened with losing their jobs to a private contractor for the management of about 3000 city-owned vehicles (Sclar 2002). On their own initiative, the public employees reorganized the service company and then outbid several other private contenders for a three-year contract. In the process, they reduced the number of employees by about one-third, bringing about a considerable savings to the city. Part of the savings went into bonuses for the employees.

Toward the other end of the spectrum is the subcontracting concept, through which the public agency retains full control over its services but simply gives out to private companies certain politically and/or economic problematic functions (Seidenstat 1999). A few case studies of this strategy, especially when it included the concept of competitive tendering, have shown that it is economically feasible, sometimes saving up to 20% of costs without reducing the level of service (Domberger and Jensen 1997). This kind of subcontracting is prevalent, for example, in large public health facilities, in which such jobs as maintenance, laundry, landscaping, and other indirect occupations are subcontracted out to companies that compete for the tender.

The fourth kind of privatization arrangement that can be found is one based on a partnership between a public body and a private entrepreneur. In many of these cases, the "private" is an illusion, as the private company is actually owned (fully or by majority stocks) by the public agency. This type of privatization is the least market-oriented, but as the private partner operates by the rules of the marketplace and not as a monopoly, it can still be considered privatization. The list of such partnerships is long, but as a rule they operate in areas that the government considers vital to its safety and well-being. The most obvious examples are national airlines, energy-related industries, and in some nations' transportation systems (Harkim et al. 1996).

A COMMON DENOMINATOR

In order to discuss how privatization would affect the area of disaster management, it is imperative to understand that there is no one single archetypical disaster management agency. In the United States, they exist at the federal, municipal, and local community levels. They run the gamut from the massive federal bureaucracies of FEMA (Federal Emergency Management Agency) and the mammoth, newly formed Department of Homeland Security to one-man shows in local communities. In other nations they are concentrated only at the federal level or are scattered in various military, police, or firefighter units. In some nations they do not formally exist or are fictitious fronts that exist on office nameplates. These variations are compounded by differences in the political economy of nations that would favor or dampen privatization. For example, in the United States, which is based on a capitalistic economy and the idealization of entrepreneurship, privatization would find fertile ground. In more socialistic countries, such as Sweden or China, this process would probably be very difficult to implement (Pestoff 1998). Despite these variations, both subtle and obvious, they all have a common denominator of being part of a larger public sector administration. This means that they are characterized as being part of a formal, complex bureaucratic structure.

Given this common denominator allows a reasonable platform from which to begin to explore the possibility of privatization. I will restrict myself to focusing on the organizational model found in most Western capitalistic countries. This does not in any way negate national variations due to ideology or political economy. The choice of the Western disaster management organizational model has two advantages. The first, as was pointed out in Chapter 1, is that most of the world's disaster management agencies are found in these nations. The second is that their link in the chain of public administration is comparable in that nearly all these units, departments, or agencies can be found at different levels of government, from the federal to the local.

PRIVATIZING DISASTERS

Given these parameters, it is necessary to formulate the alternative options that have already been used in privatization and see the degree to which they apply to public sector disaster management organizations. The most often used options are described in Figure 5. The first, "competitive bidding," occurs when a tender is put out in the private market for the operation of a specific type of service. Like most tenders, specifications are laid out that reflect the policy decisions of the contracting public sector organization and

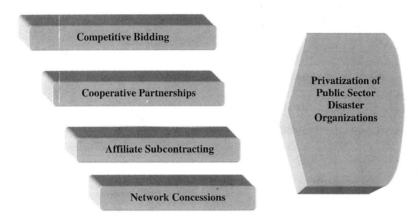

FIGURE 5   Options and strategies for the potential privatizing of disaster management.

allow monitoring of the results. It is very similar to competing for a government contract. A second type of relationship is based on "cooperative partnership," whereby both the public organization and the private company have a business partnership in providing specific services. This kind of association can be flexible, with the partners using their own organization's specialized strengths to provide services. In this case, the private company may be a marketing or production firm to complement the administrative abilities of the public agency. A third kind of association within a privatization framework is "affiliate subcontracting." In this association, private market companies that are affiliated with the public sector agency by a common type of service are subcontracted to perform that service. A good example would be the hiring of a company that provides private correctional police for guarding prisons or the electronic monitoring of offenders who are on leave from prison. (See Figure 5.)

Finally, there is the possibility of private market intervention through what has been termed "network concessions." Similar to but more complex than cooperative partnerships, the link evolves through a number of interlocking private companies that form a network based primarily on a division of labor. For example, before the Gulf War in Israel, private companies were asked to set up the organizational basis for the gas mask distribution system, devise the training program, develop the software for monitoring, and so on. The actual distribution was done by the public sector Home Front Command. In the only case of gas mask distribution in the United States, a regional office of FEMA was in charge.

PRIVATIZED DISASTER MARKET

The few studies that have focused on the public–private link in the area of disaster management have emphasized the clear-cut economic benefits of having the private for-profit sector replace the responsible government agencies (Horwich 1993). As I have already pointed out, this general trend has been going on for some time. It is now being bolstered by an economic justification that favors the development of the private market in a broad range of disasters services, but disaster service companies can make money only if they provide equitable services: "The simple fact, from an economic perspective, is that in the absence of a functioning price system [i.e., competition], neither central authorities nor well intentioned altruistic outsiders are likely to come close to knowing and responding effectively to the circumstances and preferences of afflicted populations" (Horwich 1993). As I demonstrated in the previous chapters, this inability of public sector disaster management agencies to provide services is not only economic in nature; it is also inherent in its organizational structure. One of the major reasons why this is so is that on the whole, disasters affect private property and how individuals use the market to prepare for, mitigate, or recover from a disaster. From the individual's point of view, this means buying goods in the open market that will increase his or her chances for survival. One need only recall the numerous TV news reports of people putting up large sheets of plywood to cover windows at the onset of a hurricane or hurrying to purchase gas masks or smoke alarm for their homes. Disasters can be big business.

Given the enormous flow of money involved in the area of disasters, it would seem only natural for private market firms to be attracted into this market niche. To some extent insurance companies have triggered this growth, with the largest part of the private market being taken up by specialized firms that deal in crisis reduction and risk aversion. The major buyers have included firms dealing with information technology, transportation, and energy resources. For the most part, such private disaster companies deal with disaster issues at an organizational level, focusing on specific types of industrial plants, a particular company, or corporate organization (Horwich 1993). Few if any focus on individuals, families, or communities. Only in the area of nonprofit organizations do we see an effort to deal with the victims. The extent of the penetration of private disaster consulting firms into the market can also be seen by the fact that large corporations have begun to hire in-house disaster mitigation specialists or allocate job slots and even departments to disaster and emergency management.

There is another side of privatization—probably the largest—involving ties that public sector disaster agencies have with the private market. The size of this market is an extremely difficult task to decipher, because obtaining such information, even where transparency is embedded in law and access to public records is a citizen's right, is not readily available. It would in fact mean that a detailed examination of each and every disaster management agency—public or private—would have to be made. In a public agency, this would mean fleshing out if, when, and what kind of public–private relationships were entered into. In a private agency, its relationship to public agencies and the specific kinds of disaster services provided would be needed. The sheer size of this task simply does not fall into the scope of this book.

To give just an idea of the complexity involved, FEMA, the U.S. federal disaster agency, has formal relationships with twenty-seven other government agencies, all of which probably have numerous interlocking contracts with private market firms or consultants. Add to these local and state public sector disaster agencies and their links to other private market suppliers. Some idea of the numbers involved can be gleaned from a simple Internet search of disaster-related company sites, emergency equipment suppliers, consulting firms, and so on. The majority of such links fall into the categories illustrated in Figure 3. These types of public–private dealings have long been a model in government and more recently in the area of disaster management. What has evolved is that the policy and politics of disaster management remain in the hands of the public agency, and the "dirty work" is given out to private entrepreneurs. For example, most of the cleanup activities after a flood, hurricane, or toxic spill is given to private corporations. They bring in the heavy equipment or proper detergents and do the job. Some jobs are allocated to other public agencies with appropriate budgetary compensation. Overall, disaster management agencies act as the public oversight and manager, controlling guidelines and policy affecting postdisaster recovery, but where do the victims fit into this scheme of privatization?

PEOPLE POWER

Until now I have presented one side of the privatizing coin; namely, the alternative ways in which public sector disaster management agencies have or can be privatized. For the most part, the generous funding from governments usually ends up in other disaster-related organizations. The example I previously gave illustrates this; FEMA provides funds ($21 million) through the national citizens corps to local governments and subcontractors that eventually flow into another FEMA project related to communities (Community Emergency Response Team, or CERT). What about the reverse side of the coin? If disasters are big business and involve private property, shouldn't the consumer be part of the privatization formula? The consumer in this case is the victim of a disaster, and at the end of the day the victim is the reason and justification for disaster management organizations. As consumers, the potential victims should, according to basic economic theory, affect the supply and demand of goods and their prices. As consumers, they also have a choice of what disaster survival goods and services to purchase and where to purchase them! This perspective flies in the face of regulated noncompetitive public sector disaster management agencies that decide and price what services they supply. It is probably why the private market providing disaster items and services to individuals and households stays clear of the types of services the government supplies; they simply cannot compete.

Going back to the national field study conducted in Israel will give us some idea of the place of the consumer in this privatization process. It should be recalled that the only legal public disaster agency in Israel, the Home Front Command, is required to protect the public in cases of emergencies and disasters. Its services are given without extracting a direct cost to the individual. As I pointed out in Chapter 3, this includes a series of specific missions, some of which are the distribution of gas masks, the maintenance of protective equipment and shelters, and the provision of guidelines in case of conventional and unconventional attacks by either terrorists or general war. As part of the survey, household heads were asked about their readiness to pay for a series of disaster-related services. Most of these services could be obtained free of charge through either the Home Front Command or other public agencies. In some cases, they were simply items linked to being prepared for an emergency or disaster, but the overall concept was to judge the degree to which consumers would be ready to enter the private market to purchase these critical disaster services.

READY TO PAY

The readiness to purchase disaster-related services in the private market meant that individual respondents would act upon their conviction that the private market could provide them with better disaster-related-service than that already in the public market. People were simply ready to put their money down to pay for and have these services. The use of the term *ready to purchase* was not chosen by accident, as it is as close as you can get to the actual behavioral act of purchasing This is a far cry from the problematic use of such terms that are employed in opinion polls as a *willingness* or *intent* to do something. In this sense, the question reflects potential purchasing power. In its reverse form, it also is an evaluation of the public services that they feel should be provided.

A glance at Table 1, which lists disaster-related services open for purchase, shows that about one-third of the sample indicated a readiness to enter the private market. This proportion tells a lot about the potential market for private disaster services as well as about the services already being

TABLE 1   Proportion of Households Who are Ready to Pay for Disaster-Related Services Provided by Private Organizations

Disaster service	Ready to pay
Supply food and water	31.4
Provide quality gas mask	28.3
Prepare children in schools in emergency	28.3
Have electric supply if stoppage	32.9
Evacuate to safe place if necessary	32.7
Check readiness of shelter/sealed room	28.3
Guard home in case need evacuate	27.5
Provide radio, batteries, flashlight	22.6
Psychological advise/therapy	26.7
Give detailed instructions on what to do	27.8
Materials and information on biochemical war	24.6
Materials on atomic warfare	24.4
Provide medical services	34.8

Note: The basic question, which varied by item, was formulated as "Are you ready or not ready to pay a private service organization which would provide you and your family during an emergency situation with—."

received. Looking at the services in more detail is also important, as it provides a window into what families are interested in. What seems most obvious is that the demand for private market services does not replace what is already provided by public sector disaster agencies; they in fact expand the services that are directly and indirectly related to being prepared and coping with disasters. What appears to be the case is that the "quality" ingredient of the services is most sought after. For example, there is a readiness to pay a private organization to make sure that a quality gas mask and basic supplies of food or emergency equipment are available. These are recommendations made by the Home Front Command, but are not part of the disaster service package. Also, there is no way of knowing the quality of the equipment or the item. Are they the best, the most reliable, and the most likely to help me and my family to survive? Perhaps for these reasons, there is a demand for services by private vendors or service companies to assure the respondents of the quality of the items that are critical for their survival.

SAFETY NET OF SERVICES

An additional set of private sector services was in demand by the respondents. Specifically, these services have to do with making sure that the physical protection of the family is maximized. In this case, private service organizations are sought after to prepare and qualify the readiness of a sealed room and shelter. As most respondents of the national sample had experienced the Gulf War, they were keenly aware of the threat of a biological or chemical ballistic missile attack and of its potential consequences. Seeking out this service from a private vendor provided an alternative means of making sure they were optimally protected. Along these same lines, a third of the respondents also sought out private firms that would make sure that an alternative source of electricity was available even if it was disrupted, place a guard in their homes if the need ever came to leave or evacuate, and have both the means and a place to go in case their own homes were threatened or destroyed.

Another set of safety net services that drew attention to the private market had to do with information. It can be speculated that this was related to the lack of trust in the information made available by official authorities, a point I demonstrated in Chapter 4. In any case, there was a demand for material about unconventional biochemical warfare as well as the possibility of an atomic attack. Along with this came a similar readiness to pay a private company to provide expert, detailed instructions about how to behave and what to do as the threat of a disaster (war) progressed into an actual disaster. This category of services encompassed not only providing instructions about the proper care and use of gas masks, but when and how to get the family fully prepared for the worst.

The last set of services that people felt they would be ready to pay for were in the areas of medicine and psychological therapy. Both these services are provided through public sector agencies, but it appears that despite being able to receive them at minimum direct cost there is a question as to their quality and availability. Perhaps the rationale that drives the demand for both services may be due to the fear of an overloaded and perhaps a collapsed medical system during a disaster. The readiness to purchase psychological advice or therapy before, during, and after a crisis reflects a deep understanding among the respondents that both body and mind can be seriously affected in times of great stress accompanied by potential death or injury.

WHO PAYS?

The fact that about one-third of the Israeli national sample indicated a readiness to purchase private sector disaster services also means that two-thirds did not. How can we explain why someone is ready to purchase disaster services from the private market while others are not? It should be noted that given the fact that a variety of public sector agencies as well as the Home Front Command provide most of these services gratis, it seems to be unusual that one-third should be ready to pay for private market services! What is it that attracts people to be ready to pay for services that most can obtain free of charge? A number of possible explanations come to mind. On the surface, it can argued that the rich, for example, are the ones who can afford these services and are therefore ready to pay for them, or putting the emphasis on education, that the more educated, with higher expectations in the level of consumer services, will be more ready to pay. Perhaps age and family status are the key variables! In this scenario, younger people with families are more ready to purchase disaster goods on the private market, as they may be more concerned over the welfare of children than older persons in families whose children have left the nest. All these relationships are realistic possibilities, but the best way to resolve who is ready to pay for an alternative private market source for disaster services is to simply look at the facts! (See Figure 6.)

As I have done in previous chapters, at this stage I will make use of a Pearson chi square test that seeks to find if different groups (e.g., younger or older, more or less educated) significantly differ in their choice patterns of private or public disaster services. By significant, I mean above and beyond simple random choices. If a significant difference does exist, we will therefore have an important clue about which population groups are more attracted than others to private sector services.

Wealth

Probably to the consternation of those who claim that the rich will be able to purchase better protection than the poor, we find that income has only a very

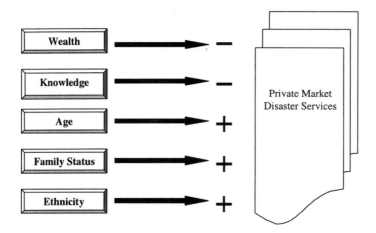

FIGURE 6 Possible group characteristics explaining a choice of private market disaster services over public sector services.

marginal impact on whether or not people are ready to pay private disaster service vendors. Based on the question that asks the sample households to rank their income in relationship to the national average (far above, above, equal to, below, far below average), the only "near" significant differences appear in paying for electric power in case of a stoppage (χ^2 8.10, p = 0.08) and receiving up-to-date information about biological and chemical warfare (χ^2 8.73, p = 0.06). Other measures of wealth, such as property (ownership of homes and automobiles), also proved not to be significant. Taken together, the conclusion is that money by itself has little impact on whether or not an individual will purchase disaster survival services from the private market.

Knowledge

Another proposition argues that people with greater knowledge have better access to up-to-date information and are more market savvy to distinguish service quality. As a result they are more likely to choose private market vendors than those less knowledgeable. An additional assumption is that private services are better than those supplied by public agencies—an assumption that seems reasonable. This does not necessarily mean that the choices of those more knowledgeable will be any better than those less so, but it does imply that the quality of the services will be a crucial determinant in their choice. With this in mind, I employed "educational attainment" as a proxy for this ability to assess the quality of a service, especially those services directly related to threats concerning disasters. In testing this proposition, it was found that the analysis discredited education as a prime suspect in why people choose private over public disaster service vendors. The fact was that this choice was not significantly different among those with higher or lower levels of education in any of the thirteen alternative services. The conclusion is that consumers of private market services are not that much educationally different from those who use public sources.

Age

We now come to a more controversial issue—age. On the one hand, some people will argue that older people have more experience with disasters, and if given a choice, would likely pay to get a better service than what they received in the past. On the other hand, older people are more likely to be set in their ways and not be bothered to start the tedious and time-consuming task of evaluating the private market for the best buy. Which is right? The analysis clearly shows that in each of the alternative disaster services, age makes a large and significant difference in the readiness to pay for private market vendors. An examination of the direction of the relationship also clarifies how age affects a choice; the older one is, the less ready he or she is to make use of the private market for disaster services. These results highlight the overwhelming impact that age has on being ready to use the private market as an alternative means for disaster survival. It also reinforces the notion that younger household heads are much more willing to try out the private market than older people. Apparently the experiences that older people have with public disaster services are satisfying enough to offset the attraction of services from the private marketplace.

Family Status

In my discussions of the family in Chapter 6, it became apparent that being a family meant a lot in terms of being prepared for disasters. Could this also be true in terms of seeking out private market disaster service vendors? Simply put, families rather than "nonfamilies" would be more interested in utilizing the private market sector for disaster services. Taking up this theme, couples forming a family were compared with nonfamily units. Families were defined for this purpose as consisting of a couple living together, whereas nonfamilies were composed of three groups of individuals (e.g., divorce, widowed, and single). In this comparison, family status proved to be a decisive factor in being ready to pay for private market services. The direction of the relationship revealed that families were more ready to make use of private market services than nonfamilies. This occurred in nine of the thirteen alternative private sector disaster services. The only areas in which family status had no significant impact on selecting private market services included the choice of the *physical protective services* (shelter χ^2 3.53 p $= 0.17$ and materials χ^2 3.99 p $= 0.14$), the need for *detailed instructions* about what to do before or during a disaster (χ^2 5.09 p $= 0.08$), or the *preparation of children in school* for upcoming disasters (χ^2 3.94 p $= 0.14$). In short, the family unit once more proves to be a selector and initiator of disaster survival behaviors.

Ethnic–Religious Differences

Focusing on ethnic–religious characteristics is another way of taking a broader view of what leads people to choose private market disaster services. Here the assumption is that certain cultural factors will predispose individuals to rely on public domain services, or in contrast, to enhance their readiness to utilize private market choices. This in itself is a very complicated issue, as it is difficult to distinguish what it is about a particular culture or religious belief that leads to a choice of disaster services. Many studies in the area of culture and ethnic behavior have grappled with these problems and have suggested various solutions (Bolin and Bolton 1986; Smith and Guest 1986). Despite these difficulties, there simply remains the benefit of peering into the mirror of larger social processes that reflect societal level determinants of behavior. In our case, I have chosen religious affiliation—being an Israeli Jew or Israeli (Arab) Muslim—to demarcate cultural differences based on the intermeshing of ethnic–religious values. I have discussed these differences in detail in Chapter 6 (see "Ethnic Hens"), but in general, the Arab Muslim culture is characteristic of traditional family–clan agrarian societies while that of the Israeli Jews is characteristic of urban–industrial modern societies.

Comparing the readiness of Jews and Arabs to pay for disaster services provided by the private or public sector markets unambiguously demonstrated that the two cultural ethnic–religious groups significantly differ in the utilization of private market services. Without exception, this difference runs throughout all the proposed disaster services. The direction of the association is also important, as it clearly shows that Muslim Arabs are not ready to pay for disaster services and prefer to rely on services from the public sector while Jews are far more ready to pay private sector vendors. Interpreting these results calls for some caution, but it seems that a case may be made for the impact of cultural background in the readiness to pay for private sector disaster services. On the one hand, persons having a strong traditional family–clan cultural background seem to rely on public sector institutional forms of disaster services. This may have been generated in the deep-rooted cultural reliance on the community or village leader to make decisions for all the family or clan. In this case, it can be argued that the government has replaced the community leader. On the other hand, modern Western capitalistic cultural values seem to prompt persons to use the private market as a viable alternative for public disaster services. Instead of reliance on community leaders has come a trend toward individualism and accountability, leading toward self-reliance and the option of the private market.

PREDICTING PAYMENTS

The analysis has so far shown that certain characteristics of consumers significantly affect whether or not they will be ready to pay for private market disaster services. Younger people, families, and Jews were found to favor private market purchases. What is still a mystery is which one of these characteristics can best predict being ready to purchase such private sector services. To answer this question requires a more sophisticated type of analysis, as the dependent variable, purchasing services in the private market is a dichotomous variable; either you purchase or don't purchase the service. This means that unlike ordinal or interval-type scales that measure various degrees of more or less, our focus will be on a zero to one scale. For this reason I will use a special type of regression called a logistic regression statistic, which is based on the log probability of an event occurring. It asks what the probability will be of a person wanting to purchase disaster services on the private market against what is provided by public sector agencies. If the answer could have been given on the basis of simply random chance, it would not be considered significant, but if the odds are not random, then there is something special about that person, or in our case his or her characteristics, that can explain a choice of a private service vendor. (See Figure 7.)

Employing this kind of logic led to the following analysis. Each of the services was individually employed as a dependent variable and a regression model for each was generated through the analysis. This meant that the choice of being ready to pay for each private service could be looked at separately as well as compared to all the various other disaster services. The analysis itself

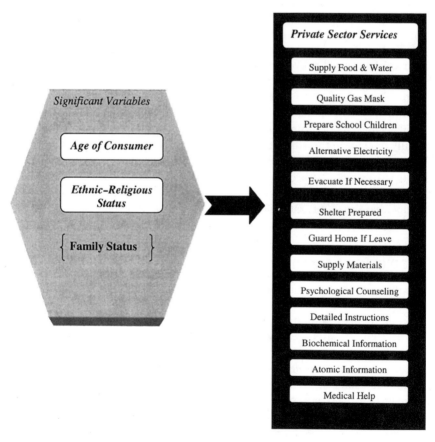

FIGURE 7   Summary results of logistic regression models for being ready to pay for private market disaster services.

provided a way of deciding what kinds of persons would be more likely to choose a private market vendor. The results are figuratively summarized in Figure 7.

To a large extent, the age of the consumer and his or her ethnic–religious status are the primary predictors of being ready to use private market disaster service vendors. Family status—being a family unit or not—also appeared, but only in the case in which a decision had to be made concerning having a private company supply a quality gas mask. Overall, it appears that among the numerous possible characteristics of the consumer that would affect his or her being ready to purchase private market disaster services, age and ethnic–religious affiliation are the most critical.

PRIVATIZATION: A RECAP

In summary, it appears that privatization of public sector disaster services makes a great deal of sense. It is an economically viable and a socially preferable alternative means to provide disaster-related services to its customers, potential victims of disasters. Based on the empirical evidence provided here, it also makes sense in light of the fact that even where such services are given out gratis, close to a third of the population is ready to put their hard-earned cash on the table to obtain similar or better-quality services from private market vendors. These disaster services cover a wide range of activities that include preparation, mitigation, and recovery. Individuals are thus interested in obtaining top quality gas masks, materials, and food stocks, as well as having their shelters and sealed rooms checked to make sure they are maximally operable.

They are also ready to pay for having up-to-date information about unconventional disasters, a way of finding alternative shelter in case of the need to evacuate, and both medical assistance and detailed instructions about what to do throughout the disaster ordeal. In short, they are ready to pay private market organizations for what they probably perceive as a better quality service. More to the point is the consistent demand for such a wide range of disaster-related services.

As the analysis has shown being ready to pay private market vendors has little to do with being rich or poor, educated or not. It was found to be linked to the age, family status, and ethnic–religious affiliation of the respondent, variables that reflect inherent behaviors associated with social norms and values. This meant that the decision to purchase private market disaster services is not so much an economic question as a social decision. It is a decision that a fairly large proportion of people are ready to make. In general, all the data strongly suggest that there is room for privatization of disaster services and that the market has potential takers.

SO WHERE TO NOW?

Taking the results of what we have learned until now opens the way to proposing a theoretical framework to approach managing disasters, but unlike most theoretical frameworks, I propose to exploit what we have learned from the empirical analysis of the Israeli national sample, especially about disaster communities, gatekeepers, and privatization. The emphasis here is on the word empirical. There is a good reason for this, as disaster management, like most other types of management, has been riddled with ideologies, changing buzzwords, and unsubstantiated theories. It has rarely been grounded in the stuff of science or empirically developed and tested theories or propositions. As a developing profession, it has sought legitimacy in the public sector that puts more relevance on organizational criteria than scientifically derived evidence. By attaching the term management to the field of disaster studies without a sound empirical base, it has exposed its major weakness. My hope is that putting back the empirical into disaster management will strengthen those who utilize this form of management to reduce deaths, injuries, and damage to people and property.

Any theoretical framework must start with a set of prior empirically based propositions and testable assumptions. On the basis of these, I will develop an outline for a social process model of disaster management. First, I assume that

1. The present public sector disaster management agencies are problematic as service organizations. The empirical evidence has shown that core disaster concepts and disaster management guidelines for effectiveness do not match those of their consumers.
2. Privatization will make disaster management more effective. Empirical evidence stresses that privatization is more consumer-oriented, fulfills a market niche, and can be substantially more economical than public sector services.
3. Disasters are social constructs having social meanings and allied social behaviors. Empirical evidence has shown that disaster behavior is affected by traditional social sources of information, socially based risk perceptions, family roles, and community social networks.
4. Disaster communities and family units are the key to surviving disasters. The evidence shows that preparing for disasters depends on the social strength of a community and the impact of family gatekeepers.
5. The key to eliminating or minimizing negative consequences of disasters lies in utilizing and directing disaster behaviors. Empirical evidence provides a set of explicit propositions related to disaster

preparedness and coping behaviors that allow such behaviors to be enhanced.

A MODEST PROPOSAL

On the basis of these assumptions and the empirical evidence that I have presented in this book to support them, I would like to propose a social process model of disaster management. This model is an attempt to open serious discussions of the place of the private market in disaster management. It is also designed to persuade disaster researchers to look more closely and systematically at the empirical links between disasters and disaster behaviors

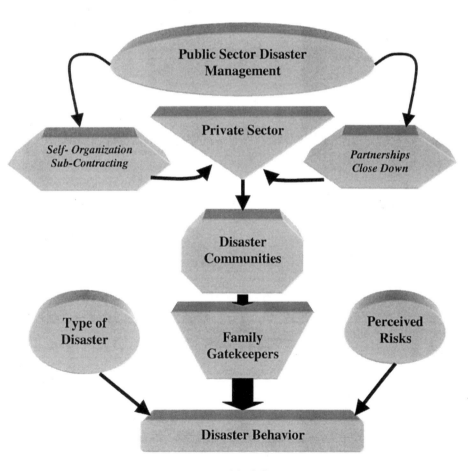

FIGURE 8   A general social process model of disaster management.

from a community and family level. Most important, it is designed to generate a framework that allows for the extension of numerous theoretical propositions of disaster behaviors to be empirically tested. Once tested, these propositions form a pool of critical information about disaster behavior that should aid disaster managers in formulating their decisions. These decisions can run from disaster preparation to recovery. The social process model (see Figure 8) has two major segments

Privatizing

The first concerns the ways and means of moving disaster management from the public sector into the private market. One of the justifications for this approach is that as the prime consumer of disaster-related services, the end user, the potential victim of disasters, should be allowed a choice of products. Rarely do such choices exist from a monopolistic provider such as a government, but they do exist in the competitive private market. From the standpoint of the public good, privatization also pays in terms of better quality at less cost. Choice and quality are the hallmarks of the privatization process.

The various means and strategies to privatize have already been discussed in this chapter. What is important to remember is that this process, even though it has been going on for some time and is generally successful, is to some extent a "hit of miss" matter; there is apparently no hard and fast formula. This is especially true in the area of public sector disaster management, in which serious and widespread efforts to privatize above and beyond contracting out specific jobs have not been made. One basic guideline for it to be successful is that it be culturally sensitive, however. The Western model of privatization, reflecting a capitalistic and individualistic culture, may not fit well into other cultures. This same principle also applies to the types of public–private market relationships that may evolve.

Behaviors

The second segment of the social process model of disaster management focuses on disaster behavior. Two empirically proven links to disaster behavior are critical to the model; namely, disaster communities and family gatekeepers. These two forms of disaster behaviors have already been discussed at length in Chapters 6 and 7, but there are certain points that should be emphasized. As the model suggests, the way to get a better understanding of disaster behavior evolves through a two-step sequence. The first derives through an understanding of the complex social nature of disaster communities. We now know that as social networks such communities have a significant impact on their members' disaster preparedness. This implies that *individual* disaster behaviors are formed within communities, making community-level analysis a critical element for understanding disaster behavior. As such disaster communities are built on the strength and intensity of social networks, a series of propositions can be formulated and tested. Each can provide an insight into what behaviors can be expected and what managerial strategies can be put in place to increase community preparedness or coping behaviors.

The second link comes from recognition that within communities, family gatekeepers are the key to survival. It may very well be that within disaster community social networks the interactive social discourse through informal communication among community members may not be enough to persuade people to use appropriate disaster survival behaviors. It is here that the family gatekeeper, or as I discovered, the mother, is a vital link in the chain affecting how we act in the face of a disaster.

Mothers in these social networks sift and digest information that is then implemented in their households. How, when, and at what levels this occurs is all grit for empirical investigation. The answers are what will provide the links between gatekeeper effects and disaster behaviors. From a managerial perspective, it should focus attention on mothers as the major players in increasing survival chances.

Type of Disaster

In the course of analyzing the data, it became apparent that the type of disaster people faced influenced their disaster behaviors. In the jargon of disaster research, disaster behaviors are agent-related. Until now and based primarily on case studies, it was argued (but never proven) that disaster behaviors are universal regardless of the disaster involved. Rare was the case in which it was possible to compare various disaster scenarios simultaneously among the same sample population to test this "universal" argument. This study has done just that and shown that natural, industrial, technological, or unconventional disasters differently affect how we prepare for and react to each. The practical implications of this finding are that we need to know more about perceptions of people toward various kinds of disasters. Such perceptions have an impact on their subsequent behaviors. Preparedness behaviors in the face of a flood, for example, are different from those for anthrax or biochemical terrorist attack!

Risk Perceptions

Similar to how types of disasters affect behavior is the impact of risk perceptions. This analysis in Chapter 5 proved to be the clearest refutation of the universal disaster behavior argument. It also demonstrated that certain types of disaster preparedness behaviors are affected by how people perceive of the risk of a disaster. There is, however, no guarantee as to how people will actually behave in the face of a disaster based solely on their perceptions of the risk; they are helpful in only certain types of disaster behaviors. Even so, the fact that perceived risks are agent-sensitive to disaster type and vary by individuals' characteristics makes understanding risk behavior an essential ingredient in predicting what people will do in disasters.

REFOCUS ON THE VICTIMS

The full social process model that I have just described is the result of systematically exploring the antecedents and consequences of disaster behavior. It certainly is not the last word! By empirically testing a series of middle-range propositions, however, some of the mystery that has surrounded disaster behaviors has been solved. In this process a model evolved that has a determined message for practitioners and scholars. The message is to refocus on what disaster management is all about—to save lives and property. To do so, I have argued that the organizational framework of disaster management must be recalibrated to get closer to its clients. One avenue to do so is to utilize various forms of privatization, but this is not enough. To simply let chaos reign by assuming the private market will take care of everything is a bit naive. The fact is that people have survived disasters for thousands of years by organizing at the community and family levels. This same principal applies today, therefore privatization should be seen as a necessary but not sufficient condition to increase our chances for survival. What privatization can provide are the disaster services that increase survival chances, but it is our choice to purchase or put aside these services that we deem critical. This ability to choose is what makes it absolutely imperative to understand disaster behavior. Being able to predict such behaviors provides the baseline for changing them. This is why social engineering through the use of powerful scientific inquiry may play a vital role in the future of disaster management.

The behavioral path by which people choose to increase their odds of surviving disasters should be the focus of disaster management. The proposed social process model takes this into account by providing where to begin looking for the middle-level propositions that can explain disaster behaviors. The model is in essence a theoretical one that can provide critical clues for practical applications. Knowing what predicts disaster behavior provides the leverage that disaster managers need in order to find practical solutions to help people make better-informed survival choices. It is not my intention here to begin to enumerate what practical solutions can be translated or derived from the results of the empirical analysis; be it sufficient to say that most of them can be made outside the walls of public sector disaster management organizations.

THE BEGINNING

This book—its message, its findings, and its implications—are only the beginning of a reassessment of the field of disaster management. It is also the first step in building a solid empirical foundation for the decisions disaster managers have to make to save lives. In the spirit of scientific inquiry, only critical thinking and the willingness to re-evaluate issues can bring about progress. This has been a first step, and as we all know, first steps are always the hardest.

References

AAP. (2000). Chemical–biological terrorism and its impact on children: a subject review. *Pediatrics* 105:662–670.

Able, E., Nelson, M., eds. (1990). *Circles of Care: Work and Identity in Women's Lives.* Albany, New York: SUNY Press.

Adams, C. R. (1981). Law: Its effects on inter-organizational authority structures in post-disaster responses. *Technical report 9. Department of Sociology.* Denver: University of Denver.

Akhter, F. (1992). Women are not only victims. In: Hossain, H., Dodge, C., Abel, F. H., eds. *From Crisis to Development: Coping with Disasters in Bangladesh.* Dhaka: University Press Ltd.

Al-Madhari, A. F., Elberier, O. M. (1996). Trends and fatality of natural disasters in the Arab world. *Disas. Prev. Mgt.* 5:27–35.

Alvarez, R. M., Brehm, J. (1998). Speaking in two voices: American equivocation about the Internal Revenue Service. *Amer. J. Pol. Sci.* 42:418–452.

Anderson, M. B., Woodrow, P. J. (1989). *Rising from the Ashes: Development Strategies in Times of Disaster.* Boulder, CO: Westview Press.

Armstrong, H., Armstrong, P., Connelly, M. P. (1997). Introduction: The many forms of privatization. *Stud. Pol. Econ.* 53:3–9.

Asgary, A., Willis, K. G. (1997). Household behavior in response to earthquake risk: an assessment of alternatives. *Disasters* 21:354–365.

Aspinall, P. J. (2001). Operationalising the collection of ethnicity data in studies of the sociology of health and illness. *Sociol Health Ill* 23:829–862.

287

Barley, S. R., Tolbert, P. S. (1997). Institionaliztion and structuration: studying the links between action and institution. *Org. Stud.* 18:93–117.

Bastida, E. (2001). Kinship ties of Mexican migrant women on the United States/ Mexican boarder. *J. Comp. Fam. Stud.* 32:549–569.

Beamish, T. D. (2001). Environmental hazard and institutional betrayal: lay-public perceptions of risks in the San Luis Opispo County oil spill. *Org. Environ.* 14:5–33.

Beck, F. D. (2001). Introduction to the special section. Struggles in building community. *Sociol. Inq.* 71:455–457.

Bedeian, A. J. (1994). Organization theory: Current controversies, issues and directions. In: Cooper, C. L., Robertson, I. T., eds. *Key Reviews in Managerial Psychology: Concepts and Research for Practice.* New York: John Wiley.

Beggs, J. J., Haines, V. A., Hurlbert, J. S. (1996). The effects of personal network and local community contexts on the receipt of formal aid during disaster recovery. *Internat. J. Mass Emerg. Disas.* 14:57–78.

Bell, D. C., Atkinson, J. S., Mosier, V. (2001). The role of gatekeepers in limiting HIV transmission. *Internat. J. Sociol. Soc. Policy* 22:47–76.

Bennett, E. (2000). Time for a change in public education, but what change? *Nature Soc. Thought* 13:181–214.

Benson, B. L. (1998). *To Serve and Protect: Privatization and Community in Criminal Justice.* Political Economy of the Austrian School Series. New York: New York University Press.

Berthoud, R. (1998). Defining ethnic groups: Origin or identity? *Patterns of Prejudice* 3:53–63.

Blaikie, P. M., Cannon, T., Davis, I., Wiser, B. (eds.). (1994). *At Risk: Natural Hazards, People's Vulnerability, and Disasters.* New York: Routledge.

Bland, S. H., O'leary, E. S., Farinaro, E., Jossa, F. (1997). Social network disturbances and psychological distress following earthquake evacuation. *J. Nerv. Ment. Dis.* 185:188–194.

Bohte, J., Meier, K. (2001). Structure and performance of public organizations: Task difficulty and span control. *Pub. Org. Rev.* 1:341–354.

Bolin, R. C. (1993). Household and community recovery after earthquakes. *Natural Hazards Research and Applications Information Center.* Program on Environment and Behavior. Monograph 56. Boulder, CO: University of Colorado.

Bolin, R. C. (1994). *Household and Community Recovery After Earthquakes.* Boulder, CO: Institute of Behavioral Sciences. Boulder, CO: University of Colorado.

Bolin, R., Bolton, P. (1986). Race, religion and ethnicity in disaster recovery. *Natural Hazards and Research and Applications Information Center.* Environment and Behavior monograph 42. Boulder, CO: University of Colorado.

Bolin, R., Jackson, M., Crist, A. (1998). Gender inequality, vulnerability, and disaster: Issues in theory and research. In: Enarson, E., Morrow, B. H. eds. *The Gendered Terrain of Disaster: Through the Eyes of Women.* Westport, CT: Praeger.

Bolin, R., Klenow, D. J. (1988). Older people in disaster: a comparison of black and white victims. *Internat. J. Aging Human Dev.* 26, 29–43.

Bolin, R., Stanford, L. (1998). The Northridge earthquake: community-based approaches to unmet recovery needs. *Disasters* 22:21–38.

Boyne, G. (2001). Planning, performance and public services. *Pub. Admin.* 79: 73–88.

Bradbury, J. (1989). The policy implications of differing concepts of risks. *Sci. Tech. Human Values* 14:380–399.

Bravo, M., Rubio-Stipec, M., Canino, G. J., Woodbury, M. A., Riberal, J. C. (1990). Psychological sequelae of disaster stress prospectively and retrospectively evaluated. *Amer. J. Commun. Psych.* 18:661–680.

Brehmer, B. (1987). The psychology of risk. In: Singleton, W. T., Hoyden, J., eds. *Risk and Decisions.* Chichester: Wiley.

Briere, J., Elliott, D. P. (2000). Characteristics and long-term sequelae of natural disaster exposure in the general population. *J. Traum. Stress* 13:661–679.

Britkov, V., Sergeev, G. (1998). Risk management: role of social factors in major industrial accidents. *Safety Sci.* 30:173–181.

Britton, N. R. (1991). Organizational and community response to a technological emergency. Case study of a major incident within a metropolitan Australian city occasional paper 6. *Centre for Disaster Management.* Armidale, Australia: University of New England.

Buckland, J., Rahman, M. (1999). Community-based disaster management during the 1997 Red River flood in Canada. *Disasters* 23(2):174–191.

Burkhart, F. N. (1994). *Media, Emergency Warnings, and Citizen Response.* Boulder, CO: Westview Press.

Burns, R., Sullivan, P. (2000). Perceptions of danger, risk taking, and outcomes in a remote community. *Environment and Behavior* 32:32–72.

Campbell, J. P. (1977). On the nature of organizational effectiveness. In: Goodman, P. S., Pennings, J. M. eds. *New Perspectives in Organizational Effectiveness.* San Francisco: Jossey-Bass.

Campbell, M. S. (1999). New trends in culture policy for the twenty-first century. *Soc. Text* 17:5–15.

Carter, T. M., Clark, J. P., Leik, R. K. (1979). Organizational and household response to hurricane warnings in the local community. *Natural Hazards Warning Systems, NHWS report series 70-0.* Minneapolis: University of Minnesota.

Casper, D. E. (1985). *Municipal Disaster Preparedness: A List of Periodical Literature 1980–1984.* Monticello, Illinois, Vance Bibliographies. Public Administration Bibliography, 1802–1808.

CDC (2000). Biological and chemical terrorism: Strategic plan for preparedness and response: Recommendations of CDC strategic planning workgroup. *Morbid. Mortal. Wkly. Rev.* 49:1–14.

Center for Research. (2000). Center for Research on the Epidemiology of Disasters. Brussels, Belgium: Universite Catholique de Louvaine.

Chang, S. (1984). Do disaster areas benefit from disasters? *Growth Change,* 1984: 24–31.

Charles, M. T., Kim, J. C. K., eds. (1988). *Crisis Management: A Casebook.* Springfield, MA: Charles C Thomas.

Chen, X., Dai, K., Parnell, A. (1992). Disaster tradition and change: remarriage and family reconstruction in a post-earthquake community in the People's Republic of China. *J. Comp. Fam. Stud.* 23:115–132.

Chilimampunga, C. D. (1997). Community's survival mechanisms in times of extreme deprivation. *Commun. Dev. J.* 32:312–320.

Clark, Y. (1995). Women and children: The key in disaster prevention in Jamaica. *Stop Disas.* 24.

Clarke, L., Short, J. F. (1993). Social organization and risk: Some current controversies. *Ann. Rev. Sociol.* 19:375–399.

Comfort, L. K. (1994). Self-organization in complex systems. *J. Pub. Admin. Res. Theory* 4:339–410.

Comfort, L. K. (1996). Self-organization in disaster response: The great Hanshin, Japan earthquake of January 17, 1995. Quick Response Report 78. *Natural Hazards Center.* Boulder, CO: University of Colorado.

Connolly, T., Conlon, E. J., Deutsch, S. J. (1980). Organizational effectiveness: a multiple-constituency approach. *Acad. Mgt. Rev.* 5:211–217.

Cosgrave, J. (1997). Are international staff hard to manage? *Disas. Prev. Mgt.* 6(4):245–251.

Couto, R. (1989). Catastrophe and community empowerment: the group formulations of Aberfan's survivors. *J. Commun. Psych.* 17:236–248.

Covello, V. T. (1983). Perception of technological risks: a literature review. *Tech. Forecast Soc. Change* 23:285–297.

Cowan, L. G. (1990). Privatization in the developed world. *Contributions in Economics and Economic History. no. 112.* Westport CT: Greenwood Praeger.

Crouch, S. R., Kroll-Smith, J. S., eds. (1991). *Communities at Risk: Collective Responses to Technological Hazards.* New York: Peter Lang.

Cuthbertson, B. H., Nigg, J. M. (1987). Technological disaster and nontherapeutic community: A question of true victimization. *Environ Behav* 19:462–483.

Cutter, S. L., Tiefenbacher, J., Solecki, W. D. (1992). En-gendered fears: Feminity and technological risk perception. *Indus. Crisis. Q.* 6:5–22.

D'Aunno, T. (1992). The effectiveness of human service organizations: a comparison of models. In: Hasenfeld, H., ed. *Human Services As Complex Organizations.* Newbury Park, CA: Sage.

Dake, K. (1991). Orienting dispositions in the perceptions of risk—analysis of contemporary worldview and cultural biases. *J. Cross Cult. Psych.* 22:61–82.

Daft, R. L. (1998). *Organization Theory and Design.* 6th ed. Cincinnati: South-Western College Publishing.

Dann, S., Wilson, P. (1993). Women and emergency services. *Symposium on Women in Emergencies in Disasters.* Brisbane, Queensland, Australia: Bureau of Emergency Services.

de Man, A., Simpson-Housley, P. (1987). Factors in perception of tornado hazard: an exploratory study. *Soc. Behav. Person* 15:13–19.

de-Silva, F. N., Eglese, R. (2000). Integrating simulation modeling and GIS: spatial decision support systems for evacuation planning. *J. Op. Res. Soc.* 51: 423–430.

DeVries, M. W. (1995). Culture, community and catastrophe: Issues in understanding communities under difficult conditions. In: Hobfoll, S. E., DeVries,

M. W., eds. *Extreme Stress and Communities: Impact and Intervention. NATO ASI series. Norwell, MA: Kluwer Academic Publishers, 375–393.*

DiMaggio, P. J., Powell, W. W. (1983). The iron cage revisited: Institutional isomorphism and collective rationality in organizational fields. *Acad. Mgt. Rev.* 21:1022–1054.

DiPrete, T. A. (1989). *The Bureaucratic Labor Market: The Case of the Federal Civil Service.* New York: Plenum.

Domberger, S., Jensen, P. (1997). Contracting out by the public sector: Theory, evidence, prospects. *Oxford Rev. Econ. Policy* 13:67–78.

Dombrowsky, W. R. (1998). Again and again: Is a disaster what we call a "disaster?" In: Quarantelli, E. L., ed. *What Is a Disaster? Perspectives on the Question.* London: Routledge, pp. 19–30.

Dominitz, J., Manski, C. F. (1997). Perceptions of economic insecurity: Evidence from the survey of economic expectations. *Pub. Opin. Q.* 61:261–287.

Douglas, M. (1986). *Risk Acceptability According to the Social Sciences.* London: Routledge & Kegan Paul.

Douglas, M., Wildavsky, A. (1982). *Risk and Culture: An Essay on the Selection of Technological and Environmental Dangers.* Berkeley, CA: University of California Press.

Douglas, P., Leigh, S., Johnston, D. M. (2000). Volcanic hazards: Risk perception and preparedness. *N. Z. J. Psych.* 29:86.

Drabek, T. E. (1969). Social processes in disaster: family evacuation. *Soc. Prob.* 16:336–349.

Drabek, T. E. (1986). *Human Responses to Disaster: An Inventory of Sociological Findings.* New York: Springer-Verlag.

Drabek, T. E., Key, W. H. (1984). *Conquering Disaster: Family Recovery and Long-Term Consequences.* New York: Irvington.

Drabek, T. E., Tamminga, H. L., Kilijanek, T. S., Adams, C. R. (1981). *Managing multi-organizational emergency responses: Emergent search and rescue networks in natural disaster and remote area settings.* Natural Hazards Research and Applications Information Center: Boulder, CO: University of Colorado.

Drakeford, M. (1997). The poverty of privatization: poorest customers of the privatized gas, water and electricity industries. *Crit Soc Policy* 17:115–132.

DRC. (2002). *Disaster Research Center.* Newark, DE: University of Delaware.

DRC, (2003). *Organizational and Community Resilience in the World Trade Center Disaster.* Disaster Research Center. Newark, DE: University of Delaware.

Drottz, S., Britt, M. (2000). Exposure to risk and trust in information: Implications for the credibility of risk communication. *Australasian J. Disas. Trauma Stud.* 4:2–9.

Dynes, R. R. (1998). Coming to terms with community disaster. In: Quarantelli, E. L., ed. *What Is a Disaster? Perspectives on the Question.* London: Routledge, pp. 109–126.

Dynes, R. R., Quarantelli, E. L., Wegner, D. E. (1990). Individual and organizational response to the 1985 earthquake in Mexico City, Mexico. *Disaster Research Center.* Newark, DE: University of Delaware.

Eade, D., Williams, S. (1995). *The Oxford Handbook of Development and Relief.* Vols. 1–3. Oxford, UK: Oxfam.

Ecevit, M., Kasapoglu, A. (2002). Demographic and psychosocial features and their effects on the survivors of the 1999 earthquake in Turkey. *Soc. Behav. Person.* 30:195–202.

Edelstein, M. R. (1988). *Contaminated Communities: The Social and Psychological Impacts of Residential Toxic Exposure.* Boulder, CO: Westview Press.

Elberier, O. H., Babiker, A., Rahman, A. A. (1998). Hazards in Africa: Implications and regional distribution. *Disas. Prev. Mgt.* 7:103–112.

Ellemers, J. E., Veld-Lengeveld, H. M. (1955). *Studies in Holland Flood Disaster 1953. Vol. 3. Study of the Destruction of a Community.* Washington, DC: National Academy of Sciences, National Research Council.

Enarson, E., Morrow, B. H., eds. (1998). *The Gendered Terrain of Disaster: Through the Eyes of Women.* Westport, CT: Praeger Press.

Enders, J. (2001). Measuring community awareness and preparations for emergencies. *Aust. J. Emerg. Mgt.* 16:45–58.

Etzioni, A. (1964). *Modern Organizations.* Englewood Cliffs, NJ: Prentice-Hall.

Ewald, F. (1991). Insurance and risk. In: Burchell, G., Gordon, C., Miller, P., eds. *The Foucault Effect: Studies in Governmentality.* London: Harvester/Weatsheaf, pp. 197–210.

Farazmand, A., ed. (2001). Privatization or public enterprise reform? International case studies with implications for public management. *Contributions in Economics and Economic History.* no. 112. Westport, CT: Greenwood Praeger.

Faupel, C. E., Styles, S. P. (1993). Disaster education, household preparedness, and stress responses following hurricane Hugo. *Environ. Behav.* 25:228–249.

Federal Emergency Management Agency. (1994). *Community Emergency Response Team Participant Handbook.* Washington, DC: Emergency Management Institute.

Federal Emergency Management Agency. (1999). *Catalog of Activities: 1999–2000.* Washington, DC: Emergency Management Institute.

Federal Emergency Management Agency (2000). *Federal Response Plan 9320.1-PL.* Washington, DC: Emergency Management Institute.

Federal Emergency Management Agency (2002). *Internet home page.* Fires.

Feigenbaum, H. B., Henig, J. R. (1990). Privatization and theories of the state. *International Sociological Association.*

Feldman, R., Masalha, S., Nadam, R. (2001). Cultural perspective on work and family: Dual-earner Israeli-Jewish and Arab families at the transition to parenthood. *J. Fam. Psych.* 15:492–509.

Fiedrich, F., Gehbauer, F., Rickers, U. (2000). Optimized resource allocation for emergency response after earthquake disasters. *Safety Sci.* 35:41–57.

Fisher, H. W. (1998). *Response to Disaster: Fact Versus Fiction & Its Perpetuation.* 2nd Ed. New York: University Press of America.

Fischer, H. W., Stine, G. F., Stoker, B. L., Trowbridge, M. L., Drain, E. M. (1995). Evacuation behavior: Why do some evacuate, while others do not? A case study of the Ephrata, Pennsylvania (USA) evacuation. *Disas. Prev. Mgt. Internat. J.* 4:30–36.

Flynn, J., Slovic, P., Mertz, C. (1994). Gender, race and perception of environmental risks. *Risk Anal.* 14:1101–1108.

Fordham, M. (1999). The intersection of gender and social class in disaster: Balancing resilience and vulnerability. *Internat J Mass Emerg Disas* 17:15–37.

Fordham, M., Ketteridge, A. M. (1998). "Men must work and women must weep": Examining gender stereotypes in disasters. In: Enarson, E., Morrow, B. H., eds. *The Gendered Terrain of Disaster: Through the Eyes of Women.* Westport, CT: Praeger.

Form, W. H., Nosow, S. (1958). *Community in Disaster.* New York: Harper and Brothers.

Fothergill, A. (1996). Gender, risk and disaster. *Internat. J. Mass Emerg. Disas.* 14:33–56.

Fothergill, A. (1998). The neglect of gender in disaster work: An overview of the literature. In: Enarson, E., Morrow, B. H., eds. *The Gendered Terrain of Disaster: Through the Eyes of Women.* Westport, CT: Praeger.

Fothergill, A., Maestas Enrique, G. M., Darlington, J. D. (1999). Race, ethnicity and disasters in the United States: A review of the literature. *Disasters* 23:156–173.

Fowlkes, M. R., Miller, P. Y. (1983). *Love Canal: The Social Construction of Disaster.* U.S. Federal Emergency Management Agency 1982–83. Report RR-1. Washington, DC: U.S. Government Printing Office.

Fried, B. J., Worthington, C. (1995). The multiconstituency approach to organizational performance assessment: a Canadian mental health system application. *Commun. Ment. Health J.* 31:11–24.

Fritz, C. (1957). Disasters compared in six American communities. *Human Org.* 16:6–9.

From Disaster Management to Sustainable Development: How the Public Sector, Private Sector and Voluntary Organizations Can Work Together. Geneva: World Health Organization.

Froud, J., Haslam, C., Johal, S., Shaoul, J., Williams, K. (1996). Stakeholder economy? From utility privatization to new labour. *Cap. Class* 60:119–134.

Gaines, S. O., Buriel, R., Liu, J. H., Rios, D. I. (1997). *Culture, Ethnicity, and Personal Relationship Processes.* London: Routledge.

Gilbert, C. (1998). Studying disaster: Changes in the main conceptual tools. In: Quarantelli, E. L., ed. *What Is a Disaster? Perspectives on the Question.* London: Routledge, pp. 11–18.

Gilbert, G. R., Parhizgari, A. M. (2000). Organizational effectiveness indicators to support service quality. *Managing Serv. Qual.* 10:46.

Gillard, M., Paton, D. (1999). Disaster stress following a hurricane: The role of religious differences in the Fijian Islands. *Australasian J. Disas. Trauma Studi.* 3.

Gillespie, D. F., Streeter, C. L. (1987). Conceptualizing and measuring disaster preparedness. *Internat. J. Mass Emerg. Disas.* 5:155–176.

Glampson, A., Glastonbury, B., Fruin, D. (1977). Knowledge and perceptions of the social services. *J. Soc. Policy* 6:1–16.

Goldhaber, M. K., Houts, P. S., DiSabella, R. (1983). Moving after a crisis: A prospective study of Three Mile Island (TMI) area population mobility. *Environ. Behav.* 15:93–120.

Goltz, J. D., Russell, L. A., Bourque, L. B. (1992). Initial behavioral response to a rapid onset disaster: a case study of the Oct. 1, 1987 Whittier Narrows earthquake. *Internat. Mass Emerg. Disas.* 10:43–69.

Goodman, P. G., Vaughan, C. E. (1988). The implications of Times Beach: a postdisaster field study in eastern Missouri. *J. Environ. Health* 51:19–21.

Gordon, P. D. (1982). *Special Statistical Summery: Deaths, Injuries, and Property Loss by Type of Disaster, 1970–1980.* Washington, DC: Federal Emergency Management Agency.

Gordon, J. R. (1996). *Organizational Behavior: A Diagnostic Approach.* Saddle River, NJ: Prentice-Hall.

Gowdy, E. A., Rap, C. A., Poertner, J. (1993). Management is performance: Strategies for client-centered practices in social service organizations. *Admin. Soc. Work* 17:3–22.

Grandjean, B. D., Vaughn, E. S. (1981). Client perceptions of school effectiveness: A reciprocal causation model for students and their parents. *Sociol. Ed.* 54:275–290.

Granot, H. (1996). Disaster subcultures. *Disas. Prev. Mgt.* 5:36–40.

Granot, H. (1999). Emergency inter-organizational relationships. *Disas. Prev. Mgt.* 8:21–26.

Gray, I., Stehlik, D., Lawrence, G., Bulis, H. (1998). Community, communion and drought in rural Australia. *J. Commun. Dev. Soc.* 29:23–37.

Grayson, C. E., Schwarz, N. (1999). Beliefs influence information processing strategies: Declarative and experiential information in risk assessment. *Soc. Cog.* 17:1–18.

Gunn, S. W. A. (1992). The scientific basis of disaster management. *Disas. Prev. Mgt. 1.*

Gustafson, P. E. (1998). Gender differences in risk perception: Theoretical and methodological perspective. *Risk Anal.* 18:805–811.

Haas, J. E., Kates, R. W., Bowden, M. J. (1977). *Reconstruction Following Disaster.* Cambridge, MA: MIT Press.

Haider, R., Rahman, A. A., Huq, S. (1991). *Cyclone 91: An environmental and perceptional study.* Daka, Bangladesh: Bangladesh Center for Advanced Studies.

Haines, V. A., Hurlbert, J. S., Beggs, J. J. (1996). Exploring the determinants of support provision: provider characteristics, personal networks, community context, and support following life events. *J. Health Soc. Behav.* 37:252–264.

Hall, R. H. (1996). *Organizations: Structures, Processes, and Outcomes.* Saddle River, NJ: Prentice-Hall.

Halualani, R. T. (2000). Rethinking "ethnicity" as structural-cultural projects(s): notes on the interface between cultural studies and intercultural communications. *Internat. J. Intercult. Relat.* 24:579–602.

Hance, B. J., Chess, C., Sandman, P. M. (1988). *Improving Dialogue with Communities: A Risk Communication Manual for Government.* Newbury Park, CA: Department of Environmental Protection. Trenton, NJ: Division of Science and Research.

Harkim, S. Seidenstat, P., Bowman, G. W., eds. (1996). *Privatizing transportation sysems. Privatizing Government: An Interdisciplinary Series.* Westport, CT: Greenwood Praeger.

Harvey, J. (1996). Productivity in professional services: To measure or not to measure. In: Halachmi, A., Bouckaert, G., eds. *Organizational Performance and Measurement in the Public Sector: Toward Service, Effort and Accomplishment Reporting.* New York: Quorum.

Harvey, J. H., Stein, S. K., Olsen, N., Roberts, R. J., Lutgendorf, S. K., Ho, J. A. (1995). Narratives of loss and recovery from a natural disaster. *Journal of Social Behavior and Personality* 10:313–330.

Hasenfeld, H. (1983). *Human Service Organization.* Englewood Cliffs, NJ: Prentice-Hall.

Hasenfeld, H., ed. (1992). *Human Services As Complex Organizations.* Newbury Park, CA: Sage.

Hawley, A. (1950). *Human Ecology: A Theory of Community Structure.* New York: Ronald Press.

Heaney, J. P., Peterka, J., Wright, L. T. (2000). Research needs for engineering aspects of natural disasters. *J. Infrastruc. Syst.* 6:4–14.

Heathcote, R. L. (1980). An administrative trap? Natural hazards in Australia: a personal view. *Austr. Geograph. Stud.* 18:194–200.

Hendrika, M., Sellers, D. E. (2000). Factors that influence personal perceptions of the risk of an acute myocardial infarction. *Behav. Med. 26.*

Herman, R. D., Renz, D. O. (1997). Multiple constituencies and the social construction of nonprofit organization effectiveness. *Nonprofit Vol. Sec. Q.* 26: 185–206.

Hewitt, K. (1995). Excluded perspectives in the social construction of disaster. *International Journal of Mass Emergencies and Disasters* 13:317–340.

Hills, A. E. (1994). Co-ordination and disaster response in the United Kingdom. *Disas. Prev. Mgt.* 3:66–71.

Hirose, H. (1979). Volcanic eruption and local politics in Japan: a case study. *Mass Emerg.* 4:53–56.

Hirose, H. (1982). Community reconstruction and functional change following a disaster in Japan. *Disaster Research Center.* Columbus, OH: Ohio State University. preliminary paper 74.

Horlick, J. T. (1995). Modern disasters as outrage and betrayal. *Internat. J. Mass Emerg. Disas.* 13:305–315.

Horwich, G. (1993). The role of the for-profit sector in disaster mitigation and response. *Internat. J. Mass Emerg. Disas.* 11:189–205.

Institute of Civil Engineers. (1995). *Megacities: Reducing Vulnerability to Natural Disasters.* London: Thomas Telford.

International Federation of Red Cross and Red Crescent Societies (1997). *World Disasters Report–1997.* New York: Oxford University Press.

Israel Central Bureau of Statistics (2002). *Statistical Abstract of Israel.* Jerusalem: Government Printing Press.

Iwasaki, N (2000). Role and functions of local communities in earthquake rescue, shelter administration and reconstruction. *Internat. J. Japanese Soc.* 9: 111–119.

Ishizuka, T., Hirose, H. (1983). Casual analysis of earthquake concern and preparing behavior in the North Izu Peninsula. *Japanese Psych. Res.* 25:103–111.

Jacobs, L., Worthley, R. (1999). Comparative study of risk appraisal: A new look at risk assessment in different countries. *Environ. Mon. Assess.* 59:225–247.

Janney, J. G., Masuda, M., Holmes, T. H. (1977). Impact of a natural catastrophe on life events. *J. Human Stress* 3:22–34.

Jayaraman, V., Chandrasekhar, R. (1997). Managing the natural disasters from space technology inputs. *Acta-Astronautica* 40:291–325.

Johnson, B. B., Slovic, P. (1994). Improving "risk communication and risk management": Legislated solutions or legislated disasters? *Risk Anal.* 14:905–906.

Jobson, J. D., Schneck, R. (1982). Constituent view of organizations: Evidence from police organizations. *Acad. Mgt. J.* 25:25–46.

Johnson, B. (1992). Knowledge and risk perception: What we don't know. *American Sociological Association.* Association paper.

Jones, R. T., Frary, R., Cunningham, P., Weddle, J. D., Kaiser, L. (2001). The psychological effects of hurricane Andrew on ethnic minority and Caucasian children and adolescents: A case study. *Cult. Div. Ethnic Min. Psych.* 7:103–108.

Julnes, P. D. L., Holzer, M. (2001). Promoting the utilization of performance measures in public organizations: an empirical study of factors affecting adoption and implementation. *Pub. Admin. Rev.* 61:693–708.

Kaniasty, K., Norris, F. H. (2000). Help seeking comfort and receiving socials support: The role of ethnicity and context of need. *Amer. J. Comm. Psych.* 28:545–581.

Kaniasty, K., Norris, F. H. (2001). Social support dynamics in adjustment to disasters. In: Sarason, B. H., Duck, S., eds. *Personal Relationships: Implications for Clinical and Community Psychology.* Chichester, England: John Wiley & Sons, pp. 201–224.

Kanter, R. M., Summers, D. V. (1987). Doing well while doing good dilemmas of performance measurement in nonprofit organizations and the need for a multiple-constituency approach. In: Powell, W. W., ed. *The Nonprofit Sector: A Research Handbook.* New Haven, CT: Yale University Press.

Karam, F. X. (2000). Investigating mutual intelligibility and language coalescence. *Internat. J. Sociol. Lang.* 146:119–136.

Karanci, A. N., Rustemli, A. (1995). Psychological consequences of the 1992 Erzincan (Turkey) earthquake. *Disasters* 19:8–18.

Karanci, A. N., Alkan, N., Aksit, B., Sucuoglu, H., Balta, E. (1999). Gender differences in psychological distress, coping, social support and related variables following the 1992 Dinar (Turkey) earthquake. *North Amer. J. Psych.* 1:189–204.

Kasperson, R., Renn, O., Slovic, P., Brown, H., Emel, J., Goble, R. (1988). The social amplification of risk, a conceptual framework. *Risk Anal.* 8:177–187.

Kauffman, S. A. (1994). *The Origins of Order: Self-Organization and Selection in Evolution.* New York: Oxford University Press.

Kelly, C. (1995). A framework for improving operational effectiveness and cost efficiency in emergency planning and response. *Disas. Prev. Mgt.* 4:25–31.

Kent, R. C. (1987). *Anatomy of Disaster Relief: The International Network in Action.* New York: Pinter.

Khoury, E. L., Warheit, G. J., Hargrove, M. C., Zimmerman, R. S., Vega, W. A., Gil, A. G. (1997). The impact of hurricane Andrew on deviant behavior among a multiracial/ethnic sample of adolescents in Dade County Florida: A longitudinal analysis. *J. Traum. Stress* 10:71–91.

Kirschenbaum, A. (1984). Segregated integration: a research note on the fallacy of misplaced numbers. *Soc. Forces* 62:784–793.

Kirschenbaum, A. (1992). Warning and evacuation during a mass disaster: A multivariate decision making model. *Internat J Mass Emerg Disas* 10:91–114.

Kirschenbaum, A. (1996). Residential ambiguity and relocation decisions: Populations and areas at risk. *Internat. J. Mass Emerg. Disas.* 14:79–96.

Kirschenbaum, A. (2001a). Mass terrorism and the distribution of gas masks in Israel: A longitudinal cohort analysis. *Internat. J. Mass Emerg. Disas.* 19:245–267.

Kirschenbaum, A. (2001b). The organization of chaos: The structure of disaster management. In: Vigoda, E., ed. *Public Administration: An Interdisciplinary Analysis.* New York: Marcel Dekker, pp. 259–286.

Kirschenbaum, A. (2002). Disaster preparedness: A conceptual and empirical reevaluation. *Internat. J. Mass Emerg. Disas.* 20:5–28.

Kirschenbaum, A., Mano-Negrin, R. (1999). Underlying labor market dimensions of opportunities: the case of employee turnover. *Human Relations* 52:1233–1255.

Kirschenbaum, A., Oigenblick, L., Goldberg, A. (2000). Well-being, work environment and work accidents. *Soc. Sci. Med.* 50:631–639.

Kletz, T. (1994). Are disasters really getting worse? *Disas. Prev. Mgt.* 3:33–36.

Krimsky, S. (1995). Dealing with risk: Why the public and the experts disagree on environmental issues. *Ann. Amer. Acad. Pol. Soc. Sci.* 554:230–231.

Kroll-Smith, J. S., Couch, S. R. (1990). *The Real Disaster Is Above Ground: A Mine Fire and Social Conflict.* Lexington, KY: University Press of Kentucky.

Kouzmin, A., Jarman, A. M. G., Rosenthal, U. (1995). Interorganizational policy processes in disaster management. *Disas. Prev. Mgt.* 4:20–37.

Laaksonen, T. (1996). Ethnicity and person perception: judging personality, language and quality of voice from accented Swedish. *Report from Department of Psychology, Stockholm University* 814:1–20.

LACDE. (2000). Local authorities confronting disasters and emergencies. *The 4th International Conference, Report and Conclusions.* Reykjavik, Iceland.

Lalo, A. (2000). Alerting the population in emergency plans: examples of local public policy in Provence. *J. Haz. Mat.* 78:281–301.

Larsson, G., Enander, A. (1997). Preparing for disaster: public attitudes and actions. *Disas. Prev. Mgt. Internat. J.* 6:11–21.

Leik, R. K., Leik, S. A., Ekker, K., Gifford, G. A. (1982). *Under the Threat of Mount St. Helens, A Study of Chronic Family Stress.* Minneapolis: Family Study Center. University of Minnesota.

Levine, A. G. (1982). *Love Canal: Science, Politics and People.* Lexington, MA: Lexington Books.

Lindell, M. K. (1994). Are local emergency planning committees effective in developing community disaster preparedness? *Internat. J. Mass Emerg. Disas.* 12:159–182.

Lindell, M. K., Perry, R. W. (1992). *Behavioral Foundations of Community Emergency Planning.* Washington, DC: Hemisphere.

Lindell, M. K., Perry, R. W. (2000). Household adjustment to earthquake hazard: a review of the literature. *Environ. Behav.* 32:461–501.

Linkie, M. (2000). The defense threat reduction agency: a note on the United States' approach to the threat of chemical and biological warfare. *J. Contem. Health Law Pol.* 16:531–563.

Lupton, D. (1999). *Risk.* London: Routledge.

Mamun, M. Z. (1996). Awareness, preparedness and adjustment measures of riverbank erosion prone people: a case study. *Disasters* 20:68–74.

Marincioni, F. (2001). A cross-cultural analysis of natural disaster response: The Northwest Italy floods of 1994 compared to the U.S. Midwest floods of 1993. *Internat. J. Mass Emerg. Disas.* 19:209–235.

Mariss, C., Langford, I., Sounderson, T., O'Riordan, T. (1997). Exploring the psychometric paradigm: Comparisons between aggregate and individual analysis. *Risk Anal.* 17:303–310.

Marks, K. S., Fritz, C. E., Quarantelli, E. L., eds. (1954). *Human Reactions to Disaster Situations.* Chicago: National Opinion Research Center. University of Chicago.

Massey, A. (1993). *Managing the Public Sector: A Comparative Analysis of the United Kingdom and the United States.* London: Aldershot.

McClure, J., Walkey, F., Allen, M. (1999). When earthquake is seen as preventable: attribution, locus of control and attitudes to risk. *Appl. Psych. Internat. Rev.* 48:239–256.

McEntire, D. A. (1997). Reflecting on the weakness of the international community during the IDNDR: Some implications for research and its application. *Disas. Prev. Mgt.* 6:221–233.

McFarlane, A. C., Policansky, S. K., Irwin, C. (1987). A longitudinal study of the psychological morbidity in children due to a natural disaster. *Psych. Med.* 17:727–738.

McLuckie, B. F. (1975). Centralization and natural disaster response: a preliminary hypothesis and interpretation. *Mass. Emerg.* 1(1):1–9.

Mileti, D. S., Sorenson, J. H. (1987). Determinants of organizationl effectiveness in responding to low probability catastrophic events. *Columbia J. World Bus.* 22:13–19.

Miller, M., Paton, D., Johnston, D. (1999). Community vulnerability to volcanic hazard consequences. *Disas. Prev. Mgt.* 8:255–260.

Millican, P. (1993). Women in disaster. *Symposium on Women in Emergencies and Disasters.* Brisbane, Queensland, Australia: Bureau of Emergency Services.

Minichiello, V. M., Browne, J. (2001). Knowledge, risk perception and condom usage in male sex workers from three Australian cities. *AIDS Care* 13: 387–402.

Morrow, B. H. (1997). Stretching the bonds: The families of Andrew. In: Peacock, W. G., Morrow, B. H., Gladwin, H., eds. *Hurricane Andrew: Ethnicity, Gender and the Sociology of Disasters*. London: Routledge, pp. 141–170.

Morrow, B. H. (1999). Identifying and mapping community vulnerability. *Disasters* 23:1–18.

Morrow, B. H., Enarson, E. (1996). Hurricane Andrew through women's eyes: Issues and recommendations. *Internat. J. Mass Emerg. Disas.* 14:1–22.

Morrow, B. H., Phillips, B. (1999). What's gender "got to do with it?" *Internat. J. Mass Emerg. Disas.* 17:5–11.

Mulwanda, M. P. (1992). Active participants or passive observers? *Urban Stud.* 29: 89–97.

Myers, M. F. (1993). Bridging the gap between research and practice: the natural hazards research and applications information center. *Internat. J. Mass Emerg. Disas.* 11:41–54.

Natural disasters and cultural responses. In: Smith, O., Guest, A., eds. *Studies in Third World Societies*. Williamsburg, VA: College of William and Mary. Anthropology Department.

Natural Hazards Research Center. (2002). University of Colorado, Boulder, CO.

Neal, D. M. (1993). Integrating disaster research and practice: An overview of issues. *Internat. J. Mass Emerg. Disas.* 11:5–13.

Neal, D. M., Phillips, B. (1990). Female dominated local social movement organizations in disaster-threat situations. In: West, G., Blumberg, R. L., eds. *Women and Social Protest*. New York: Oxford University Press, pp. 243–255.

Neal, D. M., Phillips, B. (1995). Effective emergency management: reconsidering the bureaucratic approach. *Disasters* 19:327–337.

Nehnevajsa, J. (1989). *Volunteering for Emergency Preparedness: Final Report*. Washington, DC: Federal Emergency Management Agency.

Newport, J. K., Jawahar, G. G. P. (1998). Crisis intervention by community participation. *International Journal of Mass Emergencies and Disasters* 16:363–370.

Nilson, B. G. (1981). Proposed model for crisis intervention in a community disaster. *Natural Hazards Research and Applications Information Center*. Boulder, CO: University of Colorado.

Nja, O. (1997). Emergency preparedness training as an effective consequence reducing measure. *Safety and Reliability Proceedings of the International Conference on Offshore Mechanics and Arctic Engineering. OMAE* 2. New York: ASME, pp. 33–40.

Njoh, A. J. (1994). A client satisfaction based model of urban public service delivery organizational effectiveness. *Soc. Indic. Res.* 32:263–296.

Noel, G. E. (1990). The role of women in health-related aspects of emergency management: A Caribbean perspective. In: Enarson, E., Morrow, B. H., eds. *The Gendered Terrain of Disaster: Through the Eyes of Women*. Westport CT: Praeger.

Norris, F. H., Smith, T., Kaniasty, K. (1999). Revisiting the experience–behavior hypothesis: The effects of hurricane Hugo on hazard preparedness and other self-protective acts. *Basic Appl. Soc. Psych.* 21:37–47.

Oliver-Smith, A. (1982). Here there is life: The social and cultural dynamics of successful resistance to resettlement in postdisaster Peru. In: Hansen, A., Oliver-Smith, A. eds. *Involuntary Migration and Resettlement: The Problems and Responses of Dislocated People.* Boulder, CO: Westview Press.

Oliver-Smith, A. (1986). Natural disasters and cultural responses. *Stud, Third World Soc,* 36:1–254.

Ollenburger, J. C., Tobin, G. A. (1999). Women, aging and post-disaster stress: Risk factors. *Internat. J. Mass Emerg. Disas.* 17:65–78.

Olson, R. S., Prieto, J. P. S., Olson, R. A., Gawronski, V. T., Estrada, A. (2000). The marginalization of disaster response institutions: The 1997–1998 El Nino experience in Peru, Bolivia, and Ecuador. *Natural Hazards Research and Applications Information Center.* Special publication 36. Boulder, CO: University of Colorado.

Orellana, M. F. (1999). Space and place in an urban landscape: Learning from children's views of their social worlds. *Vis. Sociol.* 14:73–89.

Pack, J. R. (1987). Privatization of public-sector services in theory and practice. *J. Pol. Anal. Mgt.* 6:523–540.

Palm, R. (1995). Communicating to a diverse population. *National Science and Technology Conference on Risk Assessment and Decision Making for Natural Hazards.* Washington, DC.

Palm, R., Hodgson, M. (1991). *After the California Earthquake Experience: Attitude and Behavior Change.* Chicago: University of Chicago Press.

Parr, A. R. (1970). Organizational response to community crisis and group emergence. *Amer. Behav. Sci.* 13:423–429.

Paton, D., Johnston, D. (2001). Disasters and communities: vulnerability, resilience and preparedness. *Disas. Prev. Mgt. Internat. J.* 10:270–277.

Paton, D., Smith, L., Violanti, J. (2000). Disaster response: risk, vulnerability and resilience. *Disas. Prev. Mgt.* 9:173–180.

Pelling, M. A., Alpaslan, Z. B., Barakat, S. B. (2002). The macro-economic impact of disasters. *Prog. Dev. Stud.* 2:283–305.

Perez, L. M. (2001). The mass media and disaster awareness in Puerto Rico: a case study of the floods in Barrio Tortugo. *Org. Environ.* 14:55–73.

Perilla, J. L., Norris, F. H., Lavizzo, E. A. (2002). Ethnicity, culture and disaster response: Identifying and explaining ethnic differences in PTSD six months after Hurricane Andrew. *J. Soc. Clin. Psych.* 21:20–45.

Perrow, C. (1984). *Normal Accidents: Living with High-Risk Technologies.* New York: Basic Books.

Perry, R. W. (1995). The structure and function of community emergency operations centres. *Disas. Prev. Mgt. Internat. J* 4:37–41.

Perry, R. W., Lindell, M. K. (1991). The effects of ethnicity on evacuation decision-making. *Internat. J. Mass. Emerg. Disas.* 9:47–68.

Perry, R. W., Mushkatel, A. H. (1984). *Disaster Management: Warning Responses and Community Relocation.* Westport, CT: Quorum.

Perry, P. W., Lindell, M. K., Greene, M. R. (1981). *Evacuation Planning in Emergency Management.* Lexington, MA: Heath Lexington Books.

Pestoff, V. A. (1998). *Beyond the Market and State: Social Enterprises and Civil Democracy in a Welfare State.* London: Aldershot.

Phillips, B. D. (1990). Gender as a variable in emergency response. In: Bolin, R. C., ed. *The Loma Prieta Earthquake: Studies in Short Term Impacts.* Boulder, CO: Institute of Behavioral Sciences. University of Colorado.

Pidgeon, N. (1997). The limits to safety? Culture, politics, learning and man-made disasters. *J. Conting. Crisis. Mgt.* 5:1–14.

Pidgeon, N., O'Leary, M. (2000). Man-made disasters: why technology and organizations (sometimes) fail. *Safety Sci.* 34:15–30.

Piette, B. (1997). Identity and language: the example of Welsh women. *Fem. Psych.* 7:129–137.

Platt, R. H., McMullen, G. M. (1979). Fragmentation of public authority over floodplains: The Charles River response. *Water Resources Research Center.* no. 101. Boston: University of Massachusetts.

Poole, R. W., Fixler, P. E. (1987). Privatization of public-sector services in practice: Experience and potential. *J. Pol. Anal. Mgt.* 6:612–625.

Quarantelli, E. L. (1985). Emergent citizen groups in disaster preparedness and recovery activities. *Disaster Research Center.* Final project report no. 33. Newark, DE: University of Delaware.

Quarantelli, E. L. (1986). Research findings on organizational behavior in disasters and their applicability in developing countries. *Disaster Research Center.* Preliminary paper 107. Boulder, CO: University of Delaware.

Quarantelli, E. L. (1988). Disaster crisis management: a summary of research findings. *J. Mgt. Stud.* 25:373–385.

Quarantelli, E. L. (1993). The environmental disasters of the future will be more and worse but the prospect is not hopeless. *Disas. Prev. Mgt.* 2.

Quarantelli, E. (1995). What is a disaster? *International Journal of Mass Emergencies and Disasters* 13:221–229.

Quarantelli, E. L. (1997). Ten criteria for evaluating the management of community disasters. *Disasters* 21:39–56.

Quarantelli, E. L., ed. (1998). *What Is a Disaster? Perspectives on the Question.* London: Routledge.

Quarantelli, E. L. (1999). Implications for programmes and policies from future disaster trends. *Risk. Mgt. Internat. J.* 1:9–19.

Quarantelli, E. L. (2001). Statistical and conceptual problems in the study of disasters. *Disas. Prev. Mgt.* 10:325–338.

Quarantelli, E. L., Dynes, R. R., eds. (1970). *American Behavioral Scientist. topical issue.* Organizational and Group Behavior in Disasters. 13(3):323–480.

Reese, L. E., Vera, E. M., Paikoff, R. L. (1998). Ethnic identity assessment among inner-city African American children: Evaluating the applicability of the multigroup ethnic identity measure. *J. Black. Psych.* 24:289–304.

Reskin, B., Padavic, I. (1994). *Women and Men at Work.* Thousand Oaks, CA: Pine Forge Press.

Robbins, S. P. (1983). *Organization Theory: The Structure and Design of Organizations.* Englewood Cliffs, NJ: Prentice-Hall.

Rogers, G. O. (1997). Dynamic risk perception in two communities: risk events and changes in perceived risk. *Environ. Plan. Mgt.* 40:59–79.

Rohe, W. M., Mouw, S. (1991). The politics of relocation: The moving of the Crest Street community. *Amer. Plan. Assoc. J.* 57:57–68.

Rondinelli, D. A. (1989). Decentralizing public services in developing countries: Issues and opportunities. *J. Soc. Polit. Econ. Stud.* 14:77–98.

Rosa, E. A., Jaeger, C., Renn, O., Webler, T. (1994). Perceiving risks: rational actor or social actor? *International Sociological Association.* Association Paper.

Ross, M. G. (1967). *Community Organization: Theory, Principles and Practices.* 2nd ed. New York: Harper & Row.

Rosse, W. L. (1993). Volunteers and post-disaster recovery: A call for community self-sufficiency. *J. Soc. Behav. Personal.* 8:261–266.

Roth, R. (1970). Cross-cultural perspectives on disaster response. *Amer. Behav. Sci.* 13:440–451.

Rubin, C. B. (1981). Long-term recovery from natural disasters: a comparative analysis of six local experiences. *Acad. Contemp. Probl.* 116 pp.

Rubin, C. B. (1985). The community recovery press in the United States after a major natural disaster. *Internat. J. Mass. Emerg. Disas.* 3:9–28.

Rubin, C. B. (1987). National origin and earthquake response: Lessons from the Whitter-Narrows earthquake of 1987. *Internat. J. Mass. Emerg. Disas.* 5:347–356.

Rubin, C. B. (2002). Timeline of Historical Disaster Events and U.S. Government Reactions. poster. Washington, DC: Claire Rubin Associates.

Ruestemli, A., Karanci, A. N. (1999). Correlates of earthquake cognitions and preparedness behavior in a victimized population. *J. Soc. Psych.* 139:91–101.

Russell, L. A., Gotz, J. D., Bourque, L. B. (1995). Preparedness and hazard mitigation actions before and after two earthquakes. *Environ. Behav.* 27:744–770.

Samson, C. (1994). The three faces of privatization. *Sociology* 28:79–97.

Scanlon, J. (1998). The Perspective of gender: a missing element in disaster response. In: Enarson, E., Morrow, B. H., eds. *The Gendered Terrain of Disaster: Through the Eyes of Women.* Westport, CT: Praeger.

Schildreman, T. (1993). Disasters and development: a case study from Peru. *J Internat. Dev.* 5:415–423.

Schmidlin, T. W., King, P. S. (1995). Risk factors for death in the 27 March 1994 Georgia and Alabama tornadoes. *Disasters* 19:170–177.

Schmuck, H. (2000). "An act of Allah": Religious explanations for floods in Bangladesh as survival strategy. *Internat. J. Mass. Emerg. Disas.* 18:85–95.

Schneider, S. K. (1995). *Flirting with Disaster: Public Management in Crisis.* Armonk, NY: Situations.

Schneider, B. J., Parkington, J., Buxton, V. M. (1980). Employee and customer perceptions of service in banks. *Admin. Sci. Q.* 25:252–267.

Schware, R. (1982). Folk Wireless: An Example of Indigenous Technology for Flood Warnings. *United Nations Research Institute for Social Development.* New York: United Nations.

Sclar, E. D. (2002). *You Don't Always Get What You Pay for: The Economics of Privatization.* Ithaca, NY: Cornell University Press.

Scobie, J., ed. (1997). *Mitigating the Millennium: Proceedings of a Seminar on Community Participation and Impact Measurement in Disaster Preparedness and Mitigation Programmes.* London: Rugby Intermediate Technology.

Scott, R. (1995). *Institutions and Organizations.* Thousand Oaks, CA: Sage.

Seidenstat, P. (ed.). (1999). Contracting out government services. *Privatizing Government: An Interdisciplinary Series.* Westport, CT: Greenwood, Praeger.

Shavit, Y., Fisher, C. L., Koresh, Y. (1994). Kin and non-kin under collective threat: Israeli networks during the Gulf War. *Soc. Forces* 72:117–1215.

Sherraden, M. S., Fox, E. (1997). The Great Flood of 1993: response and recovery in five communities. *J. Commun. Prac.* 4:23–45.

Shippee, G. E., Bradford, R., Gregory, W. L. (1982). Community perceptions of natural disasters and post-disaster mental health. *J. Commun. Psych.* 10:23–28.

Shoichet, R. (1998). An organization design for non-profits. *Nonprof. Mgt. Lead.* 9:71–88.

Sjöberg, L. (1995). *Explaining Risk Perception: An Empirical and Quantities Evaluation of Cultural Theory.* Risk Research Reports 22. Stockholm: Center of Risk Research.

Sjöberg, L., Drottz-Sjoberg, B. M. (1993). *Moral Value, Risk and Risk Tolerance.* Risk Research Report 11. Stockholm, Sweden: Center of Risk Research, Stockholm School of Economics.

Skopek, T. A. (2001). Perceptions of risk in siting nuclear waste facilities: a localized perspective. *Human Soc. Sci.* 61:29–46.

Slovic, P. (1987). Perceptions of risk. *Science* 236:280–285.

Slovic, P. (1999). Trust, emotion, sex, politics, and science: surveying the risk-assessment battlefield. *Risk Anal.* 1.19:689–701.

Smit, R. (2002). The changing role of the husband/father in the dual-earner family in South Africa. *J. Compar. Fam. Stud.* 33:401–415.

Smith, B., Pargament, K. I., Brant, C., Oliver, J. N. (2000). Noah revisited: religious coping by church members and the impact of the 1993 Midwest flood. *American Journal of Community Psychology* 28:169–186.

Smith, O., Albuquerque, A. (1986). *The Martyred City: Death and Rebirth in the Andes.* Canada: University of New Mexico Press.

Smith, W., Dowell, J. (2000). A case study of co-ordinative decision-making in disaster management. *Ergonomics* 43:1153–1166.

Solomon, S. D., Regier, D. A., Burke, J. D. (1989). Role of perceived control in coping with disaster. *J. Soc. Clin. Psych.* 8:376–392.

Sprang, G. (1999). Post disaster stress following the Oklahoma City bombing: an examination of three community groups. *J. Interpers. Viol.* 14:169–183.

Stallings, R. A. (1991). Ending evacuations. *Internat. J. Mass. Emerg. Disas.* 9: 183–2000.

Stallings, R. A., Schepart, C. B. (1987). Contrasting local government responses to tornado disaster in two communities. *Internat. J. Mass. Emerg. Disas.* 5:265–284.

Stewart, M. A. (1982). Study of Families Physical and Emotional Health Subsequent to the Woodstock Tornado. London, Canada: Department of Medicine. University of Western Ontario.

Sylves, R. T. (1991). Adopting integrated emergency management in the United

States: political and organizational challenges. *Internat. J. Mass. Emerg. Disas.* 9:413–424.

Sylves, R. T., Waugh, W. Jr. eds. (1996). *Disaster Management in the US and Canada: The Politics, Policymaking, Administration, and Analysis of Emergency Management.* 2nd ed.. Springfield, IL: Charles C. Thomas.

Szalay, L. B., Inn, A., Vilov, S. K., Strohl, J. B. (1986). *Regional and Demographic Variations in Public Perceptions Related to Emergency Preparedness.* Bethesda, MD: Institute for Comparative Social and Cultural Studies.

Tarn, J. H., David, M. S., Wen, H. J. (1998). Managing manmade system disasters with advanced cybernetics. *Human. Syst. Mgt.* 17:231–244.

Tatano, H. (1999). Risk perceptions and investment for disaster mitigation by individual households. Proceddings of the IEEE International Conference on Systems. Man. Cybern. 5:1003–1006.

Taylor-Adams, S., Kirwan, B. (1995). Human reliability data requirements. *Internat. J. Qual. Reliabil. Mgt.* 12:24–46.

Tierney, K. J. (1985). Emergency medical preparedness and response in disasters: the need for inter-organizational coordination. *Pub Admin Rev* 45:77–84.

Tierney, K. J. (1989). Improving theory and research on hazard mitigation: Political economy and organizational perspectives. *Disaster Research Center Paper 122.* Newark, DE: University of Delaware.

Torry, W. I. (1979). Anthropological studies in hazardous environments: Past trends and new horizons. *Curr. Anthro.* 20:517–540.

Tsui, A. S. (1990). A multiple-constituency model of effectiveness: An empirical examination at the human resource subunit level. *Admin. Sci. Q.* 35:458–483.

Turner, R. H., Nigg, J. M., Young, B. S. (1981). Community response to earthquake threat in southern California. *Institute for Social Science Research.* Los Angeles: University of California–Los Angeles.

Uleman, J. S., Rhee-Eun, B. N., Semin, G., Toyama, M. (2000). The elational self: closeness to ingroups depends on who they are, culture, and the type of closeness. *Asian Journal of Social Psychology* 3:1–17.

United Nations (2001). Internet Web Site. *Worlds Population.*

United Nations Economic Commission for Latin America and the Caribbean. (1985). Damage Caused by the Mexican Earthquake and Its Repercussion upon the Country's Economy. Santiago, Chile: document no. LC/G 1367.

United Nations Reliefweb (2002). Internet Web Site. *www.reliefweb.int.*

United States Government (2002). *Budget for Year 2002.* Washington, DC: U.S. Government Printing Office.

Upshur, C. C., Benson, P. R., Clemens, E., Fisher, W. H., Leff, H. S., Schutt, R. (1997). Closing state mental hospitals in Massachusetts: Policy, process and impact. *Internat. J. Law. Psych.* 20:199–217.

U.S. General Accounting Office (1991). Disaster Assistance: Federal, State, and Local Responses to Natural Disasters Need Improvement. Washington, DC: General Accounting Office.

Vernon-Wortzel, H., Wortzel, L. H. (1989). Privatization: Not the only answer. *World Dev* 17:633–641.

Vigoda, E. (2002). The legacy of public administration: Background and review. In: Vigodal, E., ed. *Public Administration—The New Generation: An Interdisciplinary Critical Analysis.* New York: Marcel Dekker.

Warrick, R. A., et al. (1981). Four communities under ash after Mount Helens. *Natural Hazards Research and Applications Informations Center.* Program on Technology, Environment and Man. Monograph 34. Boulder, CO: University of Colorado.

Weichseigartner, J. (2001). Disaster mitigation: The concept of vulnerability revisited. *Disas. Prev. Mgt.* 10:85–95.

Wenger, D., James, T. (1994). The convergence of volunteers in a consensus crisis: The case of the 1985 Mexico City earthquake. In: Dynes, R. R., Tierney, K. J., eds. *Disasters, Collective Behavior and Social Organization.* Newark, DE: University of Delaware Press, pp. 229–243.

Weyman, A. K., Kelly, C. J. (2000). Risk perception and risk communication: A review of literature. *Health Safety,* Laboratory report.

Whitfield, P. (1992). *The Welfare State: Privatization, Deregulation, Commercialization of Public Services for the 1990's.* London: Pluto.

WHO. (2002). World Health Organization Internet Home Page. *Report on Leading Causes of Deaths.*

Wiest, R. E. (1998). A comparative perspective on household gender, and kinship in relation to anger. In: Enarson, E., Morrow, B. H., eds. *The Gendered Terrain of Disaster: Through the Eyes of Women.* Westport, CT: Praeger.

Wildavsky, A. (1990). Theories of risk perception. *Deadalus* 119:41–60.

Wilson, J., Phillips, B. D., Neal, D. M. (1998). Domestic violence after disasters. In: Enarson, E., Morrow, B. H., eds. *The Gendered Terrain of Disaster: Through the Eyes of Women.* Westport, CT: Praeger.

Wink, P. (1997). Beyond ethnic differences: Conceptualizing the influence of ethnicity on individualism and collectivism. *J. Soc. Iss.* 53:329–349.

Wolensky, R. P. (1983). Power structure and group mobilization following disaster: A case study. *Soc. Sci. Q.* 64:97–110.

Zakour, M. J., Gillespie, D. F. (1998). Effect of organizational type and localism on volunteerism and resource sharing during disasters. *Nonprof. Vol. Sec. Q.* 27:49–65.

Zammuto, R. F. (1984). A comparison of multiple-constituency models of organizational effectiveness. *Academy of Management Review* 9:606–616.

Index

Academic perspective, 12
Accessible, 27, 61, 126
Accidental, 43, 81
Accidents, 62, 63, 93, 113, 119, 121,
    126, 131, 140, 148, 155, 157,
    175, 221, 287
Accumulated experiences, 159, 260
Acquaintance, 171, 194
Actions, 55, 59, 63–64, 67, 130, 174,
    181, 192, 195, 198, 200, 203,
    216, 224, 232, 256
Activities, 2, 42–45, 55, 74, 86, 94,
    96, 98, 105, 125, 140, 169, 181,
    183–184, 190, 198, 219, 221,
    228, 231, 245, 256, 270, 279
Activity, 21, 42, 50, 66, 78, 91, 191–
    192, 216, 245–246, 249, 254
Actual (or potential) delivery, 89
Actuarial accounting, 143
Adaptability, 132
Adaptation, 107
  adapted, 3, 107, 159, 198
  adapting, 37, 107–108, 138, 142,
    215

[Adaptation]
  forms of organization, 3
  mechanisms, 6, 45
  of organizations, 108
  process, 43, 132
  reorganization, 5
Administration, 3, 9, 11–12, 14–15,
    18–21, 23–25, 28, 33–35, 81,
    98, 108, 111, 217, 253, 258,
    267
Administrative, 9–10, 18, 23, 33, 39,
    53, 99, 107, 131, 136, 177, 179,
    209, 255–256, 261, 263, 268
  directives, 9, 23, 209
Administrators, 12, 15, 17–19, 23, 42
Adversaries, 137
Africa, 21, 25, 32, 234, 287
African-Americans, 205
Age, 50–51, 62, 94, 106–107, 118–
    119, 124, 160, 162, 170–171,
    274–276, 279, 287
Agenda, 14, 20, 68, 105
Agents, 56, 154–155
Agrarian society, 5

3m

DATE DUE

GAYLORD   PRINTED IN U.S.A.